TAKEOVER

TAKEOVER

FOREIGN INVESTMENT AND THE AUSTRALIAN PSYCHE

DAVID UREN

Published by Black Inc.,
an imprint of Schwartz Media Pty Ltd
37–39 Langridge Street
Collingwood VIC 3066 Australia
enquiries@blackincbooks.com
www.blackincbooks.com

National Library of Australia Cataloguing-in-Publication entry:
Uren, David, author.
Takeover : the buying and selling of Australia / David Uren.
9781863957540 (paperback)
9781925203103 (ebook)
Investments, Foreign–Social aspects. Investments, Foreign–Taxation–Australia.
Australia–Economic conditions.
332.673

Cover design by Peter Long
Text design by Tristan Main

CONTENTS

1 STRANGE BEDFELLOWS 1

Australia is uneasy about its dependence on foreign investment. Hostility is greatest on the extremes of the left and the right. While the centres of both Labor and the Coalition are more welcoming, they must each keep an eye on their factional flanks.

2 KEEPING OUT THE FOREIGNERS 17

A long history of protecting local business from foreign competition helps explain attitudes to foreign investment. Protectionism began with flour millers near Geelong in the 1850s and became the driver of economic policy in the early years of federation, when the forces of free trade were comprehensively defeated.

3 THE MONEY POWER 35

The bank crashes and depression of the 1890s shattered the dreams of a better world that had flourished in the previous decade and left a bitterness about the dominance of money power that has never really disappeared from the left.

4 MIDWIFE TO THE MOTOR INDUSTRY 53

As Labor was trying to nationalise the vilified banks, it was also nursing the Australian motor industry into existence, luring General Motors to fulfil what had been a 20-year dream.

5 HERE COME THE YANKS 62

High tariff protection made Australia an attractive market for US multinationals in the early post-war era. But their presence was not universally welcomed, with a backlash growing by the 1960s.

6 SYMBOLS FOR SALE 83

Efforts by the reviled US conglomerate IT&T to take over the company making the famous Chiko Roll in the early 1970s marked a turning point in policy towards foreign investment. Other foreign battles over brands followed.

7 MONEY FROM ROCKS 93

A sense that Australia was not getting its fair share for the sale of its natural resources has shaped attitudes towards first the American, then the Japanese and finally the Chinese investors in the resources sector. A resource tax has often been seen as the alternative to mandating Australian ownership.

8 EMBRACING GLOBALISATION 122

The 1980s gave voice to the forces of free trade for the first time since federation, as the Hawke government started rolling back the protectionist wall in a bid to modernise the Australian economy.

9 OUR LAND 143

While governments accepted greater openness to foreign investment from the 1980s onwards, strong resistance continues to foreign control of both agricultural land and residential housing.

10 THE DISAPPEARING CORPORATION 167

Companies are increasingly doing business in Australia without any significant physical presence. Companies don't need to invest if they can trade online, and they don't need to pay tax. The OECD is fighting a rear-guard action, but bitcoin may show the way to the eventual dematerialisation of the corporation.

11 CO-INVESTING IN CARS 184

The ultimately fruitless subsidies offered to the motor industry over 60 years contain lessons about using government incentives to attract foreign investment.

12 THE NATIONAL INTEREST 193

How does foreign investment affect national security and what other issues raise concerns about the national interest? Should popular opinion count?

13 POLITICAL VOICES 209

Foreign investment remains as hotly debated in parliament today as ever. Political leaders from the Greens, the Nationals, Labor and the Coalition have their say.

ACKNOWLEDGEMENTS 221

ENDNOTES 223

INDEX 235

1

STRANGE BEDFELLOWS

It was the day of the 1980 Queensland state election and tensions over foreign investment were running hot. "Queensland – beautiful one day, Japanese the next", ran a popular slogan. A call was put through to the *Morning Bulletin* newspaper in Rockhampton from someone purporting to be from the "Revolutionary Ring for the Liberation of Queensland". A bomb had just been set off at the Yeppoon tourist resort of wealthy Japanese developer Yohachiro Iwasaki and the caller claimed responsibility. No one was injured in the blast, but the damage to the project, which was still under construction, was extensive. The point had been made.

An unlikely coalition of environmentalists, fishermen and the Returned Services League (RSL) had been formed to oppose the project, which was the first major Japanese investment in Australia's tourist industry. The environmentalists were opposed to any development of untouched beach and bushland and were concerned that the leases abutted a national park. The fishermen feared that the development would disrupt their fishing grounds. The RSL had not forgiven the Japanese for the war and their Leagues Club, which was the biggest entertainment venue in Rockhampton, did not welcome the competition. All parties held dark suspicions that the development was the product of a dubious land deal with the then premier Joh Bjelke-Petersen.

It was a bit like an Agatha Christie novel – so many people had the motive and the means, but there was insufficient evidence to pin it on anyone. The RSL said they hated the project, but described the bombers as "ratbags". Labor deputy leader Tom Burns, implying that the Iwasaki was not above suspicion himself, described the developer as a "cunning old Japanese fraud". Two fishermen were ultimately tried over the attack but acquitted.

Over the next decade, Japanese honeymooners flocked to Yeppoon and other new resorts in Queensland, turning tourism into Australia's biggest single export industry by the end of the 1980s, overtaking wool. The numbers of Japanese visitors to Australia, most of whom went to Queensland, rose from 50,000 in 1980 to 250,000 by the end of the decade, with about a quarter coming either to have a western wedding or a honeymoon. Tourism minister in the Hawke government John Brown calculated that the average Japanese tourist earned as much income for Australia as 59 tonnes of exported iron ore.[1] Employment in the industry soared.

Yet the investment by Japanese businesses in expanding Australia's capacity to host this influx brought continued resentment. "The Japanese said after losing World War II that they would own Australia in 100 years. After only 43 years they are well on the way to doing just that", a letter writer to the *Courier Mail* said.[2] Popular groups opposing Japanese investment sprang up, including one calling itself "Heart of the Nation" in Surfers Paradise and "Australian Citizens Against Foreign Ownership" in Cairns. Some of the people involved were later instrumental in establishing Pauline Hanson's "One Nation" movement. The mainstream political parties also responded. Labor's Tom Burns sought the reintroduction of the wartime Aliens Act to prevent foreign ownership of land, while the National Party cabinet minister Don Lane declared elections would be lost unless the government "moves to control foreign ownership". On the left, academic Ted Wheelwright decried the investment of Japanese companies in all aspects of the tourism industry, from the duty free shops to the Lone Pine Koala Sanctuary. "Increasingly tourists from Japan fly here on their national airlines, and patronise hotels, department stores and souvenir purveyors owned by Japanese companies . . . The benefits of tourism are siphoned away from the locals to the foreign investors."[3]

The Japanese investors were ultimately successful, and a significant tourist industry was established in Australia. Although the wave of Japanese honeymooners eventually receded, it was followed by an even larger wave of tourists from China. The industry was supported by federal governments with dedicated ministers for 30 years, until the Abbott government discontinued the practice. The battles over foreign investment, however, have been repeated throughout Australia's history as the influence of foreign interests in the economy is contested.

Three forces – the protectionist right, the radical left and the free traders – have shaped Australia's approach to foreign investment. On the left, it is believed that large corporations are out to exploit their position in Australia, maximising their profits with no regard to the national interest. On the protectionist right, it is feared that better-capitalised foreign businesses will claim market share from local firms. The free traders are internationalists who believe maximising Australia's bonds with the global economy will be to the national benefit, and that protecting domestic interests can be left to market forces. These forces are deeply rooted in Australia's political history, stretching back to the 19th century, to differing conceptions of who we are and what our place is in the world.

Partisans on the left and the right of the Australian political spectrum find common ground on the issue of foreign investment to an extent unknown in any other economic policy issue. At one political extreme, the ultra-right-wing nationalist and anti-immigration Australia First Party declares it is "only under enslavement of ordinary workers that greedy multinationals can reap their massive profits",[4] using language indistinguishable from that of the left-wing Occupy movement, which rails against a government in the thrall of the richest global corporations, vowing to "fight against the corrosive power of major banks and multinational corporations over the democratic process".[5]

Closer to the political mainstream, former Greens leader Christine Milne nominated the Coalition's plan to curb foreign investment in the rural sector as one area she believed she could work cooperatively with a Coalition government led by Tony Abbott. "The Greens take a stronger position than the Coalition does, however, we would work with them to strengthen what is there already", she told the National Press Club ahead of the 2013 election.[6] The tensions over foreign investment were in full display during that campaign.

The policy of the Coalition had been strongly influenced by the National Party. At the Coalition's 2013 election launch, National Party leader Warren Truss struck a discordant note in the Coalition pitch to deregulate the economy, declaring that a Coalition government would "insist that Australia has the right to ensure investment proposals are not contrary to our national interest".[7] He said a Coalition government would expand the membership of the Foreign Investment Review Board (FIRB) to ensure farm interests were represented, while also lowering the threshold for investigation of foreign purchases of farmland and agribusinesses. It was the single-most important issue for the National Party in the election campaign.

Abbott was not entirely at ease with the policy, however, as became evident in a debate with Labor's Kevin Rudd at the Rooty Hill RSL Club in Western Sydney – a venue chosen to epitomise suburban parochialism. The two leaders were asked what each would do to control foreign investment in land. Abbott, defensive about the protectionist nature of his policy, conceded that in some circumstances, foreign investment in land could actually be good for Australia, saying "I think we've got to do what is in Australia's national interest".

Labor had previously been critical of the Coalition's plan, with its trade minister Craig Emerson claiming it would shut Australian farmers out of Asian markets. But Rudd saw an opportunity in Abbott's willingness to entertain the possibility that foreign investment might do some good. "I am a bit old fashioned on these questions and I'm not quite as free market as Tony on this stuff. I am a bit nervous, a bit anxious, frankly, about simply an open slather on this", he said. "I am looking very carefully at how this affects the overall balance of ownership in Australia."[8]

The National Party had been running hard on tightening the rules on foreign investment in the rural sector for years, with its Senate leader Barnaby Joyce setting the tone. "It would be better to knock down the Sydney Opera House to build a mine than to give up prime agricultural land", he said. "You can rebuild the Opera House, but once you destroy prime agricultural land, it's gone."[9]

Following the Coalition's 2013 victory, however, not everything went the National Party's way. Although it succeeded in getting the planned restrictions on foreign investment in the rural sector onto the official election manifesto, it did not get to keep its coveted trade portfolio. Ever since Prime Minister Robert Menzies appointed John McEwen as trade minister in 1956, the National Party (or its Country Party forbears) had held the trade ministry. National leader Warren Truss had been the last of three National Party trade ministers in the Howard government, and he expected to hold the position again. Abbott, however, had switched him to the shadow infrastructure portfolio in 2010, putting Liberal deputy Julie Bishop in charge of both foreign affairs and trade. Following the 2013 election victory, Abbott chose Liberal Andrew Robb to head a portfolio that, for the first time, included the promotion of foreign investment as an express responsibility alongside trade.

There is a deep divide in Australian rural politics, going back to the 19th century, between the large farming interests, represented by the graziers and pastoralists, and the small family farmers. The graziers have always pursued free trade, which benefited their export markets, while the small farmers, more dependent on the domestic market, organised politically to have their interests protected, ultimately forming the Country Party. The power of the Country Party reached its zenith under John McEwen who championed the cause of "protection all round", with manufacturers shielded by tariffs and farmers supported by subsidies and price guarantees for their produce. Andrew Robb, who had been executive director of the Cattle Council of Australia, reflected the other strand of Australian rural politics – the free trade interests of the large-scale producers. He was also one of the founders of the National Farmers' Federation in the late seventies, which pressed for dismantling of tariff protection and deregulation of industrial relations.

The NFF argued that high tariffs damaged the competitiveness of the economy. They generated an over-valued exchange rate, which harmed exporters and cossetted a lazy, inefficient manufacturing sector. Industries with the strongest tariff protection were those where central wage-fixing reigned supreme. With Andrew Robb as its executive director through the 1980s, the NFF became the voice for deregulating the farm sector, to the outrage of the National Party leadership.

As the first minister for investment as well as trade, Robb made it his mission to complete free trade agreements backed by an increasingly liberal treatment of investment:

> Since the First Fleet, Australia has been a country unashamedly reliant on foreign investment. It has helped build our infrastructure, grow our businesses and provide the quality of life and enviable standards of living Australians enjoy. As a big and sparsely populated continent with a thin domestic capital market, but great investment opportunities in front of us, our reliance continues today . . .
>
> As a new government in Australia, we have a clear message to global investors – we unambiguously welcome investment from abroad. We are open for business.[10]

The regulatory structure that vets foreign investment was established during the 1970s, at a time when the left and the protectionist right were both at the peak of their post-war strength. Now, in the first decades of the 21st century, the free traders are ascendant on the national stage as never before. In a carefully crafted speech in 2014, Labor's trade spokesperson Penny Wong committed her party to an open policy, backing the negotiation of regional free trade agreements and calling for a quadrupling of the threshold before foreign investments required government approval to more than $1 billion (as currently applies for several of Australia's free trade agreement partners, including the United States, Korea, Japan, China and New Zealand). Labor has staked an even more liberal position than that espoused by the Liberal's Andrew Robb. "For a country that thrives on investment, it makes no sense to impose unnecessary red tape, costs and barriers on investors looking to build businesses and create jobs in Australia", Wong said.[11] Just as the extremes of left and right converge on the issue of foreign investment, so too has the political centre.

Yet the centre is not stable. The open market stance of Andrew Robb is forever under threat from the protectionism of the National Party on his flank, while Labor's economic rationalists are exposed to undermining from the left. Wong's Labor left colleague Senator Doug Cameron doubts the merits of opening the borders. "History has shown that the benefits of so-called free trade agreements are massively exaggerated by governments and their economic advisers and the negative consequences are minimised and/or ignored."[12] On the left, there is a fear that Australia will be a loser from globalisation, as international businesses shift as many of their high-labour-cost operations as possible to developing countries. To the extent that Labor ignores these concerns, the Greens believe they are in a position to increase their vote. "Neither of the old parties are up to the challenges of globalisation and climate change", said former Greens leader Christine Milne.[13]

The fragility of the Coalition's commitment to the open borders espoused by Robb was apparent in the first months following its 2013 election victory, as Treasurer Joe Hockey considered a bid by the US grain handling business Archer Daniels Midland (ADM) for Australia's major grain company, GrainCorp. The GrainCorp board considered the bid represented good value for shareholders and would deliver benefits to growers. Chief executive Alison Watkins said ADM's larger size and global reach gave it better information on pricing and stronger customer relationships, saying "being part of a global corporation will be a positive for grain-growers".[14]

The National Party was vehemently opposed, reflecting the fear of wheat-growers that they would lose what influence they believed they had over the direction of GrainCorp if it were taken over by a global trading company. As Hockey considered the bid, deputy prime minister and National Party leader Warren Truss called for ADM's offer to be rejected. "They haven't been offering anything to Australian growers other than higher charges and potentially even an environment which would make agriculture in this country the captive of an overseas boardroom",[15] he said. Hockey was being lobbied just as aggressively by ADM. On Hockey's first visit to the United States, he was peppered in every meeting with questions about ADM, pressuring him to accept the bid. Hockey's ultimate decision to reject the bid included arguments about the impact on exports (discussed further in the next chapter), but he also acknowledged the resistance to the bid from the National Party and its regional constituents. "A further significant consideration was that this proposal has attracted a high level of concern from stakeholders and the broader community. I therefore judged that allowing it to proceed could risk undermining public support for the foreign investment regime and ongoing foreign investment more generally."[16] In other words, an unpopular foreign investment proposal could be rejected because it would make foreign investment in general unpopular.

Labor's commitment to the free flow of foreign investment in Australia was similarly challenged during the debate on the level of foreign investment in Qantas. The company was seeking to be freed from the limits on foreign investment that had been imposed on it at the time of its 1992 privatisation, arguing that it needed access to capital that only global markets could provide, to meet competition from the foreign-controlled Virgin Australia. Labor was prepared to drop the requirement that no single foreign airline could hold more than 35 per cent of Qantas, but it refused to give up the condition that Australian interests must own at least 51 per cent of the airline, or the requirements that two-thirds of directors were to be Australian, the headquarters were to be located in Australia and the majority of maintenance was to be conducted in Australia. Labor transport spokesman Anthony Albanese, from Labor's left, said the issue was "about who we are as Australians". The flying kangaroo was, he said, a source of national pride, delivering jobs and supporting Australian tourism.

"Qantas back our national teams – the Wallabies, the Australian cricket team. They do all of that because they are an Australian company." As a foreign owned company, the "flying kangaroo" would have no more meaning than the emblem of any other country, he said. "It is about Australian jobs; it is about the national interest."[17]

Such nationalism is rarely found without a taint of vested interest. Labor's stance on Qantas reflected pressure from the trade unions, which feared that a foreign owner would go further with cost-cutting measures, shifting jobs to lower-cost jurisdictions. "If the trend towards outsourcing and offshoring continues Australia will be left with virtual airlines – Australian shell companies that contract their core functions to third parties overseas. These companies are low cost, low care and high risk", a union submission to a Senate inquiry into the sale claimed.[18]

Australia is not alone in putting regulatory barriers in front of foreign investment; however, they are higher here than in most other parts of the developed world. The Paris-based Organisation for Economic Co-operation and Development (OECD) keeps track of the "restrictiveness" of national treatment of foreign investment. On the OECD's scoring of advanced countries, only New Zealand, Canada, Iceland and Korea have more restrictive foreign-investment policies than Australia. The European Union is often considered to be a regulatory minefield, but it is easier for international companies to invest in any of its member states than in Australia. Japan used to be more insular than Australia, but has recently opened its borders to foreign investment and, like the United States and the United Kingdom, is now more liberal than Australia in this regard. The regulatory barriers in New Zealand and Iceland reflect their insecurity as small economies, with fears their productive capacity will be swamped by foreign businesses, while Korea is in the process of deregulating and is acknowledged by the OECD to have achieved more progress in liberalisation than any other country over the last 15 years. Canada, which frets about economic domination by its much larger neighbour, is the only country with regulatory barriers parallel to Australia's.

Australia's need of foreign investment, however, is greater than Canada's. Unique among advanced countries, Australia has run a deficit in its trade and financial relations with the rest of the world – a current account deficit – throughout its 225-plus years of financial history. There has been the odd year or two when a surplus has been recorded, but never, as best can be deduced from historic records, a decade in the black.[19] Australia has achieved this extraordinary record because the opportunities for profitable investment have always been greater than domestic savings can finance. It is not that we're a nation of spendthrifts – over the last 50 years, only Japan, Switzerland and Norway, among developed countries, have achieved higher savings rates than Australia. The constant deficits have, instead, reflected the abundant investment opportunities, particularly in resources, but also across the economy from agriculture to manufacturing, tourism and finance.

These international deficits can either be covered by borrowing overseas or by foreign investment. At various points in Australia's history, it has been argued that borrowing is preferable to foreign investment, as it leaves Australians owning the underlying assets. If big profits are to be made from, for example, the development of resources, they will remain in the country. The downside is that debts must be serviced and repaid, even in the most difficult of global economic circumstances, whereas dividends are only returned to foreign shareholders when there are the profits to pay for them, and even then they are often reinvested. The capital that foreign companies bring into the country is for keeps, unlike debt, which must be repaid. Once the factory is built or the mine is dug, the foreign company can repatriate the profits, if there are some, but they can't take back the money they've spent. In practice, the deficits have been financed both by borrowing and investment, and foreign companies have become part of the warp and weft of the Australian economy. They are providing funeral services, bottling Coca-Cola, delivering parcels, generating electricity and making antibiotics. Historically, Australians have often resented the foreign takeover of local brands like Arnott's, Speedo and Foster's, but are happy enough buying from the large foreign companies, from Coca-Cola to Dior.

Against those who say our system of vetting foreign investment is too liberal, its defenders argue the case of economic necessity – Australia would be the poorer if it could not tap foreign savings to finance investment. Foreign investment has driven Australia's growth and prosperity, while the FIRB ensures that the national interest is taken into account.

Against those who say the system represents excessive regulation which leaves the nation poorer by deterring foreign investment, its defenders note that only a handful of foreign takeovers have been blocked in the last decade, while not many have had conditions imposed. The system puts the onus on the government to rule that an investment is against the national interest; an investing company does not have to prove it brings a net benefit, although when a bid is contested in the political domain – as was the case with GrainCorp – this makes little difference.

Australia attracts more foreign investment than can be explained by its share of the global economy, reflecting the abundant opportunities for investment, particularly in the resource sector. Australia accounts for roughly 2.1 per cent of global output, but over the six years to 2013 obtained 3.2 per cent of the world's foreign direct investment. With a more mature share market than most of the emerging world, Australia attracts an average of 5.6 per cent of the world's foreign takeovers by value.[20] But it is not easy to assess the counterfactual – would we get more foreign investment with less regulation, and how much really is deterred? The issue was well expressed in 1999 by the then Treasury secretary, Ted Evans:

> It is impossible to quantify the restrictiveness of foreign investment policy. Restrictiveness cannot be measured by the number of investment proposals rejected or even by the variations in the number of proposals received. The unmeasurable dimension is the value of investments that might have been received, but instead went to other countries or "stayed at home" without ever formally registering an interest in Australia as a destination.[21]

One stab at measuring the impact of foreign investment regulation looked at what happened to United States investment in Australia after the 2004 signing of the Australia–USA free trade agreement.[22] This raised the threshold before FIRB approval was required from $50 million to $800 million. The study found that there was $73 billion more investment in Australia between 2005 and 2010 than would otherwise have been predicted, after allowing for other factors. Certainly the Chinese government believed that the FIRB requirements were a barrier to investment, making equal treatment with the United States their principal request from a free trade agreement with Australia.

Supporters of the FIRB argue that it serves a political purpose: the public at large is satisfied that the government is in charge and will veto anything against the national interest, and therefore accepts the large flow of investment that the FIRB waves through. Public opinion polling consistently shows deep reservations about the benefit to Australia from foreign investment. The Lowy Institute's 2014 survey of public attitudes to foreign policy found that 43 per cent believed foreign investment was a critical threat to Australia's vital interests over the next decade. It was ranked ahead of China's emergence as a world power (41 per cent) or conflict on the Korean Peninsula (41 per cent) and only just behind climate change (46 per cent). The public is evenly divided about whether foreign companies ought to be allowed to invest in Australia's resource sector, while 60 per cent oppose investment in the agriculture sector or in ports and airports. Only 4 per cent support the government doing more to foster Chinese investment, while 56 per cent believe it is doing too much.[23]

Similar sentiments were tracked during the 1980s when Japanese investment was growing strongly. A survey conducted for the Japanese embassy in 1988 found that only 17 per cent of Australians thought the government should be fostering Japanese investment, while 36 per cent believed it should be doing more to discourage it. Hostility towards foreign investment has been detected in polls since the 1960s.[24] Opinion polls, though, say nothing about the strength with which views are held, or the public's comprehension of the broader economic implications of their opinions. In a set of questions about Chinese investment, the 2012 Lowy Poll found that 46 per cent agreed with the proposition that the government was allowing too much foreign investment from all countries, not just

China, while only 9 per cent disagreed. However a set of questions in the same survey about Australia's engagement with the Asian region recorded that 60 per cent believed the government should be doing more to foster Asian investment in Australia.[25] While the responses to opinion polls depend heavily upon how questions are framed, the accumulation of surveys shows a readily tapped concern.

In criticising the Coalition's plans to crack down on foreign investment in the agricultural sector after its 2013 election victory, Labor's Treasury spokesman Chris Bowen accused the Coalition of appealing to popular opinion. "Political parties have a choice; they can lead the debate on foreign investment or they can follow it. Tony Abbott's Liberal party has decided to follow it and Labor must lead it." Bowen argues that the big reforms of the 1990s, such as tariff cuts and financial deregulation, were opposed by the public at large, but that treasurer and later prime minister Paul Keating won the argument for reform both with his fellow politicians and the public.

Conservative commentator Tom Switzer has argued, on the basis of the opinion polls, that the gulf between "elite" opinion and the public at large is greater on foreign investment than on any other issue. "Not many political issues stir the emotions in the way that foreign ownership does. It is a subject that provokes deep, visceral feelings of possession, solidarity and national identity",[26] he says.

However, public attitudes do not simply reflect an uninformed xenophobia. There is a political debate on both right and left about the merits of foreign investment that both reflects and influences public views. Public opinion is built on the long histories that have shaped our political culture. Protectionism has been a powerful political current since the 1860s and was the dominant force shaping Australia's economic policy until the 1980s. The left's suspicion of global capital, or "money power", was borne in the bank crashes of the late 19th century and has shaped its attitude to global business ever since. Free trade has always been a minority stance. But it, too, has its place in Australia's history, from the early days of the settlement of New South Wales.

2

KEEPING OUT THE FOREIGNERS

Geelong is an industrial graveyard. The first Australian-assembled Model T Fords rolled out of the US multinational company's Geelong plant in 1925, but the last Ford Falcon will be built there in 2016 and the plant will close for good. International Harvester, which had built equipment for Victoria's farmers since 1938, closed in 1982, complaining that the tariff cuts of the Whitlam era had made the business unsustainable. Alcoa has closed its 51-year-old Point Henry aluminium refinery, which was no longer able to compete with Chinese suppliers. Dozens of other smaller manufacturers have quit operations in the town. Boral stopped making clinker cement, while the last major wool-combing operation, on which the town's original economy was based, shut its doors in 2003, with its plant and machinery shipped holus-bolus to a factory in the Chinese province of Shandong. Some of the businesses were foreign owned, others Australian, but all had set up operations in the town thinking it was possible to make a go of manufacturing in Australia, despite its small market and high wages, because of the protective tariff walls that kept foreign competition at bay.

Geelong was where the idea of building protective barriers against foreign competition first crystallised into a political movement. It began with Thomas Cosby Riddle, a classic 19th century entrepreneur. He landed in Melbourne from Ireland in 1842, setting up a general store with goods purchased from the ship he arrived on. Within two years he was also running Melbourne's first public baths on the banks of the Yarra, before moving to Geelong to take up a hotel licence.

He was soon making a name for himself at public meetings as an advocate for political reform, and was active in organisations such as the Geelong People's Association, the Geelong Loan Company, the Cooperative Bread Society and Bakery, the Law Reform Society and the Land Society. All were about encouraging participation by ordinary citizens in the affairs that concerned them. His view that people marginalised from affairs of the day should be encouraged to participate even found expression as he sought a piece of the action when gold discoveries set the colony alight. The Geelong correspondent of the *Argus* recorded in 1852, "Mr T.C. Riddle, of law-reform notoriety, has started a gold-digging company, in which he intends to allow a large number of *ladies* to have shares. What the gentleman's drift is, I cannot exactly ascertain ... I would recommend him to take a mangle or two up, and some scores of washing tubs".[1]

Through the 1850s, both Riddle's business and political involvements multiplied. There were fishing companies, artificial fertiliser manufacturing, sawmills, auctioneering, and wine and spirit sales. He took on the role as secretary of the Geelong Union Mill Company and, in 1856, built a four-storey wind- and steam-driven flour mill in Chilwell by the Barwon River. He became a member of the newly formed Geelong council in 1852. He was also arguing for reform of land holdings in the colony, railing against the colony's new constitution, which entrenched squatters' political power, trying to have the appointment of Geelong's first mayor ruled illegal and, crucially, building a case for government support of domestic industry.

While Riddle had been agitating on the issue of protection for local industry since the early 1850s, it became a broad political campaign from 1856 onwards. Inspired by Riddle, farmers from the Bellarine Peninsula (which includes Geelong) formed a "Farmers Cooperative and Protective Association" with the object of advancing "the protection of native industry". Riddle told the inaugural meeting that it was imperative that Victoria achieve self-sufficiency in basic food-stuffs such as wheat. "So long as this chief, this important duty of our government is neglected, so long must Victoria remain unsettled and her progress impeded instead of being advanced."[2] He argued that the problem was not fertility of soil, which the region possessed in abundance, but the high cost of labour resulting from the gold rush. This made it impossible for domestic flour millers to compete with imports. A ton of flour cost 30 pounds to produce in Australia, while it could be imported from England for 24 pounds. He argued that money spent on imports left the colony for good, whereas money spent at home could be endlessly circulated. He calculated that if Victoria depended on imports for its wheat supply, it would be sending 17.5 million pounds out of the colony over a ten-year period, leaving the colony destitute.

"By such a fearful drain of capital from our shores, it is unnecessary to declare not only will every mercantile interest, but the revenue itself must greatly diminish as the ability of the people to consume such goods as now pay duty will be reduced by the amount of capital sent out of the colony for flour, besides the immense loss sustained from the want of constant circulation of that sum."

He estimated that the loss was at least as large as the entire amount of capital in circulation by all the banks in Victoria. While free trade may be an appropriate policy for England, it was not necessarily the case for a new colony like Victoria trying to build its industry, he said.

Riddle's plea for protection drew a strong rebuttal. A letter under the name of "Colonist" to the *Geelong Advertiser* said Riddle wanted the public to pay more than fair value for their flour. "The money value of any commodity is the price for which it can be obtained, and every penny paid above the money value is a loss to the payer."[3] Far from imports draining money from the country, paying farmers a premium would generate huge public losses, the writer claimed.

Another letter writer, Charles John Dennis, a prosperous farmer, made the argument – familiar to modern debates over the protection of the car industry – that the jobs you are subsidising come from somewhere else. "Protection of native industry is a sophistry which Mr Riddle endeavours to support by resort to figures and assertions", Dennis wrote. To grow the wheat and mill the flour needed for self-sufficiency, "30,000 adults must be withdrawn from gold producing and other profitable occupations to feed the colony, and in that case it is clear that less gold (or other property exchanged for gold) will be produced in the colony. Mr Riddle labours under the supposition that the same labour can produce full quantities of both wheat and gold ... It would be equally desirable for private individuals to get their bread from a baker and yet retain the money to circulate among their friends, but narrow-minded bakers would probably object".[4]

Dennis also argued that if flour millers were granted tariff protection, "the tailor, the bootmaker, the smith, the wheelwright or any other trade [will] cry for a protective duty on their manufactures on the same grounds, viz that the wages of their men were so much higher than in any other countries that they could not compete with English or foreign production. A moderate protective duty will do no permanent good for the farmer, for profits will find their level in spite of all legislation".[5]

The *Argus* newspaper in Melbourne joined the attack, ridiculing Riddle's belief that different economic policies should prevail in a colony like Victoria to those of England. A field of ten acres in England was no different to a field of ten acres in Australia. "We hold the free trade doctrine to be quite unaffected by changes of climate or of latitude and longitude and that there are no circumstances about this new country which render it inapplicable here."[6]

This brought an intriguing response in an editorial from the *Geelong Advertiser*. The problem with the *Argus*, it said, was that its aim was to "exalt an English trading policy to the level of indisputable geometrical axioms". Free trade doctrines, however, had little in common with the sciences, and here the editorial quoted the leading social philosopher of the time, John Stuart Mill, who, notwithstanding his support for free trade, had argued that it was impossible to provide scientific proof of its benefit, since no two countries are alike in all respects except their approach to trade.

The *Geelong Advertiser* cited another speaker at the Bellarine meeting who said he paid colonial, not English, prices for his labour, his land, and the services he must buy in. "He contributes to the making of roads and is taxed for the privilege of using them and, after accepting all these colonial conditions, he is, because of free trade, forced into competition in the colonial market with foreign grown grain commodity paying nothing to the state."

The editor of the *Geelong Advertiser* was James Harrison, who was influenced by Riddle on protectionism and made it a life-long cause. As a flour miller, Riddle was clearly arguing self-interest; however, Harrison accepted that foreign competition was unfairly advantaged and took a broader perspective that protection would facilitate the development of a domestic industrial base. This was the birth of an Australian economic nationalism. Harrison (better known in Australian history as the inventor of refrigeration) took the cause of protecting local industry with him when, in the mid-1860s, he became the editor of the *Age*, whose proprietor David Syme had also latched on to the ideas of the farmers and flour millers of the Bellarine Peninsula.

By 1858, they were rallying support across the colony. "The Bellarine farmers are determined not to let grass grow under their feet", the *Argus* commented, as they established the Victorian Association for the Protection of Native Industry. "They find the principle of encouraging native industry by the imposition of import duties clearly laid down and acted upon by most of the enlightened communities of modern times."

A year later another group, the Tariff Reform League, was formed, with its first resolution declaring: "That in the opinion of this meeting the tariff of Victoria should be revised so as to place labour in every department in such a position that the working man shall not be thrown out of his usual employment by the cheap labour of countries with which he is at present brought into unequal competition."[7] As prophesied by Dennis in his letter to the *Geelong Advertiser*, the meeting pressed for duties to protect cabinet makers, harness makers, shoemakers and even monumental masons, who were being put out of business as the wealthy imported cheaper statues for their graves from the United States, where they had been manufactured using machine tools.

Protection in Victoria was associated with the forces of liberalism while free trade was the doctrine of the ruling establishment. The fight for protection was allied to efforts to upturn the privileges that squatters and merchants had obtained in the first 20 years of Victoria's settlement. Both endeavours were fiercely resisted by the upper house in the colonial parliament, the Legislative Council. To be a councillor required property holdings of at least 5000 pounds and only those with property greater than

500 pounds could vote. Positions were held for ten years.

The leader of the Legislative Council through the fights over tariffs in the 1860s was Charles Sladen, who had arrived in Victoria in the same year as Riddle, just seven years after the colony had been settled. He came from a British establishment family to take advantage of the tracts of land on offer in Victoria in the 1840s and took up 6000 acres of land that had been an Aboriginal reserve, at Birregurra, not far from Geelong. He developed the colony's premier Leicester sheep stud and also had a home in the Geelong district of Chilwell, in the same street as Riddle's flour mill. Trained as a lawyer at Cambridge, he was a deeply conservative Anglican, who did good works through the local benevolent society.

In the Council, Sladen argued that the only plausible argument for increasing taxation would be "in order that the wealthier classes should bear their fair share of the burdens of the country. The tariff would not accomplish that end, in fact it would be more burdensome to the working classes, would yield less and would cost more in collection than taxes currently in force". Sladen's refusal to allow the tariff to be 'tacked on' to an appropriations bill brought down the government, beginning what would become 15 years of constitutional crisis in Victoria as the Legislative Council, seen to represent the colonial establishment, resisted efforts of the Legislative Assembly to curb its power, with fights over tariffs, land reform and entitlements. Sladen briefly became the only member of the upper house to become premier, during one of a succession of political implosions when popularly elected governments fell after the Legislative Council blocked money bills to which land, legislative or tariff reform measures had been attached. It was an era which entrenched protectionism as a popular cause alongside democratic reform.

Following one of these crises in 1866, in which the Council had twice resisted money bills with tariff measures attached, there was an election at which the free trade party was annihilated. In the compromise that followed modest import duties were introduced. In the three decades that followed, tariffs rose substantially from 6 per cent of government revenue to 25 per cent.

Victorian protectionists claimed support from John Stuart Mill, who had, in his treatise "Principles of Political Economy", allowed that although free trade was preferable, protection may be defensible in a "new country" to allow an industry well suited to the country to get up and running. Mill was irritated that his words were being twisted to suit the cause of blanket protection, particularly in the United States.

"The passage has been used for a similar purpose in the Australian colonies, erroneously in my opinion, but certainly with more plausibility than can be the case in the United States, for Australia really is a new country whose capabilities for carrying on manufactures cannot yet be said to have been tested", he wrote in a letter published in the *Sydney Morning Herald*.[8]

Analysis of what drove the tariff increases for individual goods has found that the biggest tariffs were applied to goods with the most effective lobbyists. There was little sense that tariffs were nurturing the growth of the infant industries of the future.[9] Industries associated with the leading technology of the time – steam power – received less protection than the more labour-intensive sectors that were better organised politically.

However, protection was not simply about keeping out competitors. It also reflected a nationalist desire to create a new Anglo-Saxon society in the remote British colonies. The Victorian protectionists led the anti-Chinese campaigns in the 1870s and 1880s. At an anti-Chinese rally of 3000 people in the Melbourne Town Hall in 1880, the state's premier Graham Berry asked "what was the use of having protection if we allow the wholesale immigration of an inferior race, who would take the bread out of the mouths of our artisans".[10]

The debate in Victoria reversed the political logic of the very similar arguments that occurred in England through the first half of the 19th century over the "corn laws". Prohibitive duties on imported corn imposed in 1815 protected British landowners from competition, regardless of whether there was sufficient domestic wheat to feed the population. The high price of bread during times of crop failure in England was a source of widespread civil disturbance. Landowners, representing the old ruling order, were threatened by the rising class of new industrialists and the incipient force of a civil society represented by the Anti-Corn Law League. The landowners' control of parliament and the Conservative Party enabled them to maintain the Corn Laws through to 1846.

Free trade was an essentially libertarian philosophy. Adam Smith had argued that a nation, like an individual, wants to buy goods cheaply and sell dear. "But it will be most likely to buy cheap, when by the most perfect freedom of trade it encourages all nations to bring to it the goods which it has occasion to purchase; and, for the same reason, it will be most likely to sell dear, when its markets are thus filled with the greatest number of buyers."[11] Classical 19th century economist David Ricardo added to this his theory of comparative advantage, which argued that if one country can produce goods at a lower cost than another, both will still benefit from mutual trade. There was an internationalist aspect to the free trade movement. The *Sydney Morning Herald* editor John West argued that "humanity is broader than nationality and substantial progress is not to be sacrificed to what, after all, is but sentiment".[12] In an 1857 lecture on "the friendly intercourse among nations", West argued: "Commerce and freedom act upon each other with reflex benefits – whichever gains the field, both share the triumph. The spirit of superstition or jealous sovereignty are equally enemies to both."[13]

It was a cotton miller from Manchester, Richard Cobden, who pressed the argument for free trade in the British parliament, supported by a mass movement, the Anti-Corn Law League, eventually triumphing when the Conservatives split on the issue. As the *Age*'s David Syme observed, "The simple truth is that the Protectionist Party occupy in this country the same ground that the Free Traders do in Great Britain".[14] The protectionists in Victoria were seeking to end the privilege of the establishment, just as the free-traders were doing in the United Kingdom.

The Victorian debates over protection from foreign trade were not replicated across the border in New South Wales. As well as persuading the House of Commons of the virtue of free trade, Richard Cobden also helped frame the views of the dominant NSW political leader of the second half of the 1800s, Henry Parkes. Through the 1850s, Parkes edited a Sydney newspaper, the *Empire*, which drew on the experience of the Anti-Corn Law League to make the case for free trade in Australia. "The principles of the Manchester economists are to let industry have its own way. Never seek to bolster up a class of producers by preventing the produce of the industry of other nations from coming into competition with theirs but on the other hand do not by unjust or unequal laws tend to suppress them".[15] In 1861, Parkes went to England to promote emigration to NSW and sought out Cobden, making free trade his central concern on his return. On Cobden's death in 1865, Parkes eulogised: "The chief work of Richard Cobden was establishing that freedom of commerce which has done so much to advance England to her present position of unrivalled prosperity, and will contribute more to her glory hereafter than all her wars and victories."[16]

Through the middle of the 19th century, NSW went through a similar period of social agitation for land reform and universal male suffrage as Victoria. But where the Victorian campaign was run by the same groups calling for protectionism, in NSW this emerging civic movement was associated with calls to end transportation of convicts. The Australasian League against Transportation – hailed as Australia's first national political movement – drew directly on the organisational practices of England's successful Anti-Corn Law League.[17] Parkes was an advocate in these campaigns from the 1850s on.

Academic explanations for why Victoria and NSW set off in such different directions on trade policy have pointed to the greater resilience of the NSW government's budget, which, because of its size and because earlier limits had been placed on occupation by squatters, still benefited from large land-sales revenue. Tariff revenue was therefore less important. However, the divide also reflects the different political organisations and personalities in the two states. The cause of protection gained momentum in Victoria both from its association with the land and electoral franchise reform movements and its advocacy by people like Riddle, Harrison, Syme and the farmers of the Bellarine Peninsula. The economic argument for free trade was lost in Victoria, as the campaign for protection came to symbolise, as University of Melbourne historian Stuart Macintyre has written, "the legitimate aspirations of the bulk of the people for an outlet for energy and enterprise and to express their confidence in their ability to mould their own future. For the same reason, free trade was fatally compromised as a popular ideology by its association with wealth and privilege".[18] The tariff debate was used to break down the privilege of the Legislative Council in Victoria. In NSW, by contrast, the merchants sided with Parkes and the forces of political opening rather than with the old establishment of the pastoralists. NSW's nominated Legislative Council could be, and was, swayed to pass land reform.

On the Chinese question, Parkes took a pragmatic position, having lost his seat in 1877 because of the liberal stance he had taken on immigration. As rallies of over 50,000 people took place in the Domain protesting against the Chinese, Parkes proposed that there should be a ban on Chinese immigration altogether – in Victoria and South Australia, as well as in NSW. Free traders were in a difficult position. One, Saul Samuel, said there were "other considerations than those of free trade, and one important one was to preserve the British character of our community".[19]

With the two colonies heading in different directions on trade policy, there was interest on both sides of the Murray River in determining who was right. The two economies were similar in most other respects, and the situation appeared to establish the experimental conditions thought impossible by John Stuart Mill. Australia became a pioneer in the collation of economic statistics as both colonies sought to prove their case. By the time of federation, it was evident that neither had protection brought Victoria to its knees, nor free trade destroyed NSW's manufacturing industries. NSW overtook Victoria in the years following the gold rush; however, it has been argued this could have been due to its greater debt-financed spending on public works, lighter taxation and continued flow of revenue from land sales.[20]

In NSW, the cause of free trade was taken over from Henry Parkes in the 1890s by Geoge Reid, who led the Free Trade Party, winning NSW elections with a vow to abolish remaining tariffs and introduce direct taxation instead. Reid was influenced by the tax theories of the American reformer Henry George, who argued that exacting rent from the ownership of land was the root of all social inequality and that land taxation was the best way of raising revenue. Reid ridiculed the argument that tariffs were designed to encourage infant industries. "Believe me, these babies do not go on sucking for nothing. If the nourishment shows signs of falling off, they cry for 10 per cent more and they get it. They had not quite got hold of the maternal teat in New South Wales before I dragged them off, and, in consequence, there have been no wailings and lamentations there."[21]

In the first federal election in 1901, Reid won 28 seats, while Edmund Barton's Protectionist Party won 31 seats, and was able to govern with the support of Labor, which had 14 seats. Free traders and protectionists had both been involved in the framing of the constitution, but it reflected the views of the protectionists. It assumed that customs duties and excise would deliver the bulk of commonwealth revenue.

Barton was a fair-weather protectionist, having at various times, as a New South Welshman, sided with Henry Parkes; however, his attorney-general and successor as prime minister from 1903, Alfred Deakin, was the real thing. Deakin was a protégé of David Syme, having worked at the *Age* before entering politics. He argued the case for protection as maintaining wages against unfair foreign competition. Deakin and Syme made common cause for a much greater role for the state. Deakin promoted state investment in irrigation at Mildura, and legislation which appropriated all river waters for the Crown. He was an advocate for legislation setting maximum working hours and conditions for women and youths. "I do not deny the wisdom or necessity of employing the machinery of the state in order to cope with great injustices and injuries which at present beset our social system, provided no more efficient means of dealing with them can be found", he said.[22] In the first federal governments, Deakin's views on state intervention made him more attractive to Labor than the Free Trade Party, which advocated a minimalist role for the state.

Allied with putting up barriers to imports, the first protectionist governments also cemented the White Australia policy, Deakin introducing the Immigration Restriction Act with the declaration that "nothing less than the national manhood, the national character, and the national future that are at stake". Deakin acknowledged that there was not unanimity on the issue. "There are those who mock at the demand of a white Australia, and who point to what they consider our boundless opportunities for absorbing a far greater population than we at present possess, who dwell, if commercially minded, on the opportunities for business we are neglecting by failing to import the cheapest labour to develop portions of our continent which have not as yet been put to use." But he declared that "Unity of race is an absolute essential to the unity of Australia".[23]

Of the 21 speakers in the debate on what became known as the White Australia bill, only one, the free trader from Tasmania, Donald Cameron, was clearly opposed, arguing that the English had forced their way into China and it was only fair that the Chinese be allowed into Australia. Italians were as likely to work for cheap wages as the Chinese, he said, and coloured people were needed to develop the north of Australia, where the tropics were too hot for the whites. A white Australia, he said, was in any event an impossibility, given the substantial Aboriginal population and the large number of coloured people already in the country.[24]

In 1906, Deakin sought to cement a coalition with Labor with what he termed the "new protection". The great triumph of Australian manufacturing – the Sunshine Harvester – feared that its US rival, International Harvester, was planning to swamp its market with cut-price machines in an effort to drive it out of business. The pioneering harvesting company, established by entrepreneur Hugh Victor McKay in the 1880s, was making over 1000 machines a year and exporting to South Africa and Argentina. In his plea for tariff protection, McKay argued that International Harvester represented an "octopus trust" menacing his infant industry. When the *Argus* cast doubt on the threat to his business and suggested he should publish his profit figures, he replied, "Have you not read and published undoubted proof that a most determined effort is now being made by a confederation of American millionaires to take possession of this industry, and, if you are not assisting to add our profits to the 8 million pounds per year of John D Rockefeller and his confederates in this scheme, it would be comforting to the 3000 artisans engaged in this youthful Australian industry to know what course you would suggest to ensure success in our fight against the most avaricious confederation of trusts that has yet flaunted the pirate flag in Australia".[25]

Deakin was inclined to agree, but sought to impose the condition that companies receiving tariff protection should pay their employees fair wages. This would be effected by imposing an excise on Australian manufacturers of goods receiving tariff protection equal to the import duty. The excise would then be waived for those manufacturers offering a fair wage. McKay applied for a waiver from the excise. The judgment, by the president of the newly formed Conciliation and Arbitration Court, Henry Higgins, set a minimum wage, deemed to be sufficient for an unskilled worker to keep himself, his wife and three children in "a condition of frugal comfort estimated by current human standards". It was the first time wages had been set by the state, rather than by the employer. McKay, who vehemently opposed being told what he should pay his workers, then appealed against the constitutionality of the excise and won in the High Court. Despite his loss, Higgins preserved the notion of a fair and reasonable minimum wage in his judgements, and a state-determined minimum wage became an Australian institution. Importantly, Deakin had established the principle of a trade-off of tariffs for fair wages.

The volatile first decade of federation brought seven changes of prime minister as Labor, the Protectionists and the Free Traders vied for the numbers on the floor of parliament. This multi-party era came to an end with the historic "fusion" of the protectionist and free trade parties in 1909 to form a united front they called the Liberals, to hold back the rising tide of support for Labor. George Reid had sought to broaden the appeal of his party, styling it as the "Anti-Socialist Party" and casting his campaign against tariffs into the background. Deakin's linking of protection and state support for minimum wages had killed the political base for free trade and Reid could see this. Over the following decade, critics of protection "dwindled into a despised and detested sect suspected of nursing an anti-national heresy",[26] in the wonderful words of historian Keith Hancock. Protection was just too easy for Australians. Hancock's book *Australia*, published in 1930, identified tariff protection, the White Australia policy and the expansive role of the state – the legacy of Deakin – as the hallmarks of a society that was prepared to settle for the easy way out. "The fusion of parties safeguarded Deakin's work and made it ... the settled policy of the country."[27]

Australia was not alone in its pursuit of protection. Although the United Kingdom promoted the cause of free trade, many other similarly developed countries were using tariffs to protect their industries, most notably the United States. Australia, however, was more aggressive in protecting its industries than most. On manufactured goods, Australia collected tariff duties equivalent to 18 per cent of the value of all manufactured imports between 1875 and 1913.[28] In Denmark, France, Germany, Italy, Norway and Sweden, the average was less than 10 per cent, while in the United Kingdom it was 5 per cent. The US was the only country with higher tariffs, at around 25 per cent of imports. Australia's tariffs on agricultural goods were more in line with peer countries, with duties collected equating to 5 per cent of imports, while in the UK duties were almost at zero. Australia was unique in linking tariff protection with minimum wages – and also in barring non-white immigration. Australia was also unusual in the intensity of the debate that protectionists had with the free traders.[29]

Protectionism coexisted with an open stance on foreign investment throughout the first 70 years of federation – indeed it attracted manufacturing investment to towns like Geelong, from multinational companies that would otherwise have deemed the Australian market too small and too distant to be a base for exports.

But the latter half of the 19th century established a legitimate place for economic nationalism on the conservative side of politics – a nationalism that was prepared to promote local interest at the expense of foreign interest, and to argue the case against open borders. It has ebbed and flowed, but has never entirely left.

As noted in the previous chapter, this nationalism shaped Joe Hockey's early decision as treasurer to block the takeover of Australia's biggest grain handling company, GrainCorp, by the US-owned multinational Archer Daniels Midland. The National Party had opposed the deal, with its leader Warren Truss arguing that it would jeopardise Australia's control over its food supply and its destiny as a food-producing nation. Some wheat farmers, however, disagreed with the Nationals' position. One Mallee farmer, Chris Kelly, said the ADM takeover would bring Australian farmers much closer links to world markets because ADM had a presence in 140 different countries. "They're more than 100 years old, they're more than 10 times bigger than GrainCorp, so they're intimately well connected … that's the secret of 21st century trading. They can seamlessly move product."[30]

When Hockey ultimately blocked the takeover, part of his justification was the "infant industry" defence familiar to John Stuart

Mill and David Syme. The wheat industry had only been deregulated since 2008. Before that, there was a single seller of Australian wheat to world markets – the Australian Wheat Board – to which all farmers were required to sell and which had responsibility for handling the entire export crop. New competition was entering, with new infrastructure operators building facilities, but GrainCorp still handled 85 per cent of the crop from the eastern states.

"Given that the transition towards more robust competition continues and a more competitive network is still emerging, I consider that now is not the right time for a 100 per cent foreign acquisition of this key Australian business", Hockey said. The time would perhaps come when the Australian industry could cope with a global distributor entering the market, but not just yet. Almost 150 years after Thomas Riddle first mounted the argument that Australian flour milling should not be exposed to global competition and galvanised the wheat farmers in the Geelong district to mount a campaign for protection, the Australian government determined that the wheat industry was still not quite ready for the world.[31]

3

THE MONEY POWER

George Thornton, president of the trustees of the Savings Bank of NSW, went out onto the balcony overlooking a milling crowd of 3000 or so anxious customers packed into Sydney's narrow Barrack Street below and appealed for calm. A hush came over them as Thornton declared he had been the bank's president for over 20 years and could emphatically say the bank's funds were sufficient to meet all claims. The banks doors would remain open until 10pm to pay out all those who wanted their funds.

It was February 1892 and falling housing prices and building society failures were leading to widespread financial insecurity. The run was blamed on a speaker at the popular debating spot under the Queen Victoria Statue in Hyde Park two nights prior – an unemployed man, it was reported – who had claimed the bank was "going bung".[1] The run abated, but a few weeks later the Mercantile Bank of Australia in Melbourne failed.

Then, in April 1893, the Commercial Bank of Australia, the largest bank in the colony of Victoria, closed its doors. The Australian Joint Stock Bank in Sydney followed a few days later. Soon the crowds were massing outside the Savings Bank of NSW in Barrack Street again. A proclamation, signed by the colonial secretary

George Dibbs, was posted outside the bank declaring that depositors would be guaranteed and paid in full by the government. A bystander with a striking crop of red hair and a red beard took out a pencil and scrawled "Gone Bung!" across the notice and sauntered away.

"Plain clothes Senior-Constable Power and Sergeant Carberry were soon on his trail, and returned with him to the bank", reported the *Evening News*. "He then commenced addressing the crowd exclaiming, 'Beware men! Look after your money – the bank's going bung. You had better draw it or you won't get a cent.'"[2] The man was Arthur Desmond, editor of the newly established newspaper *Hard Cash*, which was devoted to exposing the misdeeds of the directors of failing banks and the public officials with whom they were in league. "Money rules the world", its masthead proclaimed. *Hard Cash* was associated with the Active Service Brigade, an anarchist group well to the left of the fledgling Labor Party.

Desmond was charged with damaging government property – the proclamation outside the bank, valued at threepence – and taken to the cells where he continued his harangue on the banking collapse at such volume that a doctor was called to attest to his sanity. He was fined 3 pounds and ordered to make threepence restitution for the damage or face two months' gaol. He insisted on paying the fine using bank notes issued by the Australian Joint Stock Bank, which had closed its doors a week previously. Three of his colleagues at *Hard Cash* did not get the option and were gaoled for libel, after an anonymous column alleged there was a secret tunnel under Barrack Street connecting the Savings Bank to a commercial bank opposite through which depositors' funds were being siphoned.

By the end of May 1893, 13 of Australia's 22 commercial banks had suspended operations and half of all bank deposits were frozen. With new lending suspended, house prices in Melbourne and Sydney plummeted by as much as 40 per cent. Investment, much of which had been associated with property construction, came to a standstill and unemployment soared to an estimated 30 per cent. The economic situation was made worse by the severe drought taking grip across the country, which was still overwhelmingly dependent upon rural exports. The economies of Victoria and NSW shrank by between 25 and 35 per cent.

Desmond had arrived in Sydney from New Zealand in 1892 with a reputation as a firebrand radical and a poet, and he soon fell in with the crowd at the left bookshop of William and Bertha McNamara in Castlereagh Street. It included Louisa Lawson, her son Henry, Billy Hughes and a 16-year-old Jack Lang (Lang and Henry Lawson married the McNamara's two daughters). Louisa had lost money with the Australian Joint Stock Bank, which almost sent her feminist journal *Dawn* under. Desmond blamed Jewish financiers in London, epitomised by the Rothschilds.

> The pirate bands of Panama, the plunderers of Peru,
> Ne'er pillaged richer kingdoms than the holy British Jew...
> The widow, starving slowly, and the child that feeds on crusts,
> Are melted down to dividends by vast Financial Trusts.[3]

It was a bitter time on the left of Australian politics as dreams of revolution and a better world, which had flourished through the 1880s, were trampled beneath the brutal force of a depression. The legacies from this period have shaped Australian politics ever since. The forces of labour came to realise that they could not defend their interests through industrial action alone and that engagement in the political process was needed. And the left carried forward an undying hatred of international finance that still colours its attitude to foreign investment. The strength of this conviction is explained by the magnitude of the loss that was suffered.

The world that came crashing down had been one in which working people had enjoyed the scent of power and influence for the first time. The colonial economies were growing rapidly, with a big influx of population, and demand for labour had been strong. Craft-based unions had been around since the 1840s, but in the 1880s, new unions of unskilled and semi-skilled workers were formed around groups such as the draymen, the coal lumpers and the waterside workers. They were bound by their class identification rather than their craft skills.

Deploying the industrial tools of strikes, pickets and boycotts, they forced closed shops onto reluctant employers. Labour historian Ray Markey estimates that above 20 per cent of the formal workforce in NSW and Victoria was unionised.[4]

Currents of radicalism had swept through Australia in the 1850s and 1860s. The Eureka rebellion in 1854 was born on the Victorian goldfields, but drew on English Chartism and the Irish emancipationists and a general dissatisfaction with what were seen as the colony's English overlords. By the 1880s, radicals were rallying behind what they believed to be the flag of socialism.

Revolution was in the air. In France, a revolutionary socialist movement had seized control of Paris in 1871 before being bloodily repressed, while revolutionaries had assassinated Russia's Tsar Alexander I in 1881. The threat of revolution was also felt in the United States, with four anarchists hanged in Chicago in 1887. Karl Marx's *Communist Manifesto* had been published in 1848 and translated into English two years later. Long before it was serialised in the *Worker* in 1893, its ideas began to percolate through the radical movement in Australia.

In 1888, as the rest of Australia indulged in centenary celebrations, a property boom and the afterglow of Queen Victoria's Golden Jubilee of the previous year, the *Bulletin* published a front-page editorial calling for revolution. The problem was not the need for a redistribution of wealth, said the editorial, but rather the corruption of an economic system driven by unfettered competition.

> There is no brotherhood between Capital and Labour, any more than there is a common interest between the vampire and the sleeping Indian ... We must abolish not a class but a system. The establishment of state cooperation, the nationalisation of land, the communisation of all the forces of production are the planks of the new platform ...
>
> The coming revolution is already here – the muffled trampling of its army can be distinguished amid the noises of the night, and in our streets, though faintly may be heard the rattle of side-arms and the reveille-rumblings of the drums proclaiming a new day-dawn for humanity ...[5]

Similar sentiments were to be found in all the radical papers of the day, including the *Boomerang*, the *Workman*, the *Tocsin* and the *Hummer*. In the midst of the shearers' strike in 1891, the *Worker* published Henry Lawson's poem, "Freedom on the Wallaby", the final two stanzas of which saw moves to have him tried for sedition.

> So we must fly a rebel flag,
> As others did before us,
> And we must sing a rebel song
> And join a rebel chorus.
> We'll make the tyrants feel the sting
> O'those they would throttle;
> They needn't say the fault is ours,
> If blood should stain the wattle.

The revolutionary rhetoric had little connection with the real world – there was no muffled trampling of revolutionary armies. It is somewhat reminiscent of the pamphlets that circulated on university campuses in the late 1960s and early 1970s. Many believed the revolution would simply "come" – a new ideal state would be achieved as the logic of socialism became apparent to all. The influential editor of the *Worker* newspaper in Brisbane, William Lane, was among those arguing that "every year, the number of men and women who hold socialism as a religion is growing". Eventually we would see "the Old Order melt away like a dream and the New Order replace it".[6]

Utopian idylls, styled as novels, popularised socialist thought. The most influential of these was Edward Bellamy's *Looking Backward: 2000-1887*, a best-seller which told the story of a man who had fallen asleep in 1887 and awoken in the year 2000 to a socialist utopia where all were equal, the state owned all industry and individualism was banished. In place of money, "credit cards" are distributed providing each with the same resource. Bellamy Clubs became popular political debating forums. The book was cited in the 1891 Royal Commission on Strikes as a cause of workers' "impertinence".[7]

The radicals embraced both the internationalism that had been an intrinsic part of the socialist movement since the formation of the International Workingmen's Association in London in 1864 and the nationalism that vilified outsiders, whether they were the ugly forces of capitalist oppression or the feared Chinese hordes. The Chinese and the Kanaks were villains alongside the "Fat Men", "Capitalists" and "Boodlers" in labour rhetoric of the 1880s.[8] At the same time, Australian workers raised the phenomenal sum of 36,000 pounds to support striking dockworkers in London in 1889.

With the big shearers' strikes of the early 1890s, there was a sense among some on each side that armed conflict was at hand. As boatloads of strike-breakers from the south approached in early 1891, the radical paper the *Australian Republican* declared: "The men are placed in this position – they must either have BREAD or BLOOD – WOOL or HEADS – and if the Government be not careful they will have BOTH . . . If your oppressors will not listen to reason, let them feel cold lead and steel: as they have starved you, so do you shoot them." The paper's editor, Frederick Vosper, was tried for sedition but acquitted. The *Worker* carried reports of the pastoralists' association making a bulk order of revolvers and ammunition. There were sporadic attacks at sheep stations, with crops and woolsheds burned. But with the economy slowing, strike funds giving out, non-union labour increasingly plentiful and the strike leadership thrown into gaol, the dispute petered out in a humiliating defeat for the shearers.

The labour mainstream, concluding that union militancy was too easily supressed by a hostile state, sought to build political representation through the newly formed Labor parties in the separate colonies. A commitment to socialism remained, with the Political Labour League Conference of 1896 calling for the "nationalisation of all coal, silver, copper and iron mines" and the following year's conference demanding "the nationalisation of land and the whole means of production, distribution and exchange".[9] Yet the shift of the labour movement into the political mainstream brought a pragmatic edge. It fought for conciliation and arbitration of industrial disputes, not the triumph of socialism over capitalism through revolution. By 1898, the socialist objective was described in Labor's platform as a 'statement of principle', rather than a practical goal.

While the labour movement adjusted to the new realities, its anger remained. Blame for the defeat of the striking shearers shifted from the squatters to the banks that supported them. "The squatter is just as much the slave of circumstances as the bush worker. It is notorious that the old-time squatter, who wasn't under the thumb of the banks, was a better man than the present squatter who is mortgaged to the eyebrows", said William Lane, before he headed off to Paraguay with the ambition of establishing the socialist utopia there that had evaded unionists in Australia.[10] The banks were seen as the cause of not only the defeat of the unions but also the disastrous state of the economy.

Whether the banks were locally owned or British, they were seen as part of an international capitalist conspiracy. The vilification of the banks – of "unearned wealth" or "ursury" – was at first an expression of the Marxist critique of capitalism that had inspired many in the labour movement to dream of a classless society where the state owned everything. Banks were readily identified as the primary forces of capitalism. But as those dreams of socialism faded, the attack on the forces of finance took on a life of its own.

The critique was not confined to the radicals. In his classic study of Labor's embrace of the idea that "money power" represents the real enemy of the working classes, historian Peter Love cites the Australian Workers' Union's leader, William Spence, declaring: "Usury is robbery and every private bank or finance agency are but legalised stealers of the people's labour results. The money power is the great power of the age and the sooner it is destroyed the better."[11] The anti-Semitic overtone of Arthur Desmond's attacks on the banks was widespread, with the *Sydney Worker*, for example, saying, "Jews are principally bankers, loan managers, peddlers and pawn brokers. They dress in purple and fine linen and they fare sumptuously every day – but who knows one of them that could not be spared? Did anyone ever see a Jew work?"[12]

Hard Cash lasted little more than a year, but in the mid 1890s, Desmond launched another paper, *The New Order*, with future prime minister Billy Hughes and future premier of NSW William

Holman, which painted "money power" as the root of all iniquity and poverty. "The greatest monopoly on earth is the monopoly of money for it includes all others. Cash reigns despotic and supreme. They who possess it possess land and power and slaves in countless millions. It buys all things – it rules all things. Kings are its bejewelled figureheads – presidents its executive officials and parliaments its committees of tax collectors",[13] the paper editorialised.

In place of Bellamy's utopia, the novel which caught the mood of the time was *Caesar's Column*, a dystopia by US writer Ignatius Donnelly, designed to highlight the evil of great wealth. It told a futurist story, set in 1988, in which the plutocrats own the government, the newspapers and the economy, while a struggling and starving proletariat is denied all opportunity for redress until violent revolution erupts. Donnelly established the United States Populist Party, which blamed a conspiracy of "money power" for the plight of farmers. It was a story that sold well in Australia at a time when banks were sending businesses broke, union leaders were being gaoled and unemployment was soaring.

The belief that a state-owned bank would serve the people was embedded in Labor's manifesto from the very beginning, with a vow that a Labor government would introduce a national bank, alongside a national system of irrigation and a department of labour. The party flirted with ideas of bank nationalisation in the early 1900s. In 1910, when the Labor government of Andrew Fisher achieved a majority in both houses, it legislated both for Treasury to assume all responsibility for issuing bank notes, which had previously been undertaken by the private banks, and for the establishment of the Commonwealth Bank. "The Money Power is being attacked in its vitalest spot", crowed the *Brisbane Worker*. With no private shareholders to milk its profits, the Commonwealth Bank would be able to loan out the public's deposits at the lowest possible rates. "No idler will profit by the gains of the Commonwealth Bank. The savings of workers and producers will not be made the means of exploiting other workers and producers, as is now the case in the private banks."[14]

In 1914, Labor luminary Frank Anstey wrote a book, *The Kingdom of Shylock*, asserting that British (and Jewish) financiers were the source of Australia's problems. "There is built up in secrecy and silence a Black Masonic Order of Plutocracy, cemented in all its parts by the lust of power and the cohesive power of plunder." In an updated version published in 1921, called *Money Power*, he asserted "The grip of British Capitalism upon Australia consists, not only of mortgages upon Australian Governments, not only on the overseas ownership of Australian resources, but upon the control of nearly one-third of the total depository power of the Australian people per medium of the British banks and British insurances trading within Australia".[15]

These views were deeply influential upon the Labor movement, and on John Curtin in particular, for whom Anstey was a mentor. They were given fresh impetus by the trauma of the 1930s depression. Through this period, Sir Otto Niemeyer was the avatar for all of Labor's darkest imaginings about the insidious forces of international capital. He was the emissary of the Bank of England, dispatched to review the Australian government's financial position in 1930, as it encountered difficulty in rolling over its debts as they fell due. It was akin to an International Monetary Fund (IMF) mission to a financially troubled nation today. As Niemeyer arrived with an entourage of two supporting economists and a secretary, his every move was tracked by an anxious media. What would he find? What would he say? It was said he spent his spare time writing Latin verse, and he was spotted in Adelaide reading Plato in Greek. The *Brisbane Courier* tried some doggerel of its own, reporting that:

Sir Otto came to Canb'ra
Unheralded, unsung,
The wealth of England at his back
To find if we went bung,
And how come it was we flung
Away the millions that were loaned;
And if the assets stood;
And if Australia's credit still
Was bad or fair or good.

There was little poetry in Niemeyer's findings. Australia's ability to deal with the crisis it faced was not helped by its refusal to confront it. "It is a serious problem, the principal solution of which is not rendered any easier by the natural optimism of the Australians. So long as it is generally believed in Australia that there is an unlimited market abroad for Australian goods and that something will turn up, it will be difficult to face the realities of the situation." Good prices for Australia's export commodities in the 1920s had blinded authorities to declining productivity. Protection had left Australia with an uncompetitive cost structure. "The standard of living in Australia has reached a point which is economically beyond the capacity of the country to bear without a considerable reduction of costs." Tariffs had to be lowered, costs had to be cut – meaning wage reductions – and Commonwealth and state budgets had to be brought back into balance. These, he said, were the facts. "I do not recite them in any way as a reproach, still less as a pleasure, but I believe they are the facts."[16] The *London Observer* suggested that Britain should smartly dispatch a royal tour to Australia as an antidote to Sir Otto's austerity, which compounded the misery of the depression.[17]

The left took the view that Australia's international debts were largely accumulated during the war, as Australian troops were fighting to defend England, which was now seeking its pound of flesh from those left alive. "International capital has sent its bailiff out to Australia to frighten us into paying the last fraction of interest, which it claimed was due to them. Capitalism had no conscience, men, women and children suffering made no appeal to it: interest was its first and final consideration",[18] the *Worker* recorded. The *Labor Daily* drew on the widespread misunderstanding that Niemeyer was Jewish, reporting, "The sublime impertinence of the lately-arrived emissary of Capitalism abroad – Sir Otto Niemeyer – who comes here to tell us that human misery – life even – is as nothing compared with the necessity of providing the London Jews with their fat rakes-off passes our understanding".[19]

In NSW, Labor opposition leader and Desmond's collaborator on *Hard Cash* Jack Lang campaigned in the 1930 election against Niemeyer's prescriptions. "Sir Otto Niemeyer says you are too well dressed. He says your food is too varied and must be cut out. To your little children, he says that their clothing is too good." Addressing farmers in Forbes, he said, "While he and his financiers will lend you nothing, they gave Russia tens and tens of millions to market its wheat".[20]

Lang promoted his plan for resolving the financial crisis, which was to lower interest payments to the bondholders from 5 to 3 per cent while seeking a two year moratorium on repayments to British bondholders. The Nationalist Premier Thomas Bavin warned that Lang's plan would lead to a run on the banks, and that the banks would never support his government; however, Lang triumphed at the 1930 election. Bavin's words proved prescient. Having survived two runs in the 1890s without closing its doors, the Government Savings Bank succumbed in April 1931. The bank had only three years earlier moved to grand headquarters with a pink granite façade in Sydney's Martin Place. Lang's name was engraved on the foundation stone, he having been treasurer when it was laid. Depositors understood that their bank, which invested their funds in government bonds, would be directly affected by Lang's plan to cut interest payments. The bank could not keep up with the withdrawals and the Commonwealth Bank refused to help. The bank remained closed for eight months, depriving depositors of cash at the depth of the depression. The Commonwealth government stepped in to ensure NSW's debts to British bondholders were paid in full, preventing default, but demanded Lang repay it, passing legislation to sequester the NSW government's funds from the banks. Lang responded by ordering that the entire public service operate purely on cash, which would be stored at a strong-room in Treasury, refusing to accept cheques and bypassing the banks. The state governor Sir Philip Game, a former British military officer, intervened and dismissed Lang from office.

Niemeyer's prescriptions also brought division within federal parliament. From the backbench Curtin argued that rather than cutting spending and public service wages as Niemeyer demanded, the Scullin Labor government should be obtaining funds from the Commonwealth Bank to cover the repayments due to British creditors. Cutting wages would generate deflation, reducing government tax revenues and increasing unemployment. However, the Commonwealth Bank, which was closely allied with Niemeyer and his prescriptions, had no intention of helping out. When Labor's Fisher had established the bank in 1911, he had given it an all-powerful governor to ensure it was beyond political interference; however, in 1924, the conservative government of Stanley Bruce gave it a board comprising the governor, the Treasury secretary and leading industrialists. The bank chairman, the Scottish-born Sir Robert Gibson, was a conservative businessman who took no instruction from government.

To Curtin, the Commonwealth Bank was a betrayal of the Labor principles that had established it. It had become a law unto itself run by "an interlocked group whose tentacles are fastened on to the largest of our insurance companies, the chief metal industries, the trustee agency institutions, and the principal mortgage and wholesale trading entities in the nation. The directorate of the Commonwealth Bank itself reflects this domination by the great captains of our economic life".[21] Curtin cited Henry Ford, drawing the contrast between the corrupting force of finance and the productive investment: "When money itself becomes an article of commerce to be bought and sold before real wealth can be moved or exchanged, the usurers and speculators are thereby permitted to lay a tax on production." Curtin's radical proposal was to float the currency, expand credit and bring the Commonwealth Bank under firm government control, giving it a monopoly over all Australia's international financial dealings.

As opposition leader in 1935, Curtin named Ben Chifley as Labor's representative on a royal commission into banking. Chifley's minority report argued the case for nationalisation of the banks, saying it was impossible for "any well ordered progress being made in the community under a system in which there are privately owned trading banks which have been established for the purpose of making a profit ... Banking differs from any other form of business because any action – good or bad – by a banking system affects almost every phase of national life. A banking policy should have one aim – service for the general good of the community".[22]

While defending the rights of the private banks, the majority report did call for the Commonwealth Bank to be given central banking powers under government control. The banks successfully resisted any change.

Through the 1930s and up to the beginning of the Second

World War, Curtin strongly opposed any foreign borrowing:

> The war will be won, not with money, but by men and the equipment provided for them. Only by physical things such as guns, munitions, man-power, primary production, secondary production – men or the fruits of man's labour – can this nation maintain its integrity. The money-changers cannot contribute anything other than convenience us by providing the medium whereby we can effect inter-changes between ourselves and other countries. Too long has the world worshipped at the temple of mammon. We ought not to fight this war in such a way as to enrich further the already rich when it is over.[23]

In 1947, with the war over, Curtin's successor Ben Chifley sought to make good the pledge to curb the forces of finance. After the banks resisted his efforts to give the Commonwealth Bank full central banking powers, he tabled a bill to nationalise the banks, setting off a conflict between government and business of a viciousness that would not be seen again for 60 years, when the Rudd Labor government attempted to impose a resource rent tax on the minerals industry.

The spectre of WWII still hung heavily and opposition leader Robert Menzies attacked the proposed nationalisation as the action of a Hitler, with Liberal electoral material using the swastika to illustrate the threat. In debate on the bill, Menzies declared: "The crowning point of European dictatorship was the invasion of the individual lives and affairs of individual citizens. The legislation which is now foreshadowed is the perfect example of that practice in Australia." Menzies said that giving the Commonwealth Bank a monopoly would give it absolute say over whether finance was granted to or withheld from a person or business.

"It is the very stuff of dictatorship. All the talk in the world about vested interests, as though the shareholders and directors of banks have a major concern in this matter, will not disguise these facts, and will not obscure the truth, namely, that what is being taken by the Government is not money but freedom."[24]

Chifley responded that Menzies had his history wrong. "The Leader of the Opposition said that the totalitarianism of Hitler and Mussolini started in the way that this Government is acting. I remind the honourable gentleman that, far from Hitler and Mussolini nationalising the banks, the fact is that the banks financed them. Nazism and fascism, with, their totalitarianism, were fostered by the banks." It was the banks who were the dictators, he said.

Labor backbencher Clyde Cameron (who would become minister for labour and immigration for Gough Whitlam in the 1970s) argued against compensating bank shareholders, describing them as "blood sucking parasites" and saying "We know that if it were not for the Australian Labor Party, the wage slaves of this country would still be under the heel of squatterdom and foreign-controlled financial institutions".[25] There was always the underlying suggestion that not only were the banks exploiting their control over money to bring misery to the population, but that they were also under the ultimate control of foreign interests.

The distinction was made between "financial" capital, which needed to be tightly controlled, and "productive" capital, which was seen to be responsible and did not require government direction. Chifley declared that he supported a mixed economy. As he put it, "nationalisation of hamburger stands or ice-cream shops or permanent wave establishments is not our business".[26]

Nationalisation of the banks, which seems an outrageously extreme proposition by today's standards, appeared less so in the wake of the centralised government control of the economy during wartime. A national security act enabled the Commonwealth to make laws in areas proscribed by the constitution. The Commonwealth could dictate profit margins, pay rates and prices and who was allowed to work where. There were strict limits on non-military-related employment while industrial action was proscribed, with strikers drafted into the army. Bank operations were tightly regulated, with requirements that they make available funds for investment by the Commonwealth Bank to prevent, as Curtin had put it, "the war financial policy of the government increasing the profits of the private banks and providing the basis for an unsound expansion of credit".[27]

Labor's bank nationalisation bill was rejected by the High Court and a year later by the Privy Council in London, to which the government had appealed. Chifley's attorney-general, "Doc" Evatt, represented the Commonwealth personally (in between presiding over the first general assembly of the United Nations, of which he was the first secretary) but lost to Garfield Barwick, who represented the banks. Four months later, in December 1949, Labor was heavily defeated in an election which consigned it to opposition for the next 23 years.

Labor never again attempted to take on so directly the forces of money power. Labor in government makes its accommodations with the banking sector and international capital and is genuine in its belief in open markets. But a deep suspicion of financial capital remains deeply imprinted on the party's soul.

Paul Keating is remembered as the treasurer who deregulated banking in Australia and, with the blurring of distance, is something of a hero to financiers. But Keating learned his Labor lore from Jack Lang, whom he sought out as a mentor at 18 years of age. In retirement, Lang had launched another weekly political newspaper, the

Century, which Keating helped him produce over an eight-year period. Keating, like Lang, believed banking was run by a conservative cabal and devised deregulation to break it open. "I sent these old boy networks to the grave – the thing they hated was competition – it was like a wooden stick to Dracula. Among those so-called free enterprise banks, so long as there was no real enterprise, they were happy. In those days, you'd have paid up members of the conservative parties running things."[28]

But Labor prime minister Kevin Rudd saw the era of financial deregulation over which Keating presided during the 1980s very differently. He saw it as the ultimate triumph of the forces of "neoliberalism", which he described as "that particular brand of free-market fundamentalism, extreme capitalism and excessive greed which became the economic orthodoxy of our time".[29] The global financial crisis that began in 2008 and which pitched the world into recession and an era of slow growth has fanned the embers of hostility within Labor towards the finance sector.

In an essay he wrote for the *Monthly* in 2009, while the crisis was still at its peak, Rudd called for a much stronger role for government in regulating financial markets and offsetting the inevitable inequalities resulting from market forces. The neo-liberal argument that markets were both rational and just had been exposed. "Neo-liberalism, and the free-market fundamentalism it has produced, has been revealed as little more than personal greed dressed up as an economic philosophy", he said. Arthur Desmond would have understood.

4

MIDWIFE TO THE MOTOR INDUSTRY

The shape of the motor industry might have been very different, had Robert Menzies not wanted Richard Casey out of the way and concluded that a posting as Australia's first ambassador to the United States seemed appropriately distant. Menzies had taken over the prime ministership in 1939 following the death of Joe Lyons and he saw Casey, the son of a distinguished Queensland squatter family with war-hero credentials from Gallipoli, as an unwelcome rival. The resulting by-election in Casey's seat of Corio, which included Geelong, marks a pivotal point in attitudes to foreign enterprise almost as significant as Thomas Riddle's arrival in the town a century earlier. Labor found itself advocating for the cause of the Ford Motor Company in Australia.

For the previous five years, Australian politics had been consumed by a desire for an all-Australian car. Australia was importing around 70,000 motor chassis and fully built cars a year, with a total fleet of around 500,000 vehicles. There was an active body-building and assembly industry. General Motors had taken a controlling interest in its licensed body builder Holden, which had operations in Woodville north of Adelaide, in 1931, saving it from liquidation in the depression, while Ford had established an assembly plant in

Geelong in 1925. There were also dozens of smaller players. In 1935, there were 22 manufacturers of internal combustion engines in Australia with a total output of 4,700 units. But what the country wanted was its own, all-Australian car. "The time has arrived – indeed it may be overdue – when this great industry should be established locally", the minister for trade treaty negotiations in the government of Joe Lyons, Henry Gullett, told parliament in 1936. "We have the market, we have the raw materials, we have engineering direction and artisans second to none in the world."[1] Other countries with relatively small markets such as Italy were succeeding, he said. The government introduced a bounty that would be paid on each Australian-made car, financed by tariffs on imports.

In the parliamentary debate, Labor leader John Curtin said the effect would be to stop the import of motor chassis from Canada – essentially from General Motors and Ford – in favour of fully built British cars, which were exempt from the tariffs. The two big US car-makers had established operations in Canada to gain access to the British empire market, and Labor was happy enough to treat them as fellow "dominion" car-makers. "The Canadians have treated us handsomely by reason of their trade investments in this country", Curtin told parliament, referring to their body-building operations in Geelong and Woodville, noting that the British vehicle manufacturers simply had sales networks in Australia.[2] Curtin's preference was that the government itself should start making vehicle engines, if other manufacturers were not interested. There were no takers for government's proposed bounty.

By 1939, as fears of a new war loomed, the government's view that Australia needed its own motor industry became more urgent. In May, a fortnight after taking the prime ministership, it emerged that Menzies had invited General Motors Holden representatives to Canberra for talks about the feasibility of manufacturing motor vehicles in Australia. Two weeks later he explained that no manufacturer would be offered a monopoly and that any vehicle must be "Australian in character and policy". The government had not decided whether that meant it should be wholly Australian owned, he said.

Through June to August, Menzies embarked on secret negotiations with the managing director of Australian Consolidated Industries (ACI), Bill Smith. The company was diversifying from its glass-making foundations, and Smith was prepared to give car-making a go, on the right terms. ACI was into steel fabrication, packaging, tools and engineering. Smith bought the dies to the body of the stylish American car, the Cord, which had gone out of business, thinking they would do for the new car. In December, with the country by then at war, Menzies introduced a new motor bounty bill, which provided that the government would award a manufacturer of car engines a bounty of 1.5 million pounds for the first 60,000 units produced. The government required that the manufacturer be two-thirds Australian owned and that it be equipped to make at least 8,000 engines a year. Labor supported the bill, with its deputy leader Frank Forde accusing General Motors Holden and Ford of having undermined the prospect of an Australian car industry. "We have been in the grip of huge vested interests", he said. He moved an unsuccessful amendment that required Australian ownership be raised to 75 per cent. On the Friday the bill was passed, the government invited Ford and General Motors Holden to make submissions, giving them until the Monday morning to respond.

Soon rumours began to swirl that the government was negotiating with ACI. It was suggested that, contrary to Menzies' statement to parliament, ACI was being offered a monopoly. Then it emerged that ACI's Bill Smith had, while dealing with trade and commerce minister John Lawson, offered him the lease on a racehorse. The horse, Billie, had never been particularly successful, but drew unwelcome attention to itself, its owner and its leasee by winning the Encourage Handicap at Randwick, with Lawson's prize money amounting to 300 pounds, roughly equivalent to the cost of a fine new car. It was in the midst of this heated political environment that Menzies appointed Casey to the US, bringing on the by-election in his seat of Corio. Labor leader John Curtin demanded to be shown the government's agreement with ACI, which revealed it would indeed be guaranteed a monopoly over the manufacture of cars and trucks in Australia for a period of five years, throwing doubt on the future of Ford, Geelong's biggest employer, as well as General Motors Holden in Adelaide.

Curtin threw himself into the by-election campaign. He said Lawson had concluded a deal with ACI while parliament was in recess and had used wartime national security powers to grant it a monopoly. Lawson's deal with ACI's Bill Smith on the racehorse in the midst of these negotiations was grossly improper. Labor declared that a victory for Menzies would mean the transfer of the bulk of the motor industry from Geelong and Adelaide to Sydney. Geelong's major industry was under threat. Labor suggested that Ford was not really a foreign firm, as the Geelong subsidiary came under the wing of Ford Canada and hence was from a fellow dominion. Labor advertisements in the *Geelong Advertiser* cited attacks on Ford from Menzies' attorney-general Billy Hughes, suggesting Ford was the enemy of the national interest. Hughes had said "nothing would serve Mr Ford and others better than the creating of conditions which would defeat Australian industry". Labor claimed that a third of the Geelong population gained their living either directly or indirectly from the motor industry. Menzies countered that Labor had backed the motor bounty plan and was being hypocritical in its claim to the Geelong electorate that "If you open us up you will find 'Ford' written on our hearts".[3] Menzies denied his motor industry plan would mean the death of Ford. Ford did not directly engage in the election campaign but did run a series of advertisements inviting all Geelong residents to an 'open day' at the Corio plant on the Saturday before the election.[4]

There were other big issues in the election campaign, which ended in a resounding defeat for Menzies. Among them was Curtin's demand that soldiers not be dispatched to the European war but reserved for the defence of Australia. But Menzies acknowledged that "the threat of unemployment, which was directed from every Labor platform to everyone at the Ford works and to those directly or indirectly dependent upon them, was tremendous".

Menzies was forced to bring the agreement with ACI to parliament. He pleaded that the deal was a wartime necessity. "Had Hitler not made motor cars he would never have made tanks", Menzies told parliament. "Tanks do not proceed of their own momentum; they must have some propulsive instrument. If we are to produce in Australia from our own resources tanks, armoured cars and motor transport to carry our armies over large distances – that point has a great significance for us in Australia – we must set about the business of making internal combustion engines."[5] However, Labor won the support of the Country Party for an amendment overturning the monopoly clause, leading ACI to walk away from the deal. Historian Mal Harrop says Labor's alliance with Ford and its by-election win came at a cost: "The end of any government attempt to establish a locally owned car manufacturing industry."

The effort to establish an Australian car industry had never really disappeared from the government's agenda following ACI's withdrawal of its proposal in 1941. Using war powers, the government forced manufacturers into much more sophisticated operations than had ever been attempted in Australia before, including production of a range of military aircraft. General Motors Holden found itself making aircraft engines. Curtin was looking beyond the war, establishing a ministry of post-war reconstruction in 1943, while a secondary industries commission was formed to direct the wartime manufacturers back to civilian use. In 1943 there was also a review of the requirements to establish a motor industry, which concluded that ACI would have difficulty, lacking industry knowledge. The commission recommended that government not become directly involved in manufacture, but should seek overseas assistance. Cabinet resolved that: "With regard to the establishment of new industries generally, Cabinet approved of the principle that where Australian capital is available the investment of foreign capital should not be permitted ... Where sufficient Australian capital is not available, control is not to be made too rigid with regard to foreign capital."[6]

By the end of the year the government had decided that an Australian-made vehicle should be a post-war priority. Curtin resolved there should be no monopoly and that there should be substantial Australian equity, although no decision was made on whether it should be majority Australian owned. The head of the Secondary Industries Commission, John Jensen, had worked closely with the long-time managing director of General Motors Holden, Lawrence Hartnett, in his position as head of munitions, and believed Hartnett was best placed to deliver a motor industry. In May 1944, General Motors was given permission to divert scarce staff from munitions work to drawing up plans for the post-war manufacture of motor vehicles. Companies were invited to submit proposals in October of that year, with General Motors the first to respond in early January 1945. Its bid was accepted before other companies even had the chance to respond. General Motors Holden said it would retain 40 per cent local equity through the minority shareholders in the old Holden body-building plant. It became plain that the American company would have an effective monopoly, despite Curtin's wishes. There would only be room for one local manufacturer.

General Motors' president Alfred Sloan had grave reservations about doing business with what he understood to be a socialist government, evidenced by its ownership of the railways and telephone network. Chifley, who had assumed the prime ministership following Curtin's death in 1945, had not eased Sloan's concerns by threatening that if no private enterprise took up the challenge of building a motor vehicle, the government would do so itself.

Sloan was persuaded by General Motors' Australian office that the company's investment would be secure, and in fact the investment was negligible, as the government agreed to arrange 3 million pounds to finance the development in the form of loans from the Commonwealth Bank and the Bank of Adelaide. By November 1948, the long wait for an Australian-made motor vehicle was over.

At the theatrette in the General Motors Holden plant in Melbourne's Fishermans Bend, a ten-piece orchestra quietly played a Brahms waltz as the silver curtains were drawn back to reveal an ivory-coloured FX Holden, mounted atop a slowly revolving stage. Applause rose from the crowd of 400 invited guests. Joan Ansett, the young second wife of airline millionaire Reg Ansett, sat in the driver's seat, while the wife of Liberal parliamentarian Bill Hutchinson looked on – this was a car that women could drive. Asked to pose next to the car for the afternoon papers, Chifley remarked, "She's a beauty!" as the flash-bulbs popped. In his speech, he reflected on the significance of the new industry, saying it was not only important for the national economy but also contributed to national security. The war had warned Australia of the need for an independent ability to manufacture transport vehicles at a time of crisis, Chifley said. Looking forward, he said Australia was on the threshold of "the most marvellous opportunities ever within the reach of a young country".[7]

In the shadows of the Second World War, the birth of the all-Australian car fostered hopes of a better future. "The soundness of the Australian economy is made apparent by the very great number of inquiries that we have received from overseas investors and from large companies that wish to establish new businesses or branches of their businesses here", Chifley told parliament.

"The confidence in Australia shown by the captains of industry completely refutes the statements made by some honourable members opposite or their supporters that because a Labor Government is in office, Australia does not offer great opportunities for industrial expansion and the investment of overseas capital", he said.

The economist and founding vice-chancellor of Australian National University Douglas Copland argued in 1951 that Labor needed to shake off its ancient fears of foreign debt. "We still live in fear of foreign borrowing. If capital equipment is available ... this country will be justified in borrowing lavishly if she cannot otherwise finance the purchase of it. The risks of borrowing are well covered by the prospective returns."[8] Chifley, however, backed the flow of foreign direct investment instead.

Money was coming into the country, with over 100 million pounds invested by companies from the United Kingdom, the USA and Sweden, among others. Chifley distinguished between foreign companies coming to Australia to build productive operations and what he termed "hot money", or speculative capital. "We encourage people to bring their money here for productive purposes, but 'hot' money will not be encouraged and will become 'cold' immediately on arrival, and 'cold' money may not be re-transferred without the approval of the Government."

Chifley said in 1949 that more than 200 overseas companies were investigating the possibility of establishing operations in Australia. Some had formed joint ventures with Australian-owned businesses while others had established direct subsidiaries. "All these and many other companies have added greatly to the stature of Australian manufactures and have introduced into this country the most up-to-date methods of production and technical know-how", Chifley said. "In many cases they are producing goods not previously made here."[9]

Labor remained vehemently opposed to what it saw as the malign influence of financial capital, but Chifley welcomed foreign investment in manufacturing with open arms, telling the 1949 NSW Labor state conference:

"I do not think that even the Australian people realize the enormous expansion that is taking place in secondary industries ... nor are they able to contemplate the confidence and faith which not only producers and manufacturers of this country but of other countries have in the potentialities of this country. That is true of American industrialists who want to bring factories or branches here."[10]

5

HERE COME THE YANKS

"Oversexed, overpaid and over here." John Curtin's historic pivot from the United Kingdom to the United States on New Years' day of 1942, at Australia's darkest hour, brought waves of US troops, aid and investment to our shores, not all of it appreciated. "Australia looks to America, free of any pangs as to our traditional links or kinship with the United Kingdom", Curtin had written in his New Year's message. At the peak there were as many as 250,000 Americans stationed in Australia, with up to a million US troops having passed through.

With Australian troops placed under the command of US General Douglas MacArthur, the Australian economy was swept into the task of supplying the US war machine in the Pacific. The US Lend-Lease program delivered the latest US plant and equipment to upgrade Australia's manufacturing capability for delivering everything from bomber aircraft to radios, steel, ships, clothing and tinned chilli con carne. Production of canned vegetables went from 4000 tons at the beginning of the war to 60,000 tons by the end.

Australia's trade with the US soared, with imports rising from 20 million pounds to 104 million pounds by 1944, about double the size of imports from the UK, while Australia's exports to the US had risen by a modest 20 per cent to 30 million pounds.

The relationship did not always run smoothly. The American military had little time for the unions who controlled the docks, there were disputes over who had legal authority over US troops in Australia, and Australian businesses competing with US imports were excluded from Lend-Lease assistance.

At the end of the war, a deal was cut under which Australia would pay the United States $27 million (about 9 million pounds) for the Lend-Lease equipment it was leaving behind. The war left Australia with a much larger and more sophisticated manufacturing base than it had five years before, and it also deepened links between Australia and the United States.

That the demobilisation of millions of soldiers around the world did not lead to the expected recession in the immediate post-war years, as had occurred following the First World War and the major wars throughout history, was in large part due to the discovery by US business of the mass consumer market. Tinned food and packaged soap powders, nylon stockings, vacuum cleaners sold by travelling salesmen, steam irons and, with the spread of hire-purchase, refrigerators, all came within the reach of the broad population of the industrialised world. The motor vehicle, which had been the preserve of the affluent through the pre-war years, was soon ferrying the middle-classes to their newly built suburbs. Linked to the mass market by the magic of advertising, consumer manufacturing enterprises drove global economic growth.

Major manufacturers saw sales opportunities beyond their home markets. The desire to control distribution and marketing required a local presence, while tariff protection, foreign exchange controls and other import barriers made local manufacturing profitable, even in sub-scale markets. Through the 1950s, US investment abroad rose at an average annual rate of 11 per cent a year, rising from $11.7 billion to $31.9 billion by the end of the decade. US investment was rising everywhere, but it was growing faster in Australia than almost anywhere else. By 1962, only Canada, the United Kingdom, Venezuela and West Germany attracted more US investment than Australia.[1] "Australia is the promised land", said Gillette Company of America chief executive Boon Goss. "Its stable economy, its sound political atmosphere and its people add up to an excellent guarantee for the future."[2]

US business had played a role in Australian manufacturing throughout the 20th century – Kodak started making film in Australia in 1908 and Kellogg's was selling packaged breakfast cereal from 1925, around the same time Ford set up in Geelong, while Coca-Cola and Heinz both arrived in the 1930s. But investment from the United States soared from the late forties onwards. From 1948 to 1952, the annual inflow of foreign direct investment in Australia rose from 38 million pounds to 86 million pounds, with the US share rising from 10 per cent to 33 per cent.

A survey of executives working with US-owned businesses in Australia by a young academic economist, Don Brash (who went on to become governor of the Bank of New Zealand), found that 86 per cent of firms counted the expected growth of the Australian market as one of their top-three reasons for investing, while 72 per cent cited tariff barriers and import restrictions.[3]

Australia's rapid population growth was both a key attraction for foreign business and a reason for Australia to welcome the influx of foreign investment. The shadow of war hung heavily over the country, which embarked on a huge immigration program. In a speech to parliament four days before the first atomic bomb dropped on Hiroshima, Chifley's minister for information and immigration, Arthur Calwell, said: "If Australians have learned one lesson from the Pacific war now moving to a successful conclusion, it is surely that we cannot continue to hold our island continent for ourselves and our descendants unless we greatly increase our numbers."[4] By 1950, annual immigration numbers reached 250,000 and Australia's population growth rate had doubled to 3.4 per cent. The official target, never reached, was 4 per cent growth. To employ and house such an expanded population, foreign capital was needed, whether through foreign borrowing or foreign investment.

The Menzies government, which gained office in 1949, continued Chifley's welcome of foreign investment within the constraints of an economy that had not entirely thrown off its wartime controls. A Treasury paper setting out policy on foreign investment in 1953 said growth in consumer manufacturing was outstripping the capacity of Australia's basic industries of coal, power and steel. An expected build-up in military spending would further increase the demand on these basic industries, so permission to set up operations in non-essential areas would be curbed unless they contributed to "a more balanced economy". "Subject to these general limitations, the participation of overseas capital in the development of industrial enterprises in Australia is welcomed." Investors, the paper said, would have unfettered rights to repatriate dividends, although not their capital.[5]

Political attitudes towards the wave of foreign, and increasingly American, investment were shaped by the sharpening of political division both across the world and in Australia. By 1950, Australian soldiers were again being mobilised to fight in Korea, while the threat that a cold war could go nuclear brought a paranoia to politics. While the United States and its corporations marked one pole of the new world, the rapidly rising power of the Soviet Union was the other. The depths of Stalin's atrocities were not yet known, and the miracle of Soviet economic growth rates in excess of 10 per cent a year seemed to confirm that the socialist path was a viable alternative to capitalism. The efforts by the Menzies government in 1950 to ban the Communist Party exposed deep splits within Labor between fellow travellers on the party's left and the Catholic right, which shared the conservatives' fears of the godless communists.

Just as it is hard, from the vantage point of the early 21st century, to imagine the policy environment in which a Labor government thought the answer to an expanding money supply was to nationalise the banks, it is also hard to fathom the debate in 1950 over whether the perfidious communists or the excessive profits of ruthless capital were primarily to blame for inflation, which was soaring at rates of around 20 per cent. It was precisely that debate, however, which shaped attitudes towards foreign investment over the coming decade.

Richard Casey, back in parliament and Menzies' minister for national development, said communists were trying to destroy Australia from within, with inflation as their ally. "Just as there is no easy method of guarding against the atom bomb, so there is no painless remedy against inflation", he said.[6] Moscow, he claimed, had timed its drive against the world's democracies to correspond with the inflationary trend.

In parliament, Chifley, as opposition leader, tried to separate the two issues, opposing Menzies' bill to outlaw the Communist Party while pressing for the reintroduction of wartime price controls. Labor politicians attacked what they termed "excessive" profits of businesses such as Carreras, the company behind the popular Craven A cigarettes, the Colonial Sugar Refinery and the regional trading business Burns Philp as well as General Motors and Ford. Don Brash's survey of American companies in Australia found that relatively few came here believing they would make super-profits, but it was an article of faith on the left of the labour movement that this was what the multinationals were all about.

Menzies was under pressure to deliver a policy response to the rising cost of living, but his Country Party treasurer, Artie Fadden, vehemently opposed the revaluation of the Australian currency, which economists thought was needed to gain control over inflation. Instead, Menzies announced a 15-point package of measures. It included a heavy tax on wool and the reintroduction of wartime controls on companies' ability to raise funds. The package contained a commitment to "set about destroying the influence of communists in key industries", while it also included an "excess profits tax". "As … there are certain businesses in which the acute scarcity of the commodity sold enables the sellers to obtain extravagant profits, we propose to present to parliament a bill to impose an excess profits tax. This is a novelty in time of peace", Menzies said.[7] He sought to both neutralise Labor's attack on profiteering and the high cost of living while also tying the party to the communist bogey, claiming its opposition to the abolition of the Communist Party was obstructing "one very important anti-inflationary measure".[8]

It was a message that resonated not only among the Coalition's traditional supporters but also on the right of the Labor Party, which would, in due course, split over the cause of anti-communism. A speech by one of the future members of the Democratic Labor Party, William Bourke, proclaimed, "We have the evil of monopolies on the one hand, and on the other hand we have an evil that is closely associated with monopolies – the twin evil of communism. There is no doubt that the policy of the leaders of the Communist party in this country has been to sabotage industry and production so as to force up prices and to increase the inflationary spiral so that the standards of living of the workers will be depressed to a point at which the revolutionary situation that the Communists aim at will be reached".[9]

The Catholic right of the Labor Party retained the "money power" critique of international capitalism from Labor's roots. In 1949, the conservative Catholic ideologue of the era, B.A. Santamaria, had penned a paper called "Socialisation", which, while rejecting total nationalisation of the economy under socialism, endorsed government ownership of monopolies, like the utilities, and an interventionist approach to economic management.

Menzies never enacted his promised excess profits tax, but his acceptance of the notion of profiteering in the 1950 inflation debate helped to cement its place on the political agenda. The flood of foreign investment, which Chifley had welcomed in the late forties, soon became the focus of community suspicion. Foreign companies, it was said, were exploiting Australia's liberal attitude to foreign investment and reaping usurious gains.

Labor's internal tensions over foreign investment were laid bare when, in 1953, parliament was asked to vote on a tax agreement with the United States which would stop the profits of US companies' Australian operations being taxed both in Australia and the United States.[10] Labor leader "Doc" Evatt favoured the deal, which mirrored the one his predecessor Ben Chifley had concluded with Britain, saying he wanted to foster the closer relationship between Australia and the United States. "I think we want to keep steadfastly in mind, first of all, the development of our industry and secondly, the absolute need of investment in Australia from overseas." Frank Crean – a backbencher at the time but one of the few on the Labor side with an economics degree – also spoke in favour of the agreement, though he also said foreign investment was resulting in excessive imports of consumer goods and harming the balance of payments. In general, he thought US investment would be better directed to Malaya, Burma and Indonesia where there was as yet no secondary industry. Another on Labor's right, South Australian

Albert Thompson, cited the national security imperative of population growth. "If we are sincere in our belief that Australia must increase its population and in our desire to keep Australia as a British community, we must expand our industries."

The Labor left, however, was vehemently opposed and did not mind contradicting its leader. The left's parliamentary leader, the Member for East Sydney, Eddie Ward, argued that foreign investment was based on exploitation. "I think that we will live to regret the day when we decided to encourage the domination of this country by foreign capital." Overseas industrialists did not have the same inhibitions about mixed races as Australians. "They would be willing to flood Australia with cheap Asiatic or coloured labour in order to break down Australian industrial conditions." Clyde Cameron focused on General Motors, which he claimed was making pre-tax profits larger than its wages bill. He attacked the company's introduction of 'time and motion' methods into Australian manufacturing. "Russian workers might put up with it, but free workers will not stand for a boss supervising their every movement, timing it with a stop-watch, and calculating to the exact second the time that a man takes to unscrew a nut from a bolt."

Evatt's successor, Arthur Calwell, supported the double-tax bill, saying he "would rather bring British and American industries to Australia than borrow money from Great Britain and the United States of America". He said the "know-how" brought by foreign investment bolstered Australia's security. "Only 300 miles from our shores there is an Indonesian Republic with a Premier whose cabinet is largely Communist, and if we fail to develop this country while we have the opportunity to do so, our plight will be even worse than it was when World War II broke out." He said, however, that British and American companies should stop demanding 100 per cent ownership of operations in Australia. "I suggest that

Australian citizens should be allowed to buy an equity in companies that operate in this country."

The annual profit report from General Motors Holden became a touchstone for discontent about US investment in Australia in general. Profits from its Australian operations were larger than those of any Australian company, including BHP, while travellers overseas knew that the price of a Holden car was as much as double the equivalent in the United States. In late 1959, the company decided to put an end to the controversy by buying out the remaining Australian shareholders in General Motors Holden. As a wholly owned subsidiary, it would not be required to report its profit.

Calwell declared that "General Motors Corporation is taking a contemptuous attitude towards Australian resentment against the concept of this country as a land to be exploited by American tycoons." He said the "giant foreign corporation" was "pillaging" Australia and the sooner it was required to sell down to a 49 per cent shareholding the better. "Australia is a free and independent nation within the British Commonwealth. We have no intention of becoming a satellite of any dollar imperialism."[11]

The Menzies government remained steadfastly supportive of foreign investment. Menzies' treasurer from 1958, Harold Holt, rejected suggestions that foreign companies were profiteering. "It is a matter for satisfaction that overseas interests are not only prepared to make an initial investment in Australia but also to consolidate and enlarge their investment here."[12] The impact of repatriation of profits by multinationals on the Australian economy "should not be exaggerated", he said.

The Commonwealth did, however, put pressure on state governments to amend reporting requirements so that the subsidiaries of wholly owned foreign companies would have to report their profits. There was disquiet within the ruling coalition about the level of foreign investment. As early as 1951, John Gorton, who later as prime minister would shift the policy on foreign investment, was voicing worries.

Conservative hackles were raised by the British Mirror newspaper group buying out the *Argus* newspaper in Melbourne and gaining control of the Macquarie Broadcasting Network, including a series of radio stations in both Melbourne and Sydney. In England, the *Daily Mirror* stood out as a tabloid supporting the British Labour Party. Australian Liberal Party senators darkly suggested that the chairman of the group, Harry Bartholomew, was Jewish, and that other foreign names on the board of directors suggested it was not really British at all but was controlled from "the Levant". Backbench senator John Gorton proposed that no foreigner should be allowed a controlling influence in a radio station. "In practically every house there is a radio set, which, all day long, disseminates news, views and entertainment", he said. "In other countries, in less happy circumstances, public opinion has been moulded, without the listeners really knowing that their opinions have been moulded."[13] Backing the motion, which was passed by the Senate, other Coalition senators declared that it was the government's duty to ensure that both the Australian economy and Australian culture was protected against the intrusion of foreign capital. In the mid-fifties, the sentiments of the Senate motion were translated into law.

By the late 1950s, the leader of the Country Party and deputy prime minister John McEwen was speaking out on foreign investment. McEwen was a complex figure. He had long experience in parliament, having been a minister in the pre-war Lyons and Menzies governments. He was both an internationalist and a protectionist. He chose the outstanding economist John Crawford to head the trade department and together they worked to break Australia's trade relations free from what was an effective bondage to Britain, renegotiating the 1932 deal that had given British imports privileged access over all competitors. Over the objections of many of his cabinet colleagues and the bitterness of many war veterans, McEwen pushed through a trade agreement with Japan in 1957, arguing both that Australian primary exporters stood to benefit and that it was in the interests of peace that Japan be integrated into the trading community. Yet McEwen was also persuaded that Australia needed its own manufacturing sector and that it needed protection. In his biography of McEwen, Peter Golding says he understood the economic argument that Australia's primary producers would be better off if manufacturers were not protected but thought that without a manufacturing sector, Australia could only support a small workforce and a population of 5 million. National security demanded a larger population and a protected manufacturing industry. "McEwenism" came to mean "protection all round", with manufacturers accorded tariff barriers while farmers benefitted from price supports and other subsidies. By the end of the 1950s, McEwen became convinced that foreign investment – in particular the takeover of Australian-owned concerns – was weakening our economic base. In 1960, he told the Australian American Association, "We want U.S. business here with all its magnificent skills of management at all levels. But we don't want to be taken over. We will not be taken over".[14] McEwen argued "It is not good enough for this country to live by selling a bit of its heritage every year. We do not want to see Australia have its industries unduly owned in foreign hands".[15] Over the next decade, as McEwen's public expressions of these views became more strident, Labor zeroed in on the split within the government. Calwell attacked McEwen for acknowledging the dangers posed by foreign investment but failing to do anything about it.

While Menzies backed his treasurer, Harold Holt, against McEwen on the free flow of foreign investment, he was not deaf to the concerns that were starting to be expressed by domestic business. Hostile takeovers were a particular worry. In the lead-up to the closely fought 1961 election, there was a share-raid on the mining group BH South, with Japanese investors apparently involved. Menzies told a Labor backbencher that "the rumour to which he refers has reached the Government's ears. That matter is under very close examination".[16] Within four days, the offer had been withdrawn, with Calwell darkly suggesting that Menzies had intervened for fear of it becoming an election issue. Calwell vowed that Labor would regulate to bar foreign takeovers. "The control of industry in this country must rest in the hands of Australian citizens, otherwise we are only wood and water joeys for overseas investors, whose only concern is to exploit us."[17]

By the early 1960s, the concerns expressed most volubly by Labor were starting to be shared among the Australian business elite. Academic Christopher Pokarier notes that among the voices calling for legislated Australian equity requirements were prominent stockbrokers Staniforth Ricketson and Ian Potter, along with AMP chairman Gordon Crane. One of the pioneers of investment banking, Sir John Marks, called for foreign investment in Australian companies to be restricted to passive investments in the share market. The AMP's chief economist, Harold Bell, argued that the fear that foreign ownership and control of Australian industry was too concentrated was becoming chronic and, unless well handled, risked damaging both foreign interests and the Australian economy. He suggested that US business was being short-sighted in its demand for 100 per cent ownership, and made pointed reference to the disaster that had befallen US business following the Cuban revolution the previous year.

The Victorian Chamber of Manufacturers started agitating for the government to exercise greater control over foreign takeovers.

When a multinational bought into an industry, it generally upset the cosy division of the spoils from established markets, so the rising hostility from business partly reflected the long protectionist tradition. In 1965, the national business lobby, the Associated Chambers of Manufacturers, called for all takeover bids for Australian companies to require specific government approval.[18] Don Brash was struck by how many of the executives he interviewed were hostile to US investment, notwithstanding the fact that they held senior positions in US-owned companies. He quotes one saying, "American companies are not doing us any good at all – only taking our money out of the country. They might have helped us years ago, but now we can turn out our own cars. I've always voted Country Party, but you can sympathise with Castro, can't you".[19]

The politics of defending open access to foreign investment took an unexpected twist in early 1965 when US President Lyndon Johnson imposed controls on outgoing US investment and bank loans abroad in an effort to narrow the country's balance of payments deficit, which was being inflated by the cost of financing the Vietnam War. Suddenly, the flow of foreign investment looked vulnerable, threatening Australia's ability to finance its own balance of payments deficit. Menzies wanted an exemption from the policy, as had been granted to Canada and Japan. He wrote to Johnson, reminding him of Australia's purchase of expensive F-111 aircraft to support its contribution to the Vietnam War saying that, at the time these commitments had been made, the government had no reason to expect Australia's payments position with the United States would be damaged by such unilateral decisions.[20] Australia would welcome it if US subsidiaries sought to raise capital in Australia from local shareholders, but attempts to repatriate capital would force Australia to reconsider its liberal stance on capital movement. Johnson was unyielding, saying he did not think his policies would harm Australia's interests. The government's stance on foreign investment left it looking weak. Deputy opposition leader Gough Whitlam said the American action showed Australia should pay its own way and reduce its dependence on overseas investment.[21]

Menzies asked a 1963 royal commission into the Australian economy to consider Australia's stance towards foreign investment. The commission, known as the Vernon Report, was equivocal, saying foreign investment had been vital to Australia's development but needed to be controlled. It was particularly critical of multinationals which stopped their Australian subsidiaries buying from local suppliers or exporting, arguing the Reserve Bank should ban them from importing the capital needed to set up business. Menzies said this would be tantamount to central planning and rejected the call.[22]

However, resistance to the unfettered sweep of US enterprise was emerging in economies around the world through the late 1960s. It was partly related to the US prosecution of the war in Vietnam, which bred a Marxist critique of US imperialism. The "Non-Aligned Movement" of developing countries, which was formed as early as 1955 by nations including Indonesia, Egypt and Yugoslavia, became more assertive through the 1960s, claiming that US multinationals were exacting all the rents from the primary commodities they exported, leaving nothing behind for their host nations. In Latin America, the Cuban revolution of 1959 spawned guerilla uprisings across the continent, fanned by the exploitative activities of multinational businesses such as United Fruit and the Rockefeller oil interests. The idea that the US corporate interests were indivisible from the interests of the US state was nourished by reports that the US telecommunications giant ITT plotted with the CIA to overthrow Chile's President Salvador Allende after he nationalised its operations. The unethical nature of international business was highlighted by reports of the Swiss multinational

Nestlé dressing sales people as doctors and nurses in developing countries to market their expensive baby formula in preference to breast feeding. An influential critique of the march of the US multinational by the French journalist Jean-Jacques Servan-Schreiber, *The American Challenge*, prophesied that the time was coming when the third-greatest industrial power after the United States and Russia would be US enterprise in Europe. He attributed its triumph to superior management and organisation, rather than the power of US capital. The book was serialised in *The Australian* in 1968.

The Menzies government's liberal policy towards foreign investment survived Menzies' retirement and the two years of Harold Holt's administration; however, Holt's replacement by John Gorton in early 1968 soon led to a very different approach. Since his intervention in the debate on foreign investment in broadcasting in the early 1950s, Gorton had kept close to the government's formal position on foreign investment, with none of the equivocation shown by McEwen. In a Senate debate on foreign investment in 1963 he suggested that high levels of foreign investment were essential if Australia were to realise its growth ambitions. "There is no doubt whatever in my mind that the bulk of such investment is necessarily right and that it does no harm whatever to Australia", he said, while allowing that there was room for debate about whether General Motors' dividend was too high and whether it should be forced to disclose its profits to the public.[23] In a speech in 1965, he had said Australia was under no danger of coming under foreign domination as overseas investors, including portfolio holdings, amounted to only a quarter of the capital in Australian business.[24]

The first hints of Gorton's economic nationalism came in early September 1968 when, following a visit to the mineral developments in the north and west of the country, he was asked by Labor's Rex Connor what he would do about increasing the Australian-owned stake in the resource sector. "We would wish those developments to grow with as great Australian participation as is possible", Gorton replied.[25] A few days later his minister for national development, David Fairbairn, told the American Chamber of Commerce that mining companies were ignoring the government's desire for greater local participation.

A week later, Gorton was again travelling in the north-west of the country for a ceremony at the US facilities at North West Cape. William McMahon was overseas and Gorton was acting treasurer. He received a call from Treasury, saying a complaint had been received from the Life Offices' Association about rising activity in shares of the MLC life insurance company, which had earlier in the year asked that curbs be placed on foreign participation in the life-insurance industry. A holding was being built under the anonymity of nominee shareholdings but was believed to represent a foreign interest. Treasury's advice was that the government's responsibility was to protect policy-holders, not shareholders, and that any action to protect the MLC board would "give rise to large policy issues, including issues concerning the government's general policy on overseas investment in Australia".[26] However, Gorton felt action was required. After consulting the acting leader of the Country Party, but not the Cabinet, he announced that foreign shareholdings in MLC would be subjected to a limit. "We believe that Australians will share our determination that control over their Australian savings and decisions on the investment of their Australian savings shall remain in the control of an Australian company and will not be allowed to fall under the control of overseas interests."

Gorton used the precedent of the Broadcasting Act from 1956 to limit any single foreign shareholding in the company to 15 per cent, and combined foreign holdings to 40 per cent. The move was possible because the MLC was incorporated in the ACT, which was administered by the Commonwealth, so it did not have general application in the states. However, Gorton foreshadowed further moves on foreign investment. In early 1969, travelling in the United Kingdom, he outlined a new Australian approach: "It has seemed to me that the posture of Australia in seeking overseas capital has been the posture of a puppy lying on its back with all legs in the air and its stomach exposed, and saying, 'Please, please, please, give us capital. Tickle my tummy – on any conditions.'"[27] Gorton said he wanted to see Australian participation in developments by foreign investors, and would only accept debt being raised by foreign companies in Australia if accompanied by local equity participation.

McMahon, however, fought an effective rear-guard action to preserve Australia's open-door policy to foreign investment, trying to keep the government's approach to moral suasion rather than legislative action.

McMahon may have hoped that his elevation to the prime ministership in March 1971 would bring an end to the errant nationalism of the Gorton administration; however, the pressures that had been building over the previous decade continued. On the left, the critique of foreign investment became increasingly articulate through the work of academics such as Ted Wheelwright and Heinz Arndt, who showed that multinationals were depriving Australia of tax revenue by manipulating the prices for internal group transactions, and also pointed to sham technology licensing agreements. Whitlam led a newly resurgent Labor Party promising to legislate control of foreign investment. He argued that excessive reliance on foreign investment had sapped the entrepreneurial spirit. Reversing utterly the stance of Curtin and Chifley, he emphasised "the desirability of attracting capital from overseas in the form of fixed-interest loans rather than equity investment".[28] It was an approach that would later have disastrous consequences for his own government, but was effective in building the attack on the McMahon government's continued open approach to foreign investment.

There was a pincer movement on McMahon as both the conservative business community and the left pushed for action. With an election pending, doing nothing was perilous. The Associated Chambers of Manufacturers, traditionally staunch supporters of the Coalition government, said excessive foreign investment was leading to "a transfer of ownership of resources to foreign hands or to unwelcome fragmentation of the already small Australian market". The Country Party was continuing the push against foreign investment under its new leader Doug Anthony, who argued there was so much money pouring into the country that they could afford to be selective.

Labor mustered the numbers in the Senate for an inquiry into foreign investment, which goaded McMahon into commissioning a rival report from Treasury. The latter said that provided tax and exchange-rate policies were in order, the country was a winner from foreign investment and there was no case for action. Efforts to force foreign companies to take Australian partners would simply spread the same amount of Australian capital more thinly across the economy without bringing any additional control. When the Senate report emerged, the *Age* described it by contrast as a "fire-eating, shake-'em up set of recommendations that will set racing the pulses of every red-blooded nationalist". The report called for tougher capital controls, the barring of foreign investment in sensitive sectors and steps to buy back foreign-controlled resources.

Under pressure from both the left and right, McMahon concluded he had to act. In his last policy statement before calling the 1972 election that brought Whitlam to power, McMahon announced that all foreign takeovers of Australian companies would have to be vetted by a new authority to determine whether they were in the national interest. The new authority would make recommendations, but the government would make the final decision.

"We all want the tangible benefits that access to overseas capital and skills brings us. Yet there is legitimate cause for concern", he said. "After 20 years of vigorous growth, we are today a relatively wealthy nation. We have less need to depend on overseas capital for our growth today than we did some years ago. We can afford now to trade off, at the margin, some of the benefits of overseas capital for a greater Australian share in our industry and resources."[29]

McMahon did not believe what he was saying but bowed before political forces which, eight weeks later, threw him from office. However reluctantly, he had laid the foundations for Australia's regime for controlling foreign investment. As AMP's chief economist Harold Bell remarked at the time, it was "the end of an era of an essentially laissez-faire policy on foreign investment in Australia".[30]

◆

Thirty years later, in June 2002, another Liberal prime minister, John Howard, stood on the floor of the US Congress and announced that Australia was seeking to conclude a free trade agreement with the United States. The relationship between the two nations was closer than at any time since the Vietnam War. Howard had been in the US visiting President George Bush at the time of the 2001 terrorist attacks and had committed Australian troops to Afghanistan. A free trade agreement had been talked about ever since the two nations signed the ANZUS Treaty in 1951. This new agreement would be state of the art, covering much more than simply tariff barriers to the trade of goods. The US wanted stronger protection for its intellectual property and greater freedom to set the prices of pharmaceuticals, while Australia wanted greater ability to tender for US government contracts. The US trade representative, Robert

Zoellick, said greater flows of investment would be the biggest benefit for both sides.

"With investment come ideas about how to improve productivity and how to keep the production model on the cutting edge. An FTA will put Australia in a privileged and premier position that will connect it to the central core of the growing global economy." Zoellick argued that liberalising investment would bring Australian businesses access to the world's best technology and business practice. He wanted US companies to be exempt from the Foreign Investment Review Board.

The negotiations were fraught. The US would not yield on Australian requests to lower barriers for Australian sugar and was reluctant to open its markets to more Australian beef. The Australian government came under intense political pressure over the Pharmaceutical Benefits Scheme and digital and patent rights. When the deal was finally done, in May 2004, US companies were granted a threshold of $800 million before their investments required FIRB scrutiny, compared with the $50 million threshold that applied to everyone else.

Modelling conducted for the government at the time claimed that the Australian benefit from the deal would reach $60 billion over a 20-year span, with exports to the US rising by $3 billion a year. In practice, however, in the decade following the agreement the US has slipped in importance to Australian business as China has loomed ever larger.

The share of Australia's exports going to the US has almost halved, to 5 per cent. Australian business, which had long seen the US as the easiest market to invest in, has started venturing further afield. The US share of Australian investment abroad has fallen from 40 per cent to 25 per cent.

However, US business has retained its stake in Australia.

Despite the influx of money from China and other parts of Asia, the US share of total investment in Australia has held steady at 27 per cent, by far the largest of any nation.

6

SYMBOLS FOR SALE

The straw that broke the McMahon government's resistance to regulation of foreign investment was a takeover bid for the manufacturer of the Chiko Roll, one of the first fast-food brands, based on a deep-fried pastry-wrapped cabbage roll. Dozens of corporate takeovers had gone through without rousing the government, but the 1972 bid by US conglomerate IT&T for Frozen Foods – the maker of the celebrated Chiko Roll – forced a reluctant prime minister, Billy McMahon, to bring the issue of foreign investment to the cabinet table. The discussion was sufficiently heated and the issue of how to control the wave of foreign takeovers so vexed that a special cabinet meeting had to be called for the following day to conclude the debate.

The *Age*'s finance editor Les Carlyon found it hard to credit. "The threat to Chiko is relayed in black headlines; TV interviewers furrow their brows at the gravity of it all. Federal cabinet, bless its collective heart, puts aside trivialities like electoral survival to agonise over the Chiko affair and hardly leaks a word."

"The Chiko Roll – for long a boon to weary taxi drivers and losers at the trots – is suddenly the symbol of Australian Nationalism. A symbol under siege." After all the capital that had flowed into the country over the previous decade, with the foreign takeover of the mineral fields, the foreign domination of manufacturing and the sale of half the high-rainfall land in the Northern Territory to foreign interests – over a million acres – could the humble Chiko Roll mark a signal point in the overseas investment debate, Carlyon wondered.[1]

Frozen Foods was a tiny corporate speck on the horizon of IT&T, which was the world's eighth-largest corporation. Indeed, the bid was the idea of the group's Hong Kong branch and the US headquarters knew nothing about it until the political storm exploded in Canberra. Though founded in telecommunications, IT&T had caught the management fad for conglomerates, believing its corporate magic could be applied equally in any business, from steel to fast food. IT&T was, at the time of its bid, the most vilified of US multinationals. It had been all over the papers over the previous few weeks as testimony in a US inquiry exposed its efforts, in league with the CIA, to prevent the election of Salvador Allende in Chile and, when this was unsuccessful, to bring the government down. It appeared to be the archetype of the marauding multinational.

The Chiko Roll was a local success story. Frank McEnroe, a boiler-maker by trade, had run a weekend catering business at country race meetings before the war and was impressed by the chop-suey spring rolls being sold by a Chinese vendor outside the Richmond football stadium. He thought they needed a stiffer pastry to be safely consumed with one hand while holding a beer in the other. First they were called "Chicken Rolls", but they contained no chicken, so he shortened it to "Chiko". McEnroe launched them at the Wagga Wagga show in 1951 and then teamed up with the Floyds Ice Works in Melbourne's Moonee Ponds to make frozen rolls that could be heated in a deep fryer at sports grounds. By the sixties, the business went public. During the footy season, at the half-time siren, Australians were eating a million Chiko Rolls a week. The prospect of the business being sold to Americans caused a rumbling across the political spectrum.

Senator Jack Kane, from the conservative Democratic Labor Party, led the charge. "There is a real danger that, unless a freeze is imposed pending Government action, foreign firms and corporations will endeavour to achieve substantial holdings in Australia before action is taken to prevent them doing so", he said.

Kane drew attention to the reports of IT&T's involvement in Chile: "If [IT&T] were permitted to develop its bridgeheads here in Australia to dangerous proportions, which it could well do, there would be no guarantee that it would not attempt to do in Australia what it attempted to do in Chile", Kane charged.[2]

In the House of Representatives, Labor's Al Grassby put it to McMahon that half of the top 40 food brands in Australia were now foreign controlled. "Will he take steps to halt any further takeover of the companies responsible for so much of the food on Australian meal tables to safeguard our people from monopoly exploitation by foreign corporations?"[3] Grassby asked, brandishing a list of the foreign-owned brands.

Four of the five directors of Frozen Foods, including McEnroe, voted in favour of the IT&T bid, but his partner Gordon Trewin issued a call to arms.

"The time has come when shareholders in Australian companies should be reminded that they owe a duty to future generations of Australians and that they should in their own and their country's interests, resist takeovers of important Australian industries by overseas interests."[4]

It was left to opposition leader Gough Whitlam to put a bit of perspective into the issue, commenting that "Chiko rolls are not more important to the financial wellbeing of Australians than chemicals, motor cars and metals", adding that he hoped "the present emotional debate" would not cloud the government's thinking on a clear set of rules limiting foreign ownership in Australia.

Attorney-General Ivor Greenwood attempted to defuse the situation by emphasising that the government shared the widespread concern that "this matter should not reach a situation where Australian resources are overwhelmingly in the hands of overseas interests".[5] However, he said the government would not respond in an ad hoc manner.

In fact, the first response was entirely ad hoc. Diplomatic representations following the cabinet meeting led IT&T to withdraw its bid. The US company had enough political problems on its plate already.[6] More importantly, however, the cabinet meeting over the Chiko Roll started the process which a few months later resulted in new guidelines requiring that all foreign takeovers were to be vetted by a special committee to see if they were in the national interest. This was the beginning of the regulation of foreign investment in Australia.

Forty years on, the debate over national brands still rages. Nationalist retailer Dick Smith keeps a tally of Australian-developed food brands now in foreign hands, much like the one Al Grassby brandished in parliament before Billy McMahon. It includes names like Bushells and Lan-Choo tea, Arnott's biscuits, Peters and Streets ice creams, Allen's and MacRobertson's confectionery, Vegemite, Cottee's jams, Eta peanut butter, Aeroplane Jelly and Golden Circle pineapple. It is not just foods. Swimwear brand Speedo and surfwear brand Billabong both went to overseas buyers, as did Victa lawnmowers, Esky ice-boxes and R.M. Williams.

Yet the story is not always as straightforward as the foreign company seizing control of the Aussie invention just as it is about to make good. Vegemite, the most sentimental of Australian brands, has been owned by the US-owned Kraft Foods since 1935 and would never have succeeded were it not for the two-year marketing initiative in which a jar of the thick black spread was given away with every sale of Kraft cheese. (Purchase of Vegemite could also get you entry into a raffle to win a Pontiac.) The product was originally developed by a Melbourne entrepreneur Fred Walker as a rival for the British Marmite. Walker did a deal with Chicago manufacturer, James Kraft, to manufacture and distribute his processed cheese in Australia. Kraft bought out the business when Walker died.

One of the most bitterly contested foreign takeovers – the acquisition of Arnott's Biscuits by the US Campbell Soup Company in 1992 – also had its twists. A hostile bid by Campbell's had descendants of the company's founder, William Arnott, forming a Shareholder Action Organisation, whose acronym, SAO, reflected Arnott's dried biscuit brand. Its foundation meeting of 200 or so shareholders and supporters called for a letter-writing campaign to politicians and to Campbell's to protest at the foreign encroachment. Everyone should buy Arnott's shares for their families for Christmas, while Campbell's soups should be boycotted. Arnott's family member Alice Oppen, who was an English teacher at an exclusive Sydney private school, declared "Arnott's is part of Australia's infrastructure. If we can't control our own food companies, we haven't got much hope as a nation". Sixteen-year-old Bryony Griffiths told the meeting there were fewer and fewer Australian-owned companies to give her a job when she left school. Family member Sandy Dawson, who had the previous year been dumped by the family-dominated board as company chief executive, told the meeting people could have no faith in the government to stop the bid, condemning the "Faintly Interested Review Board".[7] The family won the backing of the Australian Democrats in the Senate, arguing that a viable and established company was under threat from a foreigner that would yield no benefit to Australia. "I do not think we can look to much technology transfer in biscuit making", said Senator Cheryl Kernot.[8] The argument was really about little more than protection of the interests of those members of the Arnott's family who did not want to sell. The *Green Left Weekly* – a radical journal – took a disinterested view: "The battle for Arnott's is mainly a contest between different groups of capital owners and not much more. Inserting the nationality of the owners or the 'Australianness' of the biscuits into the question can only muddy the waters."[9]

William Arnott set up his first bakery in Newcastle in 1865 and had a thriving biscuit business within ten years. The company remained in family hands and succeeded in the mid 1960s in consolidating the other major Australian biscuit-makers, including Brockhoff and Guests, in order to resist the encroachment of the US rival Nabisco. The company went public in the mid 1970s, with the family retaining a major stake and board control. But in 1985, there was an unwelcome bid from the corporate raider Alan Bond. It was said that Bond's bid was backed by Arnott's nemesis, Nabisco. The company had an inkling that a bid was coming and had been looking for a friend among the world's biscuit-makers to defend it. The day the bid was made, Arnott's announced a placement giving Campbell's a 10 per cent holding, with the American company seeking foreign-investment approval to go to 25 per cent. Permission was granted, with Treasurer Paul Keating saying the proposal offered the prospect of a significant increase in Arnott's exports to Europe and the US where Campbell's had extensive distribution networks.[10]

When Campbell's made its bid for control in 1992, there was debate in court about just what the American company had told the government. Campbell's pitch this time was that it would use

Arnott's as a bridge for its investment in Asia, but Arnott's protested that this was just what they'd promised in 1985 and not delivered. It turned out that the chairmen of Campbell's and Arnott's had done a handshake deal, but six years later both men had gone. Industry minister John Button clarified that whatever they had said in 1985, Campbell's had given no formal undertakings to the government in return for approval. Now, facing a hostile public, Campbell's did offer the Foreign Investment Review Board undertakings that it would keep a majority of directors as Australian citizens, would retain the company's manufacturing and headquarters in Australia and would remain an Australian listed company. "Campbells' experience in the food industry and financial strength should assist Arnott's in a strategy to pursue exports in Asia. A strong asset backing will be important for Arnott's in meeting the international competition for this market and making the necessary efforts to entrench brands", [11] Treasurer John Dawkins said.

World Trade Organization researcher Bijit Bora commented that the demand that manufacturing continue in Australia was a "clear cut" breach of its global trade commitments, which forbid regulation of the location of production facilities. He noted that a decision to block the Campbell's takeover would have resulted in a queue at the treasurer's door. "Every Australian company would have the precedent to establish their claim to national icon status ... to exempt themselves from foreign takeover."[12]

Campbell's eventually moved to full ownership of Arnott's and dropped its public listing; however, it has kept its promise to retain Australian manufacturing and corporate operations and has, indeed, established both exports and regional subsidiaries. Its Indonesian offshoot makes cheese-flavoured chocolate Tim Tams, appealing to local tastes. The business has grown significantly, but it has not delivered the profits Campbell's was hoping for.

In the end, it is business. You buy or build an asset with an idea of how it might be developed and either succeed or fail in the implementation. If you fail or if someone thinks they can do better, the asset is for sale in a public market at the right price. Nothing tells this story better than the fate of Australia's most successful global brand, Foster's. Its journey from a local Victorian beer, to becoming the world's fourth-biggest brewer, to finally being sold to a South African rival is not a story of the foreigner enjoying the fruit of the hard Australian labour. Rather it is one of over-reach and serial mismanagement delivering their inevitable consequences.

Comedian Barry Humphries started it. His "Bazza McKenzie" cartoon strip in the British satirical journal *Private Eye* in the mid-sixties popularised Foster's as the quintessential Australian beer. In truth, it was barely known outside Victoria, and even there it sold less than Carlton & United Breweries' other brands including Melbourne Bitter, Victoria Bitter and later Carlton Draught. A 1972 film based on the cartoon, *The Adventures of Barry McKenzie*, was a hit in the United Kingdom, and the beer started to be exported in small quantities.

Financial deregulation in the 1980s put seemingly unlimited debt at the fingertips of entrepreneurs and one of them, John Elliott, built an empire from the jam company Henry Jones IXL that swept Carlton & United Breweries into its dominion. With clever marketing based on ocker Paul Hogan declaring Foster's tastes "like an angel crying on your tongue" and adaptation of the beer recipe to British tastes, sales took off. The company bought the British brewer Courage, and then the Canadian Carling and Molson breweries, and by the end of the 1980s global sales were almost $20 billion.

But as the 1990s recession approached and debts mounted, the business had to contract. Courage was sold but continued making

Foster's under licence. In some markets there were joint ventures, in others it used distributor agreements and in others it had its own operations. Foster's was a discount brand in Ireland but a super-premium brand in Portugal. There was no consistency to its marketing abroad, while in Australia it became a micro brand.

In Australia, too, the company was failing to manage its branding strategy. Victoria Bitter became a runaway success on the strength of its "hard earned thirst" campaign, reaching a 30 per cent market share by the early 2000s. But the company decided that it was reaching the limits of its growth in beer and diversified into wine. Paying too much for Southcorp, which controlled among other things the Penfolds brands, was a problem, as was over-paying for other wine assets. But the real problem was the entirely different business approach required for beer and wine. Beer is a commodity, whereby profit comes from cost control and throughput. Wine, by contrast, is a highly fragmented market with literally thousands of labels battling it out in the wine stores. It is also tied more closely to agricultural seasons. As Foster's took its eye off its core beer business, the Victoria Bitter market share fell to 11.5 per cent.[13] In the end, the company's market share was in retreat everywhere and it had no strategy to turn things around.

In the late 1980s South African Breweries had a monopoly in its home country but no sales anywhere else and was less than a tenth the size of Foster's. Its international expansion through the next two decades, in contrast to Foster's, was careful, well-funded, and backed up by a clear brand strategy. Foster's and SA Breweries went into China at the same time in the mid 1990s. Foster's essentially gave its operations away in 2006, having lost hundreds of millions due to poor marketing strategies, while SA Breweries (which by that time had become SABMiller) triumphed, becoming the largest brewer in China, overtaking Tsingdao. SABMiller's $11 billion purchase of Foster's in 2011 mercifully put Foster's shareholders out of their misery. Foster's business strategy had failed comprehensively under a succession of chief executives over a period of two decades.

The National Party's Barnaby Joyce could complain as foreign private equity funds circled Treasury Wine Estates, owner of the Penfolds, Lindemans and Wolf Blass brands: "The problem always is we have a Foreign Investment Review Board that will never say anything but yes." But there were few tears shed either by angels on tongues, or by long-suffering Foster's shareholders, as SABMiller wrapped up its bid with a rubber stamp from Treasurer Wayne Swan and the FIRB. "I have taken into account SABMiller's plans to strengthen Foster's brand portfolio and work with its local employees to bring its global scale and expertise to the business", Swan said.[14]

7

MONEY FROM ROCKS

Ken Henry was the closest thing we've ever had, or will ever get, to a rockstar Treasury secretary. Tall, dark, handsome and brimming with intelligence, he had an engaging story as the son of a poor woodsman from Taree in NSW who taught him the value of nature's gifts. He wore his green heart on his sleeve, taking time out from work to save endangered hairy-nosed wombats in Queensland and tending for injured animals at his rural home outside Canberra. A few days after the 2010 budget, he made an appeal to the wooden hearts of Sydney's business economists on behalf of the new mining tax that the Labor government had launched at his urging. "Australia is fortunate to have an abundance of natural resources. These natural resources are assets belonging to all Australians, including Australians not yet born. Where we undercharge for the exploitation of these resources the wealth of current and future Australians is eroded", he said.

The tax, dubbed the Resource Super Profits Tax or RSPT, with a nod to the Aretha Franklin hit, was the culmination of a career-long campaign by Henry which had started when he was an advisor in the office of Paul Keating in the mid-1980s working on a tax package that included a tax on the new offshore petroleum resources in Western Australia. His speech attempted to stop the government, which was facing a deafening howl of anger from the resources industry, from budging an inch. He warned that allowing the miners to earn anything more than the government bond rate before the tax kicked in would be entrenching a permanent taxpayer subsidy.

A sense that the state is not getting fair recompense for its ownership of the minerals in the ground has been at the heart of disputes over foreign investment in the resources industry. The mining company may be entitled to a share, reflecting the risks it has taken in exploration and investment in extracting the minerals, but the state should get a substantial part of the clear profit or "rent" (as the economists term a risk-free profit) above that.

In early 1972, as the mining industry was informed that an incoming Labor government would require 51 per cent of all new resource ventures to be Australian owned, Treasury prepared a paper arguing that the problem of Australia getting an inadequate return from its minerals should be solved by reforming mineral taxation rather than by mandating minimum local equity interests. States had been charging too little, the paper said, and adequate returns from giving up minerals should be considered the taxpayers' right, not a "windfall". "The available evidence suggests that contracted royalties could have been higher without reducing investment incentives beyond the critical point where the investment does not occur at all." The McMahon government ignored the suggestion.

Almost 40 years later, a mining tax to capture the "rent" from the extraction of resources was again on the agenda. It is sometimes forgotten that the mining industry lobby group, the Minerals Council, itself urged Ken Henry's tax review to consider a new federal mining tax to replace the array of state royalties. Royalties based on the volume or the value of sales were inefficient, the

Minerals Council's submission said: "a profits based system with an appropriate rate and base better takes account of the sharing of the risk in the joint venture arrangement".[1]

Labor's effort to introduce a resources tax in 2010 ranks as one of the greatest failures of public policy in the history of Australian government, but it has some good company in the politics of the resources industry. The efforts of the Whitlam government to raise a loan from a shady Pakistani financier to invest in Australian resource projects is an obvious stand-out.

Each wave of foreign investment in the resource industry has been met by public suspicion that Australian national interests were somehow being betrayed – first by the Americans and then the Japanese and, over the past decade, the Chinese. The hostility comes from both the anti-capitalist left and the protectionist right, whether it was columns of university students marching down the city streets in the 1970s chanting "What shall we do with Bjelke Petersen? Shove him down a Utah coal mine" or the National Party's Barnaby Joyce making television commercials declaring in 2009 as Chinese mining companies were seeking investments in Australia: "The Australian Government would never be allowed to buy a mine in China ... Stop the Rudd Government from selling Australia."

The resource industry was the primary target in the global rise of economic nationalism in the 1960s and 1970s. Newly independent developing countries saw the presence of resource companies from former colonial powers as emblematic of their former subjugation and believed that nationalisation would enable them to capture the wealth that had previously been exploited. The most dramatic manifestation of new state power over the resource industry was the 1973 oil embargo implemented by the Organization of the Petroleum Exporting Countries (OPEC), which quadrupled the oil price (from $3 to $12 a barrel). Although the embargo came at a time when the normal forces of supply and demand would have raised the oil price in any case, with rapid growth in oil consumption across the industrialised world, OPEC's success in imposing the power of a cartel on the price of the world's most important commodity inspired resource-rich nations around the world.

Often, resource companies were the only global business of substance in a country. As US academic Ray Vernon noted, once a resource company has invested in developing a mine and sunk its capital, it is in a very poor negotiating position against a hostile sovereign.[2] The terms that the company struck with the host government when investing could rapidly be rendered obsolete. Vernon's analysis led companies to look at ways of strengthening their bargaining position with investment insurance or by allying themselves to multilateral institutions such as the World Bank. But United Nations figures show the number of expropriations of foreign mining enterprises increased from 32 between 1960 and 1969 to 48 between 1970 and 1976. The share of the world's copper production mined by the seven largest multinational mining companies fell from 60 per cent in 1960 to 23 per cent by 1981.

The resource industry expanded dramatically in Australia through the 1960s and 1970s as first the iron ore fields of the Pilbara were opened, and then nickel, coal and gold reserves were developed, while major commercial finds of oil and gas in Bass Strait brought Australia close to self-sufficiency right at the time when the OPEC embargo was throwing the industrialised world into chaos. In his 1966 election speech, Harold Holt was able to boast of a resources boom, with $2 billion in investment underway. Mining rose from about 1.8 per cent of GDP in 1960 to 5 per cent by the mid-seventies, with resource investment helping to power extraordinary economic growth rates reaching almost 9 per cent in the late sixties. Australia in the early 1950s was mainly reliant on rural exports and was pinning its hopes on the tariff-protected manufacturing sector to deliver economic growth. The opening of the resource fields transformed the economy.

Iron ore exports had been prohibited from 1938, when it was feared they were assisting Japan's war preparations, until 1960, when a credit squeeze prompted a search for new sources of export revenue. Japan's rapid industrialisation through the sixties and the still-strong growth in US and European steel industries greatly expanded markets. The big operators were Hamersley Iron – a joint venture of the British Rio Tinto subsidiary, Conzinc Riotinto of Australia and the US Kaiser Steel – and the Mt Newman joint venture, which combined Australia's BHP with Japan's Mitsui and C. Itoh.

From the very outset, there was a view that Australia was not getting its fair share of the profits from the new resources, but the strength of nationalist sentiment intensified through the sixties and seventies. The starting point for the West Australian government was the idea that the Japanese steel-makers were getting all the value, with very little generated for the state by simply exporting unprocessed iron ore. It wrote into the agreements for the iron ore operators that they would conduct feasibility studies into secondary processing of the ore and, in due course, the construction of an integrated iron and steel industry in the state. The government felt that only through subsequent manufacturing could the full returns from mining be captured.

For a time, it seemed as if the West Australian government's desire for at least some of the state's iron ore to be turned into steel would be realised. BHP built a small blast furnace in Kwinana in 1967, while the Hamersley joint venture announced in 1969 it was conducting a feasibility study into building a steel mill in Western Australia. The US journal, *Business Week*, reported that the proposal for an Australian steel mill "promised to give Japanese steelmakers competition and might eventually change the world steel marketing picture".[3] Nothing came of the Hamersley plans, while BHP was talking about closing its Kwinana plant within five years and finally did so in 1982. Other high-cost efforts at further processing ended in failure, with the final ignominy being the 2013 decision by Rio Tinto to close an experimental plant for directly smelting iron ore and ship the equipment to India.

The federal government kept tight control of mineral exports. In 1966, the Holt government intervened to veto one of Hamersley's earliest contracts with Japanese steel mills, saying the price was too low. "The present price level which we are aiming to preserve represents a sharing between Japan and Australia of the economic advantage which flows from the proximity of the two countries", national development minister, David Fairbairn said. The government was concerned that the price for Australian iron ore "not be eroded".[4] The move put at risk an £18 million pellet plant that was to have been the first further processing of iron ore in West Australia. Labor's spokesman on resources, the pugnacious nationalist Rex Connor, charged that iron ore was being "literally given away". Attacking mines that had Japanese shareholding, he said "when it comes to a little bit of gentle chiselling, these people are selling their Australian production to themselves at cost", forcing the government to intervene in contracts, setting a minimum figure. "We want to sell our products, but we do not want to sell our birthright. Australia is the most notable storehouse or treasure house of mineral wealth in the world today. We should make no mistake about that", Connor said.[5] Connor noted that Australian iron ore was enabling the expansion of Japan's steel industry to the point that it was exporting to Australia, and undercutting BHP's mills operations in Port Kembla and Newcastle.

One media commentator noted that the level of foreign ownership would not be accepted in Europe. "Australia has the option of either slowing down the development of its resources to a rate which will allow internally-generated capital investment to have an increasingly significant share in the economy or to allow overseas penetration of the heights of the Australian economy to continue. The prudent overseas investor should recognize that as Australia develops into a major industrial power in the Pacific area, its people will almost inevitably come to resent foreign domination of local industry."[6]

In 1966, trade minister John McEwen floated the idea of a government-owned investment corporation that would provide development capital for Australians, and thereby reduce the need for foreign investment. It would raise funds overseas, but would be generously endowed with capital by the government. Treasurer McMahon was horrified at such a "socialist" idea and galvanised the private banks into forming a consortium bank, the Australian Resources Development Bank, to deliver the same function. Amid furious Cabinet debate, McEwen withdrew his proposal. Holt's election speech that year reflected the Cabinet tensions, acknowledging the desire for greater Australian participation in the resource sector. "There are instances in which more capital is needed to exploit these opportunities than existing Australian companies can marshal. New arrangements and facilities for the provision of capital have to be devised. This is not an easy matter, but the Government has been working actively and earnestly upon it, as have people and institutions in the world of finance."[7] Following Holt's death and the appointment of John Gorton as prime minister in 1967, McEwen prevailed, and the Australian Industry Development Corporation was established, with an ability to raise more capital than the Commonwealth or Reserve banks. One

Liberal backbencher voiced fears about what would become of the new institution under a Labor government: "We are paving the way for [Labor] to implement their policies of democratic socialism."[8]

The nationalist call was answered in a buoyant stockmarket. Geologist Ken McMahon launched the company Mineral Securities (Minsec) in 1965 with the ambition of building a major mining finance house to counter the control of global corporations like Rio Tinto. It planned to channel profits from share trading into long-term investments in development projects. One of its biggest long-term plays was the Nabarlek uranium mine in Arnhem Land in the Northern Territory. Australia's uranium mining had petered out in the early 1960s, but the belief that Nabarlek held massive reserves brought huge turnover in its shares. . It was feared it might be subject to an overseas takeover, and the chairman of its operating company obtained a meeting with Gorton to seek protection. A young Labor backbencher, Paul Keating, called for the federal government to control all uranium exports and said there should be an investigation into the activities of the world's largest uranium miner, the "Rothschild-backed Rio Tinto Zinc group". Gorton announced that no single foreign shareholder would be allowed more than 5 per cent of the Nabarlek project, while total foreign holdings could not exceed 15 per cent. "The deposits can be exploited by Australian personnel, using Australian technical knowledge and know-how and can be sold on the world market by Australia",[9] Gorton said. However, it soon emerged that the Nabarlek reserve estimates had been based on the chairman's 'gut feel', not drilling results. Minsec, which had become the biggest share-trader in the country, and had borrowed to buy into the uranium miner, collapsed in 1970. The bursting of the late 1960s resource share bubble slowed the flow of local money into the resources sector to a trickle.

As Labor took office in 1972, after 23 years in opposition, it concluded that government would have to step in. "Our objective will be to give Australians opportunities, not just to restrict foreigners", Gough Whitlam told parliament shortly before his election. "There is an alternative to government inactivity: it is government initiative. There is an alternative to relying solely upon government initiative in the negative, prohibitive sense: It is government initiative in a positive and direct way. There is an alternative to restricting private competition: It is to provide public competition." Government would become a participant in the resource sector to ensure the nation captured a fair share of the proceeds.

Although it was not until towards the end of its turbulent three years in office that the Whitlam government produced formal legislation controlling foreign investment, it was immediately obvious that the country was under new management. All tax concessions for the resource industry, including exploration, were cancelled, while a freeze on all exploration and new mining leases in the Northern Territory was imposed pending the development of Aboriginal land title. "The free-wheeling approach of the previous government is gone forever", Whitlam told the mining industry's annual dinner, adding that he did not want the foreign stake in the resource sector rising above the present 62 per cent. The government rejected a number of resource development proposals, including an alumina refinery and a steel mill in Western Australia, because the foreign shareholding would be too high.

At the heart of the new government's approach was the expansion of the Australian Industry Development Corporation's mandate to include taking controlling interests in resource companies. The goal, said trade minister Jim Cairns, was to "buy back Australia". "AIDC may come into areas subject to foreign takeover with money, rather than us just saying 'no' to the foreign investor and leaving it at that."[10] The government also planned a Petroleum and Minerals Authority, which was intended to search for and develop mineral projects in its own right. Resources minister Rex Connor envisaged the government getting into the oil business from the well to the petrol bowser, in competition with the oil majors. The Liberal's northern development spokesman said Labor was on a "socialist rampage" while Western Mining's executive director, Laurence Brodie-Hall, said it was hard to conceive of a "greater deterrent to the development of Australia's resources by the free enterprise system".[11] Views in the banking and finance sectors were no more charitable. The chief general manager of the Bank of New South Wales, Sir John Norman, repeated the strategy that had been successful in the campaign against bank nationalisation under Chifley, of enlisting branch managers with a letter to them claiming "The powers would be there for government through the AIDC to take over large segments of private industry without their consent." Legislation to establish the Petroleum and Minerals Authority was rejected in the Senate three times but passed a joint sitting of both houses following the 1974 double dissolution election, only to then be ruled invalid by the High Court.

At the end of October 1973, just ten days after the OPEC nations had ordered huge production cuts and imposed an embargo on oil deliveries to supporters of Israel, Gough Whitlam flew to Japan, which had a greater dependence upon imported raw materials than any other industrial power. He told the shell-shocked Japanese that the government's objective was "full Australian ownership in development projects involving uranium. We also regard this as a desirable objective in oil, natural gas and black coal". He said the government understood that the resource industry needed access to global expertise but hoped to obtain that through licensing agreements and long-term contracts. Japan's foreign minister Masayoshi

Ohira said it would be "unfortunate for both countries if a series of policies taken by the Australian government ... should affect smooth transactions of resources between the two countries".[12]

The OPEC crisis demonstrated the possibility of shifting market power from the manufacturing industry of the advanced world to largely developing country producers of raw materials. It was seen to herald what became popularly known as a "New International Economic Order". Jamaica led a copycat effort to mount a cartel of bauxite producers. Australia – the world's biggest bauxite producer – signed up. Jim Cairns said Australia would be a voice of reason in the group and would ensure that prices were not hiked excessively at the expense of consumers.

The seventies also brought new focus on the limits to the world's non-renewable resources. A disparate group of industrialists and academics from Europe and the US, calling themselves the Club of Rome, produced a text – *The Limits to Growth* – which argued that rapid industrialisation, population growth, depletion of mineral resources and environmental degradation were setting the scene for a social cataclysm. It became a bible for the growth of green groups worldwide. Safeguarding the environment became a new imperative in controlling foreign investment in the resource sector. Whitlam, who had appointed the first minister for the environment, Moss Cass, ruled that resource projects would not be granted export licences unless they completed environmental impact statements. The resource sector struggled to deal with the political hostility it confronted. The head of the Australian Mining Industry Council, M.W. Howell commented, "without minerals we would not be here today. We would have fallen prey to the wild animals the good Lord sent here to try us".[13]

OPEC's success in lifting the oil price brought the Arab states revenue in US dollars far in excess of what they could spend. Vast pools of "petro-dollars" accumulated in the British and other European financial markets, attracting borrowers around the world. Frustrated by the High Court in setting up his Petroleum and Minerals Authority, resources minister Rex Connor conceived the notion of tapping this pool to fund a suite of ambitious projects. He calculated that the Arab states had to find takers for $65 billion in petro-dollars a year. There was to be a $400 million pipeline bringing gas from the north-west of Australia to Melbourne and Sydney, a uranium enrichment plant, upgrades to the coal ports and a fleet of oil and bulk carrier ships, all funded from a petro-dollar loan of $5 billion. "To maintain and increase ownership by the people of Australia of our own resources calls for immense sums of money", Connor told a sceptical parliament, egregiously misquoting and mis-attributing to an anonymous Australian poet lines of the American poet Sam Walter Foss, which he read into the Hansard record as:

> Give me men to match my mountains,
> Give me men to match my plains,
> Men with freedom in their vision,
> And creation in their brains.[14]

Connor declared that the next election would be fought on the issue of "who will own Australia", but in fact it was his dealings with shady financiers which brought about an end, not only to the dreams of using the government's financial muscle to buy back resource projects from foreign owners, but also to the Whitlam government.

In the 1930s and 1940s, Curtin and Chifley had both preferred foreign equity to foreign debt, having blamed the stranglehold of Australia's overseas creditors – the forces of money power – for

Australia's suffering during the depression. Their hostility to financial capital drew on long Labor traditions. Whitlam, however, saw debt as an almost free ride. It was readily available, and not too expensive. When Whitlam promoted "the desirability of attracting capital from overseas in the form of fixed interest loans rather than equity investment", he wanted to capture the upside profits from Australia's resources. The palpable failure of the government to even raise the finance, much less run the resource industry, left the country back where it was, dependent upon foreign investment to fund its growth. However, the nation wasn't happy about it.

The new profiteer was Utah Mining. Having come to Australia in the 1950s as a construction firm, Utah made a fabulous discovery of rich steel-making coal reserves in Queensland, just as Japan's steel industry was entering its burst of rapid growth. The reserves, which could be accessed by open-cut mining, were among the richest in the world, with the lowest cost to mine. By the late seventies, Utah had overtaken BHP as Australia's most profitable company. Labor's new resource spokesman, Paul Keating, who replaced Connor in 1975, said that while there was a place for companies like Utah in Australia, it was "making the best of a good thing. They're making a positive contribution, but this is a deal running in their direction. While we need a proportion of foreign capital, the control and ownership of Australian resources ought to be the prime requirement of Australian resource development policy",[15] he said.

Utah's sense of the public pressure over its profits was sufficient that it fielded a series of television advertisements featuring Australian Hollywood actor Rod Taylor (Hitchcock's *The Birds*) and opera star Joan Sutherland, and made a $250,000 donation to the Australian Opera. "I've learned there's enough coal up here to last for hundreds of years so development can continue to grow, the towns are going to continue to grow larger and the jobs are going to be increased", said

Taylor with an unfortunately strong American accent. "Utah is going to spend a lot more money in Australia as will other industries. Utah believes in backing Australia."[16]

In the Whitlam government's final few months, it legislated to limit foreign investors in resource projects to 50 per cent ownership. Foreign investments above $1 million would require approval from a new Foreign Investment Advisory Committee to determine whether they were in the national interest. The legislation was accompanied by additional policy requirements that were thought too hard to put into law. Foreign governments and their agencies had to seek approval for any investment, as did any foreign purchase of media companies.

Whitlam's successor Malcolm Fraser kept this policy largely in place, extending the 50 per cent rule beyond mineral resources to farming, forestry and fishing. In a statement early in the Fraser government's first term, Treasurer Phillip Lynch commented: "In past decades of high immigration, and rapid industrial development, there was a general presumption that all foreign investment should be welcomed. This is no longer the case. The Australian community quite properly demands that government today take a more discriminating and mature attitude towards foreign investment."[17]

In practice, the Fraser government was torn between the nationalism of its prime minister and a perceived need to appease some potent international mining interests with strong local representation. There was some flexibility in the 50 per cent minimum local stake – a foreign company could buy now and sell down later, however, a number of major transactions were blocked. Australia's abundant reserves of coal received much greater global attention. Among the deals blocked by the Fraser government was a bid by Japan's state-owned Electric Power Development Corporation for a 19 per cent stake in a Queensland coal mine. The treasurer, John

Howard, argued that majority owner CRA had not tried hard enough to find a local partner. Rio Tinto, which had major investments in Australian iron ore, uranium and bauxite, found its ambitions to expand into coal and diamonds were facing political barriers. It negotiated a deal under which its subsidiary, CRA, in which Australian shareholders had a 27 per cent stake, would be granted a new status as a "naturalising" company, with an agreement to move to 50 per cent Australian equity over an indeterminate period of time, and this enabled it to make investments and takeovers without foreign investment approval, as if it were an Australian company. In his doctoral thesis, academic Christopher Pokarier notes that the Fraser government faced strong resistance to the granting of "naturalising" status from Australian-owned companies including CSR, BHP, Western Mining and Peko-Wallsend, all of which gained from the requirement that foreign companies offer equity stakes to local investors.[18] The nationalist demand for local equity had created a tribe of rent-seekers.

Oil prices had soared following the Iranian revolution in 1979 and the second OPEC oil crisis. With oil companies in Australia being allowed to raise the price of their local oil from a government-controlled level to parity with the new and astronomic world prices, bringing huge one-off profits, the Coalition announced in its 1977 budget that it was examining a resource tax. Said Treasurer Phillip Lynch: "The Government believes that not all the additional profits resulting from these decisions [parity pricing] should remain with the producers, and that the community should obtain a return from the exploitation of these resources which adequately reflects their value."[19] However, the resulting backlash from resource companies was sufficient for the government to retreat, with the Fraser government citing sensitivity to the views of foreign investors. With the government also winding down Labor's export levy on coal, it was vulnerable to attack from Labor's Keating, who charged that "even with exceptionally profitable ventures, [the Fraser government] has not attempted to maximise the benefits to the Australian people". The failure to introduce a resource rent tax meant the only way Australia could gain its fair share was through increased Australian ownership, he said.[20] The time had passed when Australia needed access to foreign technology and capital to develop its mineral resources. "We have the money, the know-how and the markets ... What we need is a government with national pride and imagination, a government with confidence in Australians and Australian institutions. What we have for a government is a cringing, crawling bunch of sell-outs – unimaginative drones."[21]

In opposition, Keating had vowed to introduce a resource rent tax on all minerals, replacing state government royalties, acknowledging it would be a tough negotiation but saying the Commonwealth could threaten to withdraw untied grants to states that did not tow the line.[22] In government, however, he was not prepared to have that battle, with states having a clear constitutional right to resources. But a resource rent tax was imposed on new offshore oil and gas finds, as the continental shelf is Commonwealth territory. It was set at 40 per cent of profits, once they were 15 per cent above the government bond rate. The tax was intended to replace oil levies and it also exempted existing oil fields, notably Bass Strait. However, the oil industry was up in arms. "The leakage of BHP funds overseas could well increase as a consequence",[23] BHP Petroleum's head of exploration, Bryan Griffith said, while the Australian Petroleum Exploration Association said it would result in exploration spending drying up. It argued that all taxation on the oil industry should be removed, and instead a consumption tax be introduced with a standard rate for all goods and services. Resources minister Gareth Evans countered that the profit-based tax would help make projects more economic. "The only point about it is that it means that great dollops of cream cannot be scooped off from the big bonanza windfall projects, which resource companies regarded as their right to collection, notwithstanding that they then whinge their heads off in times of low profitability and demand the reduction of production based taxes as a result."

Keating justified his 1988 decision to remove the requirement for Australian nationals to hold at least half any oil or gas project by suggesting that this was no longer needed, given that the country now had a resource rent tax on the oil industry. In truth, the winding back of controls on foreign investment under the Hawke and Keating governments was mainly due to the internationalisation of the economy, following the floating of the currency, and also to balance of payments crises that showed the country needed capital inflow and could not afford to be too choosy about the terms. The FIRB remained, with its vague test of whether a transaction contravened the national interest. The demand for 50 per cent local participation in mining was the last to go, at the beginning of 1992, as the economy was struggling with recession.

The 1983 removal of capital controls, along with the float of the dollar, made Australian businesses more international, including in the mining industry. In 1984, BHP bought Utah's international mining operations, including not only its Australian coal mines, but also iron ore in Brazil and a stake in the huge Escondida copper deposit in Chile. The petroleum division became a major world operator. The same international forces drove a merger of Rio Tinto with its CRA subsidiary, with the combined entity listed on the share market both in Australia and London. The Keating government approved the merger, subject to a series of undertakings, including that a third of the board would be Australians, that substantial management would continue to be located in Australia and that the global exploration operations be Australian based. The internationalisation of the mining industry has continued. Following BHP's merger with Billiton in 2001 (for which conditions were imposed requiring that the business remain headquartered in Australia, with the chief executive and finance director having their primary residence in the country), the company is now the world's largest mining company, with Australian domiciled shareholders owning 24 per cent. Rio Tinto, the world's second largest minerals group, has not kept to the undertakings it gave the Keating government and all its head-office functions are in London. Australian shareholders own 16 per cent.

During the Coalition's 13 years in opposition, John Howard had, both as opposition Treasury spokesman and opposition leader, pressed for further deregulation of foreign investment, vowing in the lead-up to the 1987 election to abolish the FIRB altogether.[24] In government from 1996, he left the structure of foreign investment regulation largely intact, besides removing Labor's requirement that uranium mining be controlled by Australians. However, in 2001, the FIRB had a difficult transaction to consider: a $10 billion hostile takeover bid by Shell for the operator of the North West Shelf project, Woodside. The development of gas fields 100 kilometres off the West Australian coast was the biggest commercial project ever undertaken in Australia. Woodside was the operator of the field. Shell was building its portfolio of gas projects through the Asia-Pacific region. Critics of the takeover bid argued it would allow Shell to pick and choose which of its Asian projects would proceed. Ill-considered comments from Shell chief executive Raoul Restucci underlined these concerns: "If Shell wins control after the shareholder vote, probably in late March or April, it will aim to stop Woodside from competing directly with Shell, as it has in liquefied natural gas receiving terminals in China and India."[25]

Labor backbencher David Cox highlighted that Shell was also negotiating a stake in the Korean state gas company, Kogas, with the objective of gaining its stake in the Russian Sakhalin gas project. This would be a direct competitor to the North West Shelf. There were more fundamental political forces at work. Woodside was West Australia's largest company and West Australian Coalition parliamentarians argued strongly for government protection. "If we wanted a laissez-faire system of enterprise in this country, one has to ask why we have the Foreign Investment Review Board",[26] one asked. The Liberal government in Western Australia fell at the polls in February 2001, while a federal election was due later that year. "I am concerned to ensure that this country does not become a branch office economy", Howard commented following the West Australian poll loss. "My commitment to globalisation – my commitment to open markets – does not blind me to the reality that economic sovereignty and economic independence and economic dignity is a very important part of political independence and political dignity."[27] The FIRB was split on the issue, but the Howard government's treasurer, Peter Costello, resolved to block the Shell bid, saying, "It is in the national interest for the operator of this project to develop the resource to its maximum and for sales from the North West Shelf to be promoted in preference to competing sales from projects in other parts of the world".[28] He said he could not conceive of effective conditions that could be imposed on the Shell bid that would ensure this was the case.

Political interest in the resource sector has always run in tandem with commodity prices. The late sixties boom, driven by the rise of Japan and the opening of Australian iron ore, bauxite and nickel reserves, inspired McEwen's Australian Industry Development Corporation. The opening of Queensland's coal reserves and the surge in coal prices following OPEC's embargo in the mid seventies gave the market background to the Whitlam government's efforts to maximise Australian control. Fraser made the prospect of a resources boom the centrepiece of his 1980 election campaign, and at the same time became stricter on foreign investment. The dramatic industrialisation of China through the 2000s pushed the issues back into the limelight.

In its last years before losing office in 2007, the Howard government was content to let the company tax receipts from the mining sector roll in, rising in the space of just four years from $2.7 billion to $8 billion, as Chinese demand pushed prices for iron ore and coal to historic heights. For a while the Howard government contemplated a "strategic economic partnership" with China while it initiated negotiations on a free trade agreement. When China's biggest aluminium company, the state-owned Chinalco, bid $3 billion to develop the Aurukun bauxite leases in Queensland in 2007, Treasurer Peter Costello welcomed it as a sign of the strength of Australia's relationship with China. For a brief period, following the election of the Rudd Labor government, it appeared that nothing would change. Treasurer Wayne Swan waved through FIRB approval for the first hostile takeover bid by Chinese state-owned Sinosteel for Midwest Minerals, which was developing an entirely new field of iron ore in West Australia, near Geraldton. But when Chinalco raided Rio Tinto's London share register in February 2008, foreign investment policy suddenly jumped to the top of the new government's priorities. Rio Tinto was in play, with BHP-Billiton having made an informal takeover offer for it two weeks before the 2007 election. Chinalco's raid was an attempt to stop the merger of its two biggest iron ore suppliers.

Kevin Rudd came to government keenly aware that he had a deeper knowledge of China than any other western leader, at a time when China was emerging as the world's number two power. In a speech to the Brookings Institution several months before the 2007 election he said China's leaders aspired to national wealth and power but did not have a clear vision of how they intended to use it. A benign future could not be assumed. Rudd saw the rise of China as the greatest geopolitical challenge of the times and regarded China's advance in Australia's minerals fields as a strategic move by the Chinese state, rather than the commercial action of individual state-owned companies.

Uppermost was the concern that China, as a customer of Australian resources, might gain inside knowledge which would be to its advantage in pricing negotiations. A customer owning the supplies of such a key export commodity would dilute the market power of the other suppliers. Rudd also wanted to know if there were broader security implications, and referred the issues raised by Chinalco's share raid to the Cabinet's powerful National Security Committee.

The only public outcome of that work was the spelling out of the guidelines by which investment proposals from state-owned companies would be judged. These included whether the enterprise operated at arm's length from its owner government, and whether the government had the ability to influence the direction of the business, whether through governance arrangements or through control of funding. Corporate governance would be considered. Although this was only making public what had long been the guiding principles for the FIRB, it was seen in China as a new policy aimed at warning its investors off.

Chinalco had behaved badly – it had been told by its legal advisors that the Australian government would expect it to seek prior approval before buying Rio Tinto shares, but it believed this was impractical ahead of what was the largest share raid in the history of the UK market. It was being tricky by taking advantage of

Rio Tinto's dual listings in the UK and Australia. This prejudiced its relationship with the government. Because the stakes were so high, it inevitably coloured the bilateral relationship. Rudd sought to calm matters by declaring that the guidelines were not discriminatory and that he had received no negative response in discussions with Chinese authorities. However, WikiLeaks later reported a discussion between FIRB's executive officer Patrick Colmer and a US embassy official, recording that the guidelines had intentionally "signalled a stricter policy aimed squarely at China's growing influence in Australia's resources sector" and that the government privately wished to "pose new disincentives for larger scale Chinese investments".

Next, Sinosteel sought to buy out Murchison Metals, which held the neighbouring leases to Midwest Minerals. This would give it full ownership of the new Geraldton iron ore deposit. The FIRB ruled it could only take 49 per cent of Murchison, saying the government preferred that significant new resources should be open to multiple investors. The government did not want Sinosteel to be the sole customer for the project. The idea that Australia wanted a diversity of customers was a new element in foreign investment policy and reflected the work of the National Security Committee.

The impression that the government wanted to limit the equity of state-owned entities in resource projects was fanned by a speech given by Colmer to the Australia China Investment Forum. "In the resources industries ... government has expressed a preference for projects which are joint projects in various forms, and in particular we are much more comfortable when we see [foreign] investments which are below 50 per cent for greenfields projects and around 15 per cent for major producers", he said. Colmer added that many approvals had been given to projects that did not meet these targets; however, his speech was interpreted as new policy.

Chinalco raised the temperature further in 2009, with a complex joint venture proposal with Rio Tinto that would have left the Chinese company with 19 per cent equity, and higher stakes in several of the operating businesses, including in iron ore. BHP-Billiton argued in a confidential submission to the government that it should see Chinalco's prospective deal with Rio Tinto as part of a pattern of investments by Chinese state-owned companies. "The risk of coordinated action seems particularly real when one aggregates the proposed acquisitions by Chinalco with existing Chinese investments in Australian iron ore companies and/or assets."[29] The Chinalco deal with Rio Tinto brought widespread opposition. Barnaby Joyce made television advertisements, funded by maverick businessman and political activist Ian Melrose. The Coalition leader at the time, Malcolm Turnbull, said that Chinese companies should be privatised if they wished to execute deals of that sort in Australia. The Greens said the deal would result in a "communist dictatorship" pulling strings in the Australian resources sector, while the Australian Workers Union said having a foreign government as both the producer and the consumer of iron ore was a conflict of interest.

The Chinalco deal was ultimately scuppered by Rio Tinto's UK institutional investors and its board, who concluded too much was being given away. However, it was BHP itself which took the heat out of Chinese investment in Australian resources. BHP succeeded in shifting the basis of iron ore marketing from long-term fixed-price contracts, which were hammered out in tortuous annual arm wrestles between Australian miners and Chinese steel mills, to the spot market, where anonymous bidders and vendors traded iron ore daily, with the prices reported by independent third parties.

It had not been a figment of BHP's imagination that there were forces within the Chinese government that were extremely aggrieved by the stratospheric price of iron ore, and believed that, as the leading customer, China should take steps to strengthen its bargaining power in the annual contract talks. Once the trade shifted to spot markets, and there were no more contract negotiations, all question of political influence over prices disappeared, and with it, any reason to fear ulterior motives behind China's investment in Australian resources. Ownership of Australian resources would bring no influence over the price.

But Treasury continued to believe that the Australian people were not getting full return from the prices China was paying for our minerals. "Australia's current resource charging arrangements fail to collect an appropriate return for the community from allowing private firms to exploit non-renewable resources, mainly because these arrangements are unresponsive to changes in profits", was the blunt conclusion of the review of the tax system conducted in 2008-09 by Treasury secretary Ken Henry. Henry had worked on the original petroleum resource rent tax as a junior Treasury officer in Paul Keating's office and, like many tax economists, believed a rent tax was the best way to achieve a proper return to the state. The argument made by the Minerals Council in its submission to the Henry Review was that royalties taxed mining production, whether it was profitable or not, and therefore discouraged investment. Henry argued that royalties failed to capture the upside during price booms, and produced a chart showing minerals taxation had dropped from as much as 45 per cent of mining company profits at the beginning of the 2000s to just 15 per cent. It is probable that Treasury expected the review's recommendations to be exposed to a period of consultation; however, Wayne Swan wanted to take a tax package to the 2010 election, with a new tax on the resource industry paying for a series of tax concessions he believed would be electorally popular.

The Resource Super Profits Tax, unveiled a few days ahead of the 2010 budget, was seen by the mining industry as an attempt by the government to expropriate 40 per cent of everything they had built. Companies would be allowed to earn a return equal to the government bond rate (6 per cent at the time the tax was unveiled), and deduct depreciation, but the government would take 40 per cent of everything above that. If the project failed, the government guaranteed it would provide tax credits equivalent to 40 per cent of the costs. In this way, it was argued, the tax was like the government taking a 40 per cent equity stake with exposure to the downside as well as to the profits. However, the mining companies said that the government was taking its share of mines based on their written-down value, which was a fraction of their true worth, while the promised tax credits would be worthless. Fortescue Metals chief executive Andrew Forrest captured the industry's sentiment. "This is a nationalisation of 40 per cent of the mining industry and the first step towards where the despotic economies go when they start nationalising industry."[30] The government may have thought that the mining industry was too remote from the electorate to become a political danger; however, the industry funded an aggressive television advertising campaign devised by Neil Lawrence, who had been responsible for Labor's winning 2007 election campaign. With a theme of "keep mining strong", the campaign, on which $22 million was spent, claimed the tax would hurt the economy at large, illustrating it with the person in Whyalla renting his house to a miner and the young geologists believing in their mission as they tramp through the outback. With the Coalition running a blistering campaign against the tax, the government's poll ratings began to wilt. Many other factors contributed to the downfall of Kevin Rudd, but the launch of the mining tax without any consultation with the industry (or Cabinet) was one of them.

His replacement, Julia Gillard, quickly dealt with the issue, negotiating a new resource rent tax that met most of the industry's objections. The terms of the new tax were hammered out in an extraordinary four-day session in which Treasurer Swan and resources minister Martin Ferguson sat opposite the chief executives of Rio Tinto, BHP-Billiton and Xstrata. Both sides kept their advisor staff in adjacent rooms. The concessions were large – the tax rate was now an effective 22.5 per cent, it applied on profits greater than the bond rate plus 7 per cent, with the base for this calculation being the greater of market price or historic cost. Companies were allowed to exclude profits earned from transporting, crushing or any other processing of minerals. The tax would only apply to iron ore and coal, Australia's biggest two minerals exports. The government was able to claim the resulting fall in revenue would be modest, because it had massively inflated the estimates of commodity prices.

The International Monetary Fund (IMF) had seen Australia's adoption of a full resource rent tax as model for the world, particularly for the developing world where natural resources were poorly managed and lightly taxed. "There are few areas of economic policy making in which the returns to good decisions are so high – and the punishment of bad decisions so cruel – as in the management of natural resource wealth", the fund's then managing director, Dominique Strauss-Kahn, had said.[31] The fund regretted the backdown by Swan and Gillard from the original design and expressed a hope that the tax's coverage would be extended again to cover all minerals. There was a sense that one reason the mining companies fought the original tax so hard was their very fear that it would be rolled out across the rest of the world with backing from bodies like the IMF.

Although the industry could live with the revised tax, the Coalition kept its campaign against it burning and made its repeal one of the first orders of business following its election in September 2013. In the end, the tax yielded almost nothing. A crucial error in drafting the agreement with the three mining companies allowed all state royalties to be deductible from the resource rent tax. Swan and Ferguson had intended this to include royalties applying at the time the tax was launched, not all future royalties. This oversight, however, enabled the states to jack up their royalty rates, arguing that it would all be deductible from the Commonwealth's resource rent tax. Increased production and increased royalty rates meant that over a five-year period, state government income from minerals almost doubled from $4.8 billion to $9.3 billion. Revenue from the mining tax, which was forecast to raise $3.5 billion in 2013-14, in fact yielded just $100 million. Treasury had miscalculated the size of the deductions that mining companies would be able to claim for their existing investments. However, estimates made by Deloitte Access Economics for the Minerals Council show that the original Resource Super Profits Tax wouldn't have made any money either, given the fall in commodity prices from their 2011 peaks, because it had proposed refunding resource companies for all their state royalties. The reason a profits-based tax has worked well in the offshore oil and gas industry is because there are not royalties to be paid in addition.

So do the resource companies pay enough to the state for their exploitation of the nation's resources? Mining is an industry which, throughout history, has enjoyed brief and fabulous booms and long periods of hard work, where the margin between the world price and the cost to extract and ship can be very tight. It is during the booms that royalties seem to deliver inadequate returns to the state for the magnificent profits being returned to shareholders. In 2007, Treasury decided that this boom was different: China's growth would deliver super-profits to the resource sector for another two decades. This gave it the urgency to find a better way of taxing resources, but the never-ending boom was not to be. As prices crashed back to long-term averages and below, many a foreign investor, particularly in Australia's coal and iron ore industries, was left licking their wounds from loss-making ventures.

When the resource industry suggested to the Henry Tax Review in 2009 that Australia should switch from royalties to a profit-based resources tax, it was thinking about the long lean periods. The need to pay royalties when prices are low or when a venture is just starting up is, as the Henry report identified, a barrier to investment. The projects that get up are less likely to be the marginal ones. The best projects will still go ahead.

Royalties do provide state governments – the constitutional owners of minerals in the ground – with a steady income stream. Their budgets are less subject to the wild swings of the resource cycle than if they were dependent on resource company profits. Estimates by Deloitte Access show royalties were only 13 per cent of resource company pre-tax and pre-royalty profits in 2010-11, at the peak of the boom. By 2012-13, they were up to 24 per cent and rising. The return to the state, as the owner of natural resources, is less in the boom-time than it would be with a resources tax, but is greater during the long and lean periods.

The nation has gained from the rise of the resource industry, with almost $1 trillion invested between 2005 and 2015. Mining has risen from 5 to 10 per cent of the economy over the space of a decade, and up from barely 2 per cent in the mid sixties. The Reserve Bank estimated that including the suppliers to the resource sector raised its influence on the economy to 20 per cent. Until the early 1960s, Australia's major role in the world mining industry was as the biggest source of lead. It is now the biggest source of global trade in iron ore, coking coal, gold and bauxite, while still also being the biggest supplier of lead. It will soon be the biggest seaborne supplier of liquefied natural gas (LNG). Canada also has great mineral wealth, but is not on the scale of Australia, either in its contribution to Canada's growth or its weight in world trade. Mining is the unique national competency that Australia does bigger and better than anyone else. The foreign share of the resources industry has risen from the 62 per cent, which Whitlam wished to set as an upper limit, to about 82 per cent in 2015, by the Reserve Bank's reckoning. It will rise further as the predominantly foreign-owned LNG projects are completed. Foreign investment has driven the growth of the industry.

The majority ownership of BHP-Billiton and Rio Tinto may be global now, but there is still a solid Australian stake and, with more than half their assets here, their fortunes are inextricably linked with our own. Mining has driven the internationalisation of the Australian economy. Japan overtook the United Kingdom as Australia's most important export market in 1967, with iron ore the biggest export. Total iron ore exports reached 16 million tonnes in that year, up from only 2 million tonnes two years previously. They were up to 84 million tonnes by 1973 and reached 700 million tonnes in 2014. China has now surpassed Japan as trading partner, but minerals into the Asia-Pacific region now account for 60 per cent of Australia's exports. Australians wondering about their share of this bounty should reflect upon their standard of living, with average incomes and wealth among the highest in the world.

8

EMBRACING GLOBALISATION

The most unexpected result of the 1983 decision to float the Australian dollar, allowing financial markets rather than the government to set the exchange rate, was the assault waged by Australian entrepreneurs upon global markets. John Elliott set out to "Fosterize the world", John Spalvins' tugboat operations went global, Robert Holmes à Court became the biggest theatrical entrepreneur in London, Christopher Skase was buying the Hollywood studio MGM and Alan Bond had gold and telecommunications businesses in Chile, brewing interests in the United States, and huge property holdings in Hong Kong and England. "There were no real limitations when it came to where you could go in business, so long as you were prepared to take on the task and plan it properly",[1] said Bond. There'd been nothing like it since the Seekers, Bee Gees and Easybeats hit London in the sixties.

Until 1983, it had been very difficult to get money out of the country. Regulation was designed to ensure that Australian savings were invested at home and that foreign money flows could not influence Australian interest rates. Portfolio investment abroad was banned until the late 1970s, while direct investments overseas had to be approved individually. In general, foreign investment was something multinationals did to us, not what we did to anyone else. The banks were active in New Zealand and around the Pacific islands, as were trading companies, of which Burns Philp was the biggest. But until the 1970s, the only Australian company with a truly global presence was Kiwi Boot Polish, which had established an English subsidiary before the First World War and started manufacturing in the United States in the late 1940s. With the float of the currency, capital controls had to go.

The 1980s deregulation of banking meant that debt was readily available seemingly for any global project, and the removal of capital controls that accompanied the float of the Australian dollar took away the barriers. The stock of Australian equity investment abroad had risen from just $1 billion in 1979 to $5 billion by 1982 as a few companies worked through the bureaucracy for approval. Brambles, for example, formed a joint venture in London in 1974, which led to global distribution of its humble wood pallets. But following the float of the dollar, Australian investment abroad increased tenfold to $52 billion, or 15 per cent of GDP, by 1989. It would rise another tenfold to $500 billion, or 35 per cent of GDP, over the next 20 years, reaching a point at which Australian direct equity investment abroad matched foreign investment in Australia.

International investment flows were rising rapidly everywhere. It started in the 1970s following the floating of the US dollar, after American president Richard Nixon broke the dollar's link to gold. Big US balance of payments deficits – the result of massive increases in oil prices and of financing the Vietnam War – resulted in large pools of US dollars accumulating offshore. The deregulation of banking in both the United States and the United Kingdom in the mid-1980s powered the rise of global capital markets. Capital flows rose, from 17 per cent of global GDP in 1980 to 54 per cent by 2008.

The eighties were an economic watershed worldwide. By the mid-1970s, the policies implemented in the wake of the Second World War were failing, with the most obvious symptoms being slow growth, weak productivity and high inflation, which reached 13 per cent in the United States and 25 per cent in both the United Kingdom and Australia. Margaret Thatcher was elected UK prime minister in 1979 and Ronald Reagan US president in 1981 on very similar policy platforms, including cutting income tax and public spending, rolling back regulation and reining in inflation. Inflation would be managed, not through the price and wage controls that had been tried by their predecessors, but by curbing monetary supply, in line with the theories of economist Milton Friedman.

The idea that the state could control the economy through management of the budget and regulation, which had influenced post-war development throughout the world and led to an expansion in the role of the state, had been contradicted by the economic turmoil of the 1970s. Friedman argued that government's useful roles were limited to defence, enforcing contracts and preventing crime, and that any attempt to control the economy would only result in inefficiency. Inspired by Friedman, Thatcher also embarked on an ambitious privatisation program, reversing the widespread nationalisation of industry that had occurred in the United Kingdom throughout the post-war period. Another economist, the Austrian Friedrich Hayek, also became hugely influential. His 1944 book *The Road to Serfdom* argued that state planning was bound to end in totalitarian disaster and that democracy flourished where individuals were free to make choices in competitive markets.

There was no trace of this agenda in the 1983 election manifesto of Bob Hawke, which instead featured a corporatist vision in which, if unions agreed to limit wage claims, companies would limit price increases. An economic summit of business and union leaders was promised to achieve such an accord. However, sitting on the bookshelf in the office of the new treasurer, Paul Keating, was his predecessor, John Howard's copy of the Campbell Report – an inquiry into the financial system commissioned under the Fraser government and delivered to Howard in 1981. The first financial system inquiry since the 1936 review (of which Ben Chifley was a member), it called for the unwinding of the web of regulation that had enveloped the financial system since the Second World War.

Where Treasury had argued the system of regulation enabled it to control the economy, the review concluded that the effect was to spread inefficiency. "The committee's study of the efficiency aspects of these issues has led it to recommend the immediate or ultimate abandonment of a wide rage of direct controls and a shift to almost total reliance on open market methods of intervention in domestic financial markets."[2] The review argued that adequate and vigorous competition was essential for efficient financial markets.

The Campbell committee struggled over the exchange rate. The secretariat pushed for a float but Treasury secretary John Stone wished to preserve Treasury's hold on this lever of economic power for as long as governments were unwilling to run sound budgets. The big banks flew Milton Friedman out to present to the committee and he proved persuasive on the currency. The report argued that if the authorities "get it wrong" in defending a particular level for the exchange rate, the result would be greater financial instability. The report called for a free float and the abolition of exchange controls. It said the regulation of interest rates suppressed competition and resulted in shortages of credit at times of rising rates. It argued that banking should be opened to foreign competition, saying that this would "give existing banks a greater incentive and capacity to compete with each other and with non-banks and make bank status more attractive to new entrants".[3] The document was too radical for the Fraser government, which failed to act on the vast majority of its recommendations, although Fraser and Howard dispute who is to blame. Some of the Campbell committee's recommendations were resisted by Treasury, and others by the banks. Commentary at the time pointed to the National Party's leaders Doug Anthony and Ian Sinclair for persuading Fraser to "pigeonhole" the Campbell Report. A few recommendations, such as allowing the market to set the bond rate for government borrowing, were implemented.

Keating was not an instinctive deregulator, much less a "Friedmanite". He was critical of the Fraser government's tariff policy, which he said defended the inefficient, rather than channelling resources into areas with long-term prospects. But he believed the state had a strong role in shaping the economy. "There must be available to the national Government tools such as exchange controls, export controls, trade practices, the Foreign Investment Review Board, the banking controls and the Prices Justification Tribunal. These are all tools which people from both sides of politics believe are necessary to regulate the Australian economy and to make it work in a much more socially desirable way that is more akin to the national interest",[4] he told parliament in 1978.

He was in many ways a Labor leader in the tradition of John Curtin. He shared the traditional Labor hatred of "money power" but was open to the workings of a competitive market economy. Monopoly was a far greater enemy than foreign ownership. In a 1977 speech to parliament which Keating himself cites as a pointer to the attitudes he brought to the Treasury portfolio, he blamed the increasing foreign domination of Australia's burgeoning coal industry upon the laziness of the Australian banks.

"The monopoly in banking given to Australia's handful of private and public banks has produced the most conservative banking community in the world", he said, adding that the only way Australian resource developers could obtain capital was to sell out to foreign companies. "There is just no point in the government talking about minimum Australian equity requirements when it knows damn well that these hopeless institutions in Australia stand in the way of a growing level of Australian corporate ownership."

"One wonders what the answer to this problem is. Perhaps it is the opening up of the banking licences in Australia to world banking competition so that some of the smug executives in Australia will have to get out and compete instead of having their business given to them on a plate by the provisions of the Banking Act."[5] It was the belief that the big banks were a cosy cartel protected by the regulation and statute that disposed Keating to the deregulatory agenda outlined by Campbell.

However, Keating was also persuaded by the intellectual force of the Campbell Report's arguments. These were ahead of their time – the big deregulation of UK banking did not occur until 1985, four years after the Campbell Report's completion, while it was also the mid-eighties before the US was goaded into action by the widespread failure of savings and loans institutions. The Campbell Report had an able secretariat, led by a young Treasury officer Fred Argy, who went on to a successful academic career, and he drew on the expertise of up-and-coming finance academics such as Tom Valentine at Macquarie University, Peter Swan at UNSW and Bob Officer at Melbourne University. There was also support from within John Howard's office, from his advisor John Hewson.

For free traders believing in the power of unfettered global commerce, the seventies brought a political flowering after a long drought that had begun with the 1909 fusion of George Reid's Free Trade Party with Alfred Deakin's Protectionists. There had always been a few isolated voices pleading for Australia to open up to the world, but there was no political base.

Economist Edward Shann, a professor at the University of Western Australia from 1912, argued against the "hermit state" which wrapped business in protection, breeding a lazy economy.

"The voice of the special pleader is never stilled. New protection, developing through wages fixation, tariff schedules, Navigation Act restrictions and subsidies on export has wrapped Australian industry in a net of legal rules. The Australian business man is tempted to become a suave concessionaire exploiting his small corner while yet the system admits it, but explaining that he would gladly treat his clients better if the newest board would but give him a little larger scope and check the unpatriotic greed of others."[6]

As chief economic adviser to the Bank of NSW, Shann was influential in shaping responses to the depression, including greater flexibility for the exchange rate, and deregulation of business markets, while pressing for governments to balance their budgets.[7]

The great historian Keith Hancock wrote that protection had become a cult that was "interwoven with almost every strand of Australia's Democratic nationalism". Australians saw menace in the poverty of its neighbours and regarded protection as the bulwark defending their high living standards "against the onslaughts of frugal and unscrupulous foreigners",[8] he wrote.

At a popular level, Tariff Reform Leagues had a small but dedicated following in the 1920s and '30s.[9] They provided earnest letters to the editor, engaged in public debates and provided a consumer voice before the Tariff Board. Senator Hal Colebatch was president of the Melbourne branch of the league and he had a few fellow senators who felt the same. However, belief in free trade found no traction at a policy level from either Labor or conservative governments.

Perhaps surprisingly, there were members of the Tariff Board, appointed to give effect to the policy of protection, who began to question its cost as early as the 1920s, expressing concern that its determinations were being swallowed whole by trade unions, pushing up their wage claims to match the tariffs. Among the doubters on the board in the late '20s and early '30s was a South Australian farmer, Stan Kelly, who argued inefficient industries were being coddled by the system. His parliamentarian son Bert Kelly helped to erode the political base for protectionism through the seventies.

The independence of the Tariff Board was a source of angst for its political masters, particularly John McEwen as trade minister through the 1950s and 1960s. He appointed and then battled with its chairman Leslie Melville, who was among the tribe of economists who mixed public service and academic brilliance from the 1930s onwards. Infuriated by Melville's determination to reject blatant rent seeking from companies seeking protection, McEwen increasingly bypassed the Tariff Board to offer protection to firms he favoured. Melville resigned and was replaced by a public servant whom McEwen thought he could control, the head of customs, Alf Rattigan. However, by the 1960s, forces driving a greater openness to the world had begun to coalesce. Rattigan found support in the work of economist Max Corden, who demonstrated that tariffs on business inputs rendered local manufacturers uncompetitive with imports and massively increased costs to consumers. In parliament, Bert Kelly became a formidable opponent of John McEwen from the backbench. *Australian Financial Review* editor Max Newton sent a young economics graduate, Alan Wood, to Canberra to report on what became an epic struggle between Rattigan and McEwen over the cause of free trade.

Though a vehement protectionist, McEwen had himself helped prise open Australia's door to the world. Under the influence of another brilliant academic economist-cum-public servant, John Crawford, whom he'd appointed his department head, McEwen could fairly claim credit for cutting Australia's exclusive commercial ties with the United Kingdom and opening Australia's trade relations with Japan. Crawford had in 1938 delivered a revolutionary speech attributing the growing military aggression of Japan to the attempts by western powers to exclude it from their markets. Growth in Australia's traditional markets was limited, while Asia held great prospects. "Japanese trade expansion may be expected to be industrial in form, and makes that country potentially a greater importer of foodstuffs and raw materials", he said. Post-war, Crawford was helped by the terms of the 1941 Atlantic Charter, sealed between the United States and the United Kingdom, to which Australia acceded as part of the mutual aid agreement it reached with the United States in February 1942, as part of John Curtin's historic pivot from the United Kingdom to the United States. The charter pledged that nations would, at the end of hostilities, work to eliminate commercial discrimination, reducing tariffs and other barriers to trade. Economist Peter Drysdale writes "at the time, the Australians had little choice but to accede to these principles in return for military assistance".[10] Within less than ten years of signing McEwen's trade deal, Japan had replaced the United Kingdom as Australia's largest export market.

Australia's opening to the world took a leap forward with the election of Gough Whitlam in 1972. This brought about the abolition of the White Australia policy, the recognition of China, a formal dialogue with ASEAN and the start of negotiations of a friendship treaty with Japan that would assure it of equality of treatment in investment, immigration and supply of resources. While maintaining a staunchly nationalist approach to foreign investment in the resources sector, Whitlam's internationalism translated into economic policy with the 25 per cent tariff cut in 1973. Whitlam had been the main champion of lowering protection within Labor since the late 1960s, arguing it hurt both Australian consumers and workers in developing nations.[11] In 1973, as inflation was rising, Whitlam asked Rattigan to head an investigation into whether across-the-board tariff cuts would lure imports and lower domestic price pressures. Whitlam was supported in his resolve to act by his economic advisor Fred Gruen, who believed it was a rare moment in which both economic and political conditions favoured a lowering of protection. However, there were recriminations when, in the following year, the global oil price crisis sparked a downturn, with both unions and business saying the tariff cut had made conditions worse.

Opposition leader Malcolm Fraser was relentless in his criticism of the tariff cut, making it the base for a successful campaign in a by-election in the Tasmanian seat of Bass where textile mills were struggling. He attacked the "unreasonable across-the-board tariff cuts which have led to great unemployment in a number of areas, in towns such as Launceston where 2000 people are out of work".[12] In his successful campaign at the 1975 election, Fraser promised: "We will give Australian industry the protection it needs. We would sooner have jobs than dogma."[13] He was true to his word, offering additional help for textile clothing and footwear and the motor industries. He later justified his preservation of protection saying it was "almost impossible" for a country like Australia to gain reciprocal access to other markets in return for lowering its own trade barriers other than through multilateral trade negotiations.[14] He preserved the Foreign Investment Review Board and extended the demand for at least 50 per cent Australian ownership from the resources sector favoured by the Whitlam government to agriculture and fishing.

However, within his party, the ghost of federation's free-trading George Reid was stirring. Bert Kelly lost preselection in 1977, but other Coalition backbenchers influenced by his views, led by a West Australian backbencher John Hyde, began meeting and advocating. The "dries", as they called themselves, wanted to roll back the influence of the state.

Milton Friedman had provided the intellectual argument against the Keynesian idea that government spending could ameliorate unemployment. There was no trade-off between unemployment and inflation as was believed by Treasury – inflation was simply a consequence of the amount of money in circulation. The dries in parliament latched on to Friedman's thinking, and more generally critiqued the idea that the state could shape prosperity. They attacked the industrial relations system, which was seen as a club of unions and employers, they were hostile to the cosy monopolies in markets like air transport, and they sought to dismantle the edifice of tariff protection. Hyde estimated that he could rally at least 20 of his parliamentary colleagues. Eleven crossed the floor on a vote preserving the two-airline monopoly agreement. "We believe in individual liberty and with it, individual responsibility. We believe in the market. We've got much more faith in the market than we have in bureaucratic decision-making. This is only another way of saying we trust the people to identify their own interests and act on them and are not prepared to play god with other people's interests", Hyde said.[15]

There was no sense that the dries were responding to a popular movement – there was no equivalent even of the Tariff Reform Leagues of the 1920s and 1930s. However, the debates were in the public domain. Milton Friedman had done a successful public speaking tour in Australia in 1975, followed the next year by Friedrich Hayek. Both appeared on the popular ABC show, *Monday*

Conference (as did Keynes' Cambridge University associate Joan Robinson). Their views were echoed among academic economists, in some corners of the business world and the media, and among a number of Treasury and Reserve Bank officials. A view that industries with the greatest tariff protection were also those with the worst industrial relations helped drive the creation of the National Farmers' Federation, which lobbied for the dismantling of protection, in direct opposition to the views of the Country Party. A Sydney schoolteacher, Greg Lindsay, won business backing to establish a think-tank – the Centre for Independent Studies – inspired by the Mont Pelerin Society founded by Friedrich Hayek, Ludwig von Mises, Karl Popper and Milton Friedman. The long-established Institute of Public Affairs adopted the new current of libertarian philosophy under the leadership of Rod Kemp (son of its founder Charles Kemp) from 1982.

It was a time before the cost-cutting of the 1990s, when major corporations still had inhouse economics teams that informed their participation in public debates. Shell Australia's chief economist Doug Hocking was taken by an essay of a German academic working at Australian National University, Wolfgang Kasper, portraying contrasting scenarios for Australia – one in which existing mercantilist policies of protection and central wage fixing were maintained and another in which libertarian reforms were implemented, arguing a doubling in income growth was possible. Hocking commissioned Kasper to expand it into a book with a series of co-authors. The result, *Australia at the Crossroads*, published in 1980, became a manifesto for libertarians, with regular meetings of what became known as the "Crossroads Group". "We began to write op-ed pieces advocating heresies, such as the complete removal of all capital controls, the gradual, but across-the-board lowering of all tariffs, vouchers for socialised services, lower, simpler taxes and balanced budgets. All of a sudden, I enjoyed the imaginative, inspiring and energetic camaraderie of people of a truly liberal mindset", Kasper said.[16]

These libertarians had no reason to hope that the election in March 1983 of Labor, led by the most successful advocate the union movement had ever seen and a young treasurer best known as Labor's parliamentary attack dog, would help realise their ambitions. Labor's election platform had been shorn of the left's preferred capital gains tax and total ban on uranium exports, but it retained a requirement that all mineral resources would have to be majority Australian owned. The platform declared that "increasing foreign domination" endangered national sovereignty and eroded "the authority of the elected government". Key sectors should be preserved for excusive Australian ownership and control. In his election speech, Hawke promised to keep industry protection, particularly for the textile and the motor industries, while vowing the government would help to create a steel industry of global stature.

In the last weeks of the Coalition government, invitations had been issued to foreign banks wanting to enter Australia, with application dates after the election. Incoming treasurer Paul Keating suggested they should not bother. Labor's attitude towards the Campbell Report was expected to be influenced by the critique of it coming from the, at the time left-leaning, Melbourne Institute for Applied Economic and Social Research, which had argued the deregulation agenda would come at the cost of social hardship. "Judgments about the financial system we want in Australia cannot be separated, as the committee has tried to separate them, from value positions in regard to the type of Australian society we seek", a Melbourne Institute critique said.[17]

The new Hawke Labor government was immediately confronted with the instability created by the managed exchange rate as capital fled Australia, fearing a re-run of the Whitlam years. Soon, even greater problems would be created by capital flooding back. While Treasury remained as opposed to a free float as ever, Keating had plainly absorbed the arguments of the Campbell Report when, two months after gaining office, he asked Reserve Bank governor Bob Johnston to prepare a "war book" on how a float would be managed. At the same time, he commissioned a review of the Campbell committee's recommendations. By the end of the year, foreign capital was coming into the country, much of it driven by the self-fulfilling speculative hope that the government would be forced to revalue, delivering an easy profit. Treasury secretary John Stone urged the government to tough it out to punish the speculators, but both Hawke and Keating believed the managed exchange rate was dysfunctional and needed to be replaced with the float. "The decision to float now means the speculators will be speculating against themselves, rather than against the Australian government via the Reserve Bank", Keating said.[18]

The decision provoked uproar within the Labor Party. Left backbencher and former academic Andrew Theophanos said the float "handed over control of Australia's monetary system to foreign banks and corporations" and would eventually result in reduced productive investment and undermine government planning.[19] Keating received a stream of protests from ALP branches protesting the decision and opposing any entry for foreign banks, including one from the ACTU.[20] But by the new year, Keating was flagging that new banks would be required, apart from anything else, to deepen the foreign exchange market to manage the newly floated dollar.

Foreign investment continued to be managed under the regime Labor had inherited. Keating rejected a number of foreign takeovers, including an unfathomable ban on US-owned Citibank buying out its British partner, Grindlays, in a merchant bank they jointly owned. However, two weeks after the float of the currency, Keating indicated that the government would not be toughening foreign investment guidelines in line with Labor Party election policy but would continue with the Fraser government's foreign investment stance, itself an extension of the Whitlam stance. Where left academics like Ted Wheelwright had dominated the debate on foreign investment during the Whitlam era, it was now the new libertarians who argued that the Hawke government should build on its removal of capital controls by abolishing restrictions over foreign investment. An influential paper by Wolfgang Kasper argued Australia faced a choice about whether it wanted to "develop an open, competitive, achievement-oriented society or remain mercantilistic, protected and regulated, gradually and irrevocably overtaken by others, clinging to xenophobic attitudes and the illusory security of a wall of tariffs and foreign investment controls".[21] Tariffs had prevented Australia from reaping the full benefit from foreign investment by fostering the development of "tariff factories", or plants that operated at way below economic scale with foreign companies abandoning competition in favour of "oligopolistic peace". In the resource sector, controls on foreign investment limited the number of participants and increased the super-profits the lucky handful were able to obtain.

The Coalition's response to Labor's financial deregulation was to protest that it was not going far or fast enough. In early 1984, the opposition announced an economic platform including entry of foreign banks, further banking deregulation, and a sweeping program of privatisation including the Australian Industry Development Corporation, which, as commentators noted, was a National Party creation. "The Liberals have saddled themselves with a policy approach which will not be supported by its junior Coalition partner", one noted.[22] It was a dynamic that continued through the 1980s.

The deregulation of foreign investment occurred in stages. In September 1984 Keating announced that foreign banks would be invited to apply for licences and at the end of the year controls on foreign investment in stockbrokers were relaxed. In February 1985, Keating shocked the finance industry by announcing that 16 proposed foreign controlled banks would be awarded licences – 10 more than anyone expected.

In October of that year there was the first general relaxation of foreign investment, abolishing demands that vendors of businesses demonstrate that they have given Australian companies ample opportunity to bid. The threshold for gaining government approval was also increased. From Menzies' time, Australia had been running current account deficits of around 2 per cent of GDP but had accumulated very little debt, as most of the deficit was funded by direct foreign investment. But with the decline in Australia's competitiveness through the seventies, the deficit was blowing out to more than 4 per cent, with a lot of it funded by debt. Keating explains:

"I took the view that not only was it imperative that we leave the country open to funding the current account by more than simply portfolio investment but by direct investment as well, and that therefore, we had to take a more liberal attitude to foreign ownership of various sectors of the economy. It was for those reasons [that I liberalised foreign investment] and my general philosophic view of overturning the whole Deakin legacy, which it was my job to do, including tariffs, central wage fixing and the rest. Part of that was dealing with the phobia about foreign investment and more than a phobia – a direct retardant to economic growth."[23]

Through the mid-eighties, Australia suffered a balance of payments crisis. Prices for exports had fallen but recovery from the recession of the early 1980s meant imports were rising rapidly. The resulting blowout in the deficit sent the currency plunging, prompting Keating to declare that unless Australia acted to raise its competitiveness, it would become a "banana republic". As the currency dropped to a low of US57c, Keating announced that foreign investments in manufacturing, tourism and the non-bank financial sectors would no longer need local participation. Proposals would automatically be approved unless they were considered "contrary to the national interest". This reversed the onus of proof. There was another round of liberalisation in 1987, freeing investment almost everywhere except mining and real estate, while in 1992 mining was at last exempted from the requirement for 50 per cent Australian participation. Thresholds for FIRB approval were raised from $5 million to $50 million.

While this succession of investment policy liberalisation was consistent with moves the government was taking to open financial markets to competition more generally in the wake of the Campbell Report, it also reflected the government's strategy of strengthening Australia's international economic relationships. A paper written in 2002 by former academic (and now Labor frontbencher) Andrew Leigh says the seeds of the Hawke government's trade liberalisation were sown with the appointment of Ross Garnaut as the prime minister's economics adviser in 1983.[24] Garnaut saw dismantling protection as essential to Australia's integration with the Asian region. Hawke set out his views in a speech in early 1984. "There is quite wide appreciation within Australia that it will be necessary gradually to reduce Australian protection levels if we are to achieve the goal of a more efficient, export oriented manufacturing sector."[25]

The government did not move quickly on tariffs – there was a lot of economic reform underway, placing strain on the government's accord with the union movement, and it was five years before dismantling trade protection began. In 1986, the Hawke government initiated the Cairns Group of 19 agricultural exporters, which successfully pushed agricultural trade onto the table of multilateral negotiations to update the post-war General Agreement on Tariffs and Trade. This underlined the government's commitment to trade liberalisation.

In 1988, Keating unveiled the beginning of what would become the unilateral demolition of Australia's wall of industry protection. With carve-outs for textiles and motor industries, tariffs in excess of 15 per cent would be cut to that level while everything else would be brought to 10 per cent. "In the past many of the so-called industry assistance arrangements introduced by successive governments have been anything but of assistance. Their legacy is a less flexible economy, too reliant on protection and regulation", Keating said.[26] The package also included cutting the company tax rate from 49 to 39 per cent.

This was followed in 1991 by what must be the most politically audacious economic statement in Australia's history. In March of that year, the unemployment rate stood at 9.2 per cent, having risen from under 6 per cent, with almost 400,000 people losing their jobs in the space of 18 months as recession gripped the economy. Despite the prospect that further jobs could be lost in heavily unionised sectors of manufacturing, Hawke and Keating announced that tariffs on cars would be cut from 35 to 15 per cent, sharply reduced to 25 per cent for textiles and to 5 per cent for everything else. "The package of measures announced today ends forever Australia's sorry association with the tariff as a device for Australia's industrial development", Keating said.[27] Most countries negotiate tariff reductions in multilateral trade deals in order to obtain some sort of quid pro quo. Australia's unilateral reductions, however, were all about improving competitiveness and opening up to the world. Hawke told parliament his government sought "an outward-looking community, enmeshed with the dynamism of the Asia

Pacific region, and capable of taking on the best the world has to offer – and winning."[28]

Andrew Leigh argues the government was helped by a constructive approach from the unions, which, while opposed to much of the government's deregulation agenda, saw the merits of targeted industry assistance plans over general tariff protection. ACTU delegates went on a mission to Scandinavia in 1986 to understand how its lightly protected manufacturing was prospering, and penned a report, *Australia Reconstructed*, advocating interventionist industry policy. Further to the left, Labor's policies were vilified for "surrendering to the multinationals", but without the backing of the union mainstream the criticism of Labor's "economic rationalism" carried no political weight.

The opening of the Australian economy to the world was not confined to the lowering of barriers for capital, goods and services. Hawke made the strengthening of relations with Asia a priority from early in his administration. Asia was becoming an economic force, with the rapid growth of the economies of South Korea, Hong Kong, Singapore and Taiwan earning them the epithet of the "tiger economies". A desire to capture the economic opportunity in the region inspired the amalgamation of the departments of foreign affairs and trade in 1987. Hawke's foreign minister, Gareth Evans, commented that "the Hawke Government, more than any previous Australian Government, has brought trade concerns into the mainstream of foreign policy and has abandoned the artificial distinction between trade policy and foreign policy".[29] In Hawke's first overseas trip in November 1983 he floated before an ASEAN meeting in Bangkok the idea of a regional economic association in the event of failure of multilateral trade negotiations. Australia leapt at the opportunity when the Japanese suggested forming a regional economic forum across the Pacific. Japan asked Australia to take the lead, conscious that its wartime efforts to create a "Greater Asian Co-Prosperity Sphere" were not forgotten.[30] APEC, which started as a ministerial-level forum for economic cooperation, was then elevated to a leaders' forum. Paul Keating, as prime minister, did much to engineer this, and was also influential in getting APEC members to agree to unilateral reduction of trade protection.

As the eighties progressed, the opening of markets around the world, the conquering of inflation and relative international peace brought an acceleration of global growth from the sub-2 per cent managed through the 1970s to just under 4 per cent. The editor of *Harvard Business Review* (*HBR*), Theodore Levitt, popularised the term "globalisation" with a 1983 article, arguing that the future belonged not to multinationals tailoring their products to individual markets but to global corporations offering the same low-cost product around the world. Another *HBR* article in 1989, by the head of McKinsey's Tokyo office, Kenichi Ohmae, asserted that business now lived in a "borderless world". "On a political map, the boundaries between countries are as clear as ever. But on a competitive map, a map showing the real flows of financial and industrial activity, those boundaries have largely disappeared", he wrote.[31]

From the mid-1980s, the average level of tariffs around the world dropped from 26 per cent to 8 per cent, while over a 30-year period, until the global financial crisis, trade grew at rates more than double that of global output. The rising interconnection between advanced countries and the emerging world brought an unprecedented advance in living standards across much of the world.

In Australia, the pressure of tariff reductions brought huge dislocation in the manufacturing industry as businesses such as clothing and footwear were undercut. Manufacturing had been declining as a share of GDP from the beginning of the 1970s, when it accounted for a quarter of national output, but the slide accelerated over the

1980s and 1990s. It is now little more than 6 per cent of GDP. An unexpected side effect of the unwinding of protection, however, was the growth of manufactured exports, which rose from 10 per cent of the total to about 30 per cent between the end of the 1990s and the beginning of the 2000s (a share that has since fallen as resource exports have surged). Suddenly, Australia was exporting pharmaceuticals, components for the Airbus and computer hardware.

The changes of the 1980s opened Australia to the world. Foreign investment poured into the country, doubling its share of the economy. Investment by Australian companies abroad soared even more remarkably, rising from 5 per cent of GDP before the float to 35 per cent by the end of the 1990s. The combined value of investments by Australian companies overseas exceeded the foreign investment in Australia.

In 2009, the Liberal Party held celebrations for the 100th anniversary of the "fusion" of George Reid's Free Trade Party and Alfred Deakin's Protectionists in a new group – the Commonwealth Liberal Party – designed to keep Labor out of power. Reid had resigned as it became obvious that the pro-protection forces would triumph. A century later, there was a consensus, at least at the apex of both the Labor and Liberal parties, that free trade and opening to the world provided the foundations of Australia's prosperity.

9

OUR LAND

The political centre may have decided to embrace globalisation, but the forces traditionally opposed to foreign investment on both the left and the right still carry their torches. Land is the new battleground. Agricultural land has been a political flashpoint for foreign investment over almost 200 years, while sensitivity around foreign investment in residential real estate has forced even the most determined globalisers to tread warily. The internationalisation of the Chinese economy has brought fresh investment to both rural and urban property markets in Australia. It has not been welcomed.

"Foreign land grab on Aussie farms and brands to secure local food supply", read a headline in the *Daily Telegraph* in late 2010. The growth of China had not only generated astronomic prices for coal and iron ore; the increasing affluence and number of China's middle classes were contributing to surging prices for food commodities. Poor seasonal conditions in various parts of the world, including drought in Australia, had also contributed to a rundown in food stocks, while increasing production of biofuels was diverting some land use away from food production. There was a 70 per cent lift in prices for globally traded food commodities between 2009 and early 2011. World Bank president Robert Zoellick warned, "This is the biggest threat today to the world's poor, where we risk losing a generation. We are one shock away from a full blown crisis".[1]

The United Nations trade and investment body, UNCTAD, reported that foreign investment in agriculture was soaring, having tripled to $3 billion from 1990 to 2007, although this was only a tiny fraction of global investment flows.[2] The *Daily Telegraph* story captured the mood of the moment. "Foreign investors have snapped up tens of billions of dollars of Australia's prime agricultural land and rural enterprises – and no one is keeping watch. A swag of government-backed entrepreneurs – mainly from China, the Middle East and Singapore – are sizing up potential investments as global powers move to secure food supplies."[3]

The argument ran that these countries were seeking to shore up the security of their own food supplies by buying up farm production in Australia and elsewhere, with the implication being that Australia's own food security would be jeopardised as a result. "What people don't realise is that if someone buys prime agricultural land, we can't force them to sell us the food from that land. They can ship the food from the land directly to their country and I think that should be looked at", said nationalist businessman Dick Smith.[4]

On the same day the *Daily Telegraph* article appeared, Liberal senator Bill Heffernan – a farmer from Junee in NSW – tabled a petition in the Senate, signed by 1384 citizens, calling for foreign consortia with any government interest to be barred from purchasing freehold agricultural land, because of the "risk to national food security and national security generally posed by acquisitions by foreign entities of Australian agricultural, horticultural and other farming land".[5]

The hostility to foreign investment in the farm sector crossed party lines. A week later, Greens leader Christine Milne and independent Nick Xenophon launched a private members' bill in the

Senate that would require Foreign Investment Review Board approval for any foreign purchase of more than 5 hectares of agricultural land, matching the restrictions imposed in New Zealand. "We used to say 'Australia rode on the sheep's back' but now it seems we're selling the wool, the sheep and the land", Xenophon said.[6]

The National Party and the Greens jointly supported referring the bill to a Senate inquiry. There were widespread calls for the threshold for FIRB scrutiny of foreign purchases of agricultural businesses to be drastically lowered from the $231 million applied to businesses in other industries. In November 2010 the newly elected Gillard government sensed there was a political tide flowing and commissioned the Australian Bureau of Statistics and its agricultural industry advisory body, ABARES, to conduct studies into the actual level of foreign investment in the agricultural industry.

Hostility to foreign investment in agricultural land runs through Australia's history. The very first foreign private investment was in agricultural land and brought a strong nationalist reaction. In return for the promise of an investment of private British capital of up to a million pounds, the Australian Agricultural Company (AAC) was to be granted a million acres of the best pastoral land that its managers could find in New South Wales. For nearly two decades, the pioneer of the Australian wool industry, John Macarthur, had nursed the dream of attracting British capital through a joint stock company. In 1820, he found a receptive audience with the British Colonial Office, which believed the venture would help fund the convict settlement. The company's charter, modelled on that of the British East India Company, received royal assent in 1824.

"The Report of the Directors to the Proprietors of the Australian Agricultural Company occupies a large space in our paper of this day", the editorial of *The Australian* newspaper read on 1 April 1826. "Our Readers will be pleased at being put in possession of the details which this report contains, as they will learn from this the precise character of the monster that is let loose amongst them." Macarthur had his enemies. Among them was William Wentworth, who, along with a journalist Robert Wardel, had established *The Australian* as the colony's first independent newspaper in 1824. The son of a former convict, Wentworth was excluded from the Sydney establishment of which Macarthur was a leading pillar; Macarthur had vetoed Wentworth's proposal of marriage to his daughter Elizabeth. As a campaigner for the rights of freed convicts and small landholders, Wentworth took aim at the AAC, decrying "the merciless rapacity which distinguishes this Company's proceedings". The foreign investors had presented themselves as advancing the interests of the colony. Larding the sarcasm, Wentworth wrote: "The innocent creatures, like true philanthropists, had nothing else but the general weal at heart; and, harmless as the lambs they were to breed, were primarily attached to the 'growing of wool.'" Wentworth continued that the company's first annual report had revealed itself to be "a report for England – for this company, not for the good people of New South Wales". The paper accused the AAC of obtaining favoured access to convict labour and land, and of using its market power to squeeze small settler farmers out of business.[7]

The division between the interests of the large pastoralists, many of whom were associated with British interests, and the small settler farmers runs through the next two centuries, shaping the cleavage between economic nationalism and the embrace of globalisation. While the large graziers were strongly represented in conservative politics, the growth of grain and dairy production by small farmers led to the formation of farmers and settlers associations in the late 1800s and early 1900s. They were formed partly in reaction to the unionisation of rural workers, but they also wanted statutory or government-controlled marketing of their produce, to cut out middlemen, and state provision of rail, bulk grain terminals and irrigation. If manufacturers were to have tariff protection, the farmers wanted the government to underwrite their production. The farmers also wanted tariff-free entry for farm equipment and fertiliser. When in 1913 the West Australian Farmers and Settlers' Association debated forming a political party, they considered, but then rejected, a motion that would place the party firmly on the side of free enterprise and opposed to socialism. "If the motion were carried in the face of the platform in regard to the bulk handling of grain, it would make the association appear ridiculous", one delegate argued.[8] By the beginning of the First World War, there were state-financed meat freezing facilities, state-financed butter factories, state credit for farmers, state dams and irrigation and state agricultural colleges. Farmer representatives, independent of the major parties in state and federal politics, would soon establish the Country Party.

Opposition to the big pastoral companies also helped to define the left. During the bitter shearers' strikes of the 1890s, the pastoral companies were seen to be either British owned or British financed. With the memories of the shearers' strike still fresh, the first Labor government in Queensland, elected in 1915 and led by T.J. Ryan, set out to establish a vast array of state-owned enterprises, including cattle stations, freezing works and butchers shops, in a bid to undermine "the meat trust" – the foreign, mainly US, companies which controlled the meat export industry, and which were believed to be responsible for high domestic meat prices during the First World War.

From the early 1910s through to the mid-1960s, the vast holdings of the British Vestey family across Northern Australia were emblematic of the foreign-owned pastoralist in the eyes of the left. There was a general strike in the Northern Territory in 1919 over claims of corruption involving the Vestey's hiring of a former senior official and their attempts to seize pastoral leases from competitors. There was outrage at the company's exploitation of the territory's tax-free status to avoid tax on their meat exports. Its land management practices were the subject of successive government inquiries from the late 1930s, but the most searing battle was over its treatment of its Aboriginal stockmen and their families. Strikes for equal pay in the mid-1960s were defeated, as was the first claim for land rights over a portion of the Vestey's Wave Hill Station. In the 1970s, this was the land that the Whitlam government awarded to the Gurindji people in the first acknowledgement of Aboriginal land rights.

In the 1960s, the arrival of US beef producers, such as the International Packers from Chicago and King Ranch from Texas, and a big cattle station purchase by US entertainer Art Linkletter, coincided with the rising economic nationalism of the time. In the 1966 election, Labor leader Arthur Calwell attacked the permissive approach to foreign investment, brandishing a Canadian newspaper advertisement proclaiming that land in Australia could be bought at "never-to-be-repeated" prices. It was not as if cattle grazing was an industry in which Australia had no expertise and nor were the sums being invested beyond Australia's own financial resources, he argued.[9]

The Whitlam government was more concerned with foreign investment in resources than in any other sector; however, in the early eighties, rural land again became a hot issue across the political spectrum. On the right, Western Australia's agriculture minister Dick Old, and Queensland's lands minister Bill Glasson, both from the National Party, were calling for a register of foreign land owners, while on the left, NSW agriculture minister Jack Hallam and the Labor opposition's federal rural affairs spokesman, John Button called for the foreign investment guidelines to be reviewed for farm purchases.[10] The West Australian government instructed its agent in London to discourage investment proposals which appeared primarily about achieving capital gain. Hallam called for a rural representative to be included on the FIRB, complaining that much of NSW's best farmland, with top-soil metres deep, was being bought by foreigners. He said there were "deeply disturbing trends", including "the importation of investment which precludes Australian ownership in the future ... and the possible creation of a peasant class of Australian farm managers and workers under absentee foreign landlords".[11] Australian farmers were in danger of becoming sharefarmers for the "gnomes of Zurich" he said.[12] In January 1982, the Fraser government responded, extending the Whitlam government's requirement for 50 per cent Australian ownership in mineral resources to rural and fishing industries. These limitations were rolled back by the Hawke government alongside the general liberalisation of foreign investment controls through the mid-eighties. First, wholly owned investment in farms worth less than $3 million was permitted, provided a third again was invested in capital upgrade, and then that requirement was dropped as well.

A backlash did not take long in coming. The eighties had brought boom conditions to the Japanese economy and increasing affluence to its middle classes who, as import barriers were lowered, developed an appetite for imported beef. The Hawke government had put a lot of energy into improving access for Australian beef into the Japanese market, as Japan had signed a preferential agreement with the United States, which was a threat to Australia's market. Beef sales to Japan had doubled over the 1980s, partly as a result of the Hawke government's efforts. Japanese traders, meat processors and growers started investing in Australia.

It was not long before there were calls for them to be banned. "At the end of the day, the Japanese could have a monopoly control or at least a major influence on every facet of the cattle industry because of their existing role in shipping and importance as an international consumer market", Labor backbencher Keith Wright said. The Cattle Council of Australia, which might have been expected to welcome the attention from its biggest growth market, called for each Japanese investment to be vetted carefully. It preferred foreign investments to take place in joint ventures with majority Australian control. Approval should be conditional on reciprocal access to the investors' home market.[13] National Party leader Charles Blunt said these proposals were not a "xenophobic reaction" to the increased foreign activity. "It is a rational reply to the short term policies of the government who are happy to keep selling off the farm to prop up falling living standards of non-rural voters."[14] The United Graziers Association and the Australian Cattlemen's Union both called for Japanese purchases of pastoral property to be blocked.[15] The concern was that through vertical integration, Japanese buyers would undercut Australian exporters. It was muttered darkly, however, that race had a role. At a Gold Coast public meeting called to discuss the issue, there were cheers among the crowd of 1300 as a woman read a poem dwelling on the racial inferiority of the Japanese.[16]

The Hawke government toughed out the criticism, emphasising the potential gains from the Japanese market, which were realised as its purchase of Australian beef rose a further 70 per cent over the 1990s. The Coalition opposition had, under the leadership of John Howard, sought to outflank the government by arguing it was not going far enough with its economic liberalisation. Its policy document "Future Directions" called for the FIRB to be abolished. The row over Japanese investment caused deep divisions within the Coalition with the National Party wanting vetting of foreign investment to be intensified, not dropped. It contributed to the overthrow of Howard by his rival Andrew Peacock in 1989.

The hostility to Chinese investment in rural Australia in 2010 was therefore springing from well-tilled ground. The campaign for action gained momentum with a report in *The Australian* about the Chinese state-owned coal mining group, Shenhua Watermark, purchasing 43 rural properties in the Gunnedah region of NSW where it was planning to develop a mine. The company had paid huge prices – a farmer received $5.2 million for 600 hectares he had bought seven years earlier for $376,000. A 183 hectare property sold for $1.9 million, up from a previous sale price of $350,000. The Gunnedah mayor Adam Marshall commented: "It's perfectly legal, and some of the people have been able to make some very, very good money out of their properties and are very, very pleased. The concern is more that the Foreign Investment Review Board allows overseas-owned companies – and in this case an overseas state-owned company – to buy Australian land, to mine Australian resources and take them out of our country."[17] The Nationals, on the right, and the Greens on the left, were united in their opposition. Barnaby Joyce – at the time the Coalition's regional development spokesman in opposition – said prime agricultural land should be off-limits for mining.

"Once it's gone, it's gone forever and prime agricultural land is really the agricultural form of the Opera House. It is unique and Australia has some of the best in the world and that should always be quarantined from any event that would destroy its nature", he said.

The Greens leader Bob Brown said food production should have priority over mining. "Shouldn't we be making sure we do have secure and growing food production for a planet that's heading for nine to 10 billion mouths to feed in three or four decades?" he asked.[18] Conservative broadcaster Alan Jones mounted his own campaign against foreign mining companies buying farmland, while the NSW state government announced that the terms of Shenhua's exploration licence were being tightened. Opposition leader Tony Abbott appointed a working group chaired by National Party leader Warren Truss and co-chaired by deputy Liberal leader Julie Bishop to develop a policy on foreign investment in agriculture.

The Australian Bureau of Statistics' finding that only 1 per cent of the almost 140,000 agricultural businesses had foreign shareholding and that 11 per cent of farm land, predominantly in the dry north, had foreign ownership did little to quiet the debate, as critics highlighted methodological flaws in its survey. If a property was owned by a nominee company, who really stood behind it? The ABS did not inquire. The Coalition's discussion document called for a national register of foreign ownership of land to be established and for the threshold for FIRB scrutiny to be lowered to $15 million. It also called for the FIRB to consider agriculture a "sensitive" sector, similar to defence or telecommunications, and receive closer monitoring. Echoing the calls from cattlemen in the 1980s, it recommended the appointment of someone with agricultural expertise to the FIRB. However, implementation of the policy was to be kept away from the National Party and would remain in the hands of Treasury spokesman Joe Hockey.

The tensions that had always existed within the Coalition between the free traders keen to promote foreign investment and the protectionist sentiments of the Nationals broke into the open in mid-2012 as a Chinese buyer emerged for the vast Cubbie Station – a cotton property covering 130 square kilometres in Southern Queensland that had been sent into administration with $320 million in debts by the drought of the first decade of the 2000s. In a good season, the property holds as much water as Sydney Harbour, putting water rights at the centre of the debate. When Treasurer Wayne Swan gave foreign investment approval for the sale of the property to China's textile giant, Shandong Ruyi, Barnaby Joyce condemned the decision as a "bloody disgrace", saying the Chinese owner would add nothing to the property. "The big issue is that, under this deal, a company with clear connections to another nation's government will own Australia's biggest farm by value."[19] Other Nationals joined the chorus of opposition. The Coalition's agriculture spokesman, John Cobb, said Swan's approval had been "just a tick and flick by one of his Treasury bureaucrats" adding that food security should be the key consideration. However, Treasury spokesman Joe Hockey rebuked them, saying he spoke for the Coalition on matters of foreign investment policy and that "some people are freelancing". Hockey's intervention had the apparent backing of Abbott who said he could understand why the Queensland senator felt strongly about the Cubbie Station sale but the Coalition had a "clear and distinct policy" to support foreign investment.[20]

An ANZ study released while the Cubbie debate was at its peak made the obvious point that foreign investment might actually help the Australian agricultural sector make the most of its opportunities. There was the potential to double the volume of agricultural exports into Asia over the next 40 years, capitalising on the rapidly growing middle classes there, but it would take an investment of $600 billion to achieve it. Simply maintaining the status quo would require $400 billion of investment as the rapidly ageing generation of farmers made way for the next generation.[21]

The executive director of the rural industry funded think-tank, the Australian Farm Institute, Mick Keogh, says the idea that foreign investment in agriculture might jeopardise food security is beyond comprehension. "Presumably the fear is that ... in a future time of food shortages, Australians could go hungry while others enjoyed Australian-produced food." Australia, he notes, is the world's fourth-largest net exporter of agricultural products, shipping between half and two-thirds of its food production. The largest landholder is still, after 190 years, Australian Agricultural Company, which controls just over 1 per cent of the land area and a considerably smaller portion of agricultural output. It would take at least 50 operations of similar scale to divert all the fruits of their production offshore before there was the least concern about inadequate domestic supplies. Keogh similarly dismisses the notion that foreigners are pricing the next local generation out of the market, saying foreign purchasers are looking for businesses worth $20 million or more.[22]

Yet logic has little purchase in the emotional argument over agricultural land. Noting that a coal mining company had paid $13.9 million for Kurrumbede near Gunnedah in NSW – the property where Dorothea Mackellar wrote the poem "My Country" – the broadcaster Alan Jones declared: "When you start turning Dorothea Mackellar's property, or, indeed, R.M. Williams' property at Hodgson Vale near Toowoomba, into slag heaps, surely the nation must wake up."[23] The national land-use survey shows that mining affects only a microscopic portion of agricultural land.[24] The total area covered by mines and tailings deposits across Australia is 273 square kilometres, most of which is in arid zones. This generates 67 per cent of Australia's export income. By contrast, improved grazing pastures (as opposed to the vast unimproved outback grazing lands), cropping and horticulture cover 1 million square kilometres, a greater area than France and Germany combined.

Following his election in September 2013, Tony Abbott kept a lid on the firm views of his National Party colleagues about foreign investment in agriculture while his investment minister Andrew Robb negotiated a free trade agreement with China.

China's President Xi Jinping signed the free trade agreement after the Brisbane G20 meeting in November 2014 and followed his trip to Canberra with a visit to Tasmania, along with the business delegation that had come with him. Tasmanian authorities regarded it as a coup that promised much-needed investment and tourism. But radio host Alan Jones was not impressed. With Tony Abbott on his show trying to explain the benefits of the free trade agreement, Jones burst out with, "By this time next week who's going to own little Tasmania? The public are very, very angry about this, prime minister, I can tell you".

Once the China deal was done, Abbott moved to implement the restriction on foreign investment in farmland to $15 million before FIRB approval was required and announced that the Australian Tax Office would have responsibility for compiling a register of owners of farmland. "Foreign investment is important to us, but it's got to be investment that serves our national interests. It can't just serve the investors' interests", he said. Although the new low thresholds were written into the free trade agreements with China, Japan and South Korea that were concluded in 2014, they could not be retrospectively applied to agreements with the United States, Chile and New Zealand, whose citizens could spend up to $1 billion on agricultural land without requiring FIRB approval. Labor investment spokeswoman Penny Wong said the restriction appeared aimed at Asian investors. The Business Council condemned the move, saying agriculture would need capital far beyond the reach of Australian savings over the coming decades.

The trickier part of the new Coalition policy was a plan to cut the threshold for investment in "agribusiness" by 80 per cent to $55 million. But what is an "agribusiness"? The ABS defined an agribusiness as directly involved in farming. So a piggery or a vineyard would be caught but not a sugar mill or cotton gin, both of which are defined as manufacturers. Barnaby Joyce made it clear he wanted all food processors and handlers of agricultural produce, such as GrainCorp, to be caught. Treasury and trade minister Andrew Robb wanted the narrower definition. With no one agreeing on just why special rules were needed for the agricultural industry, the issue was thrown open to consultation. Joyce prevailed, and Cabinet agreed to the new threshold applying to downstream manufacturers in the food industry as well as to farm producers. It was an unqualified victory for the National Party. "We have heard the Australian people, fought for changes and now have delivered", Joyce said.

Attitudes towards foreign investment in residential property are, if anything, less rational than those towards agricultural land. When Treasurer Joe Hockey commissioned a parliamentary inquiry into the issue in 2014, there was a steady flow of submissions vilifying the Chinese. "The uncontrolled buy-up of our properties by desperate offshore Chinese buyers flush with money but lacking confidence in their own country's economy – instead they want to hijack Australians out of their homes and replace them with their own people, who will be in control of Australia's biggest asset: its homes. Australians, so displaced will put pressure on more affordable homes and drive those home owners further down the scale to a new class of poor Australian home owners", wrote D. O'Sullivan, while Mitchell Rilington declared: "The circumstances in which people from China and other Asian countries are flooding into Australia is deeply disturbing. We are experiencing mass immigration from Asia, especially China. These people are often cashed up; they are buying properties in our country and intent on buying more, competing with us, evading our already relaxed immigration and investment laws, and are causing catastrophic repercussions on both Australia's standards of living for younger generations and our long term economic stability."[25]

The language is not so florid, but there is a resemblance to the lines about the Chinese penned in 1888 by socialist William Lane in his newspaper, the *Boomerang*: "They skin our goldfields, they debauch our children, they undersell our merchants, shopkeepers, and producers, availing themselves of trade-tricks and subterfuges such as no honest community could descend to, in order to achieve the white man's ruin more happily."[26]

Asian and particularly Japanese investment in residential housing sparked similar hostility in the mid-1980s. Asia was becoming a part of the Australian world for the first time. Prime Minister Bob Hawke spoke of Australia's "enmeshment" with Asia as he sought to strengthen relations with the region. Asian migration had risen from about 5 per cent of the annual intake in the mid-1970s to about a third by the mid-1980s and half by the end of the decade. Japan's global influence was at its zenith and the yen was trading at an all-time high. "The feared yellow hordes of Asia are not flooding southward – but their capital is", wrote the *Sydney Morning Herald*'s Max Walsh as the level of Japanese investment in Australian real estate rose from $500 million to $2.1 billion in the space of 12 months.[27] Both historian Geoffrey Blainey and the then opposition leader John Howard voiced concerns that the level of Asian immigration was excessive. The grizzled president of the RSL, Bruce Ruxton, did not want anyone to let go of wartime enmity. "No way will the Australian people accept the buying of Australian real estate by Japanese nationals. In fact, their buying of Australian real estate can be equated to the plundering of the Spanish Main by British pirates, centuries ago", he wrote.[28]

For the most part, the Japanese investors were buying apartment blocks in the Gold Coast and prime harbour-side Sydney real estate, but there was a sense that they had a hand in the surge of real estate prices everywhere. "In the last four months over 50 per cent of our sales were to overseas buyers", said Sydney celebrity auctioneer, Andrew Gibbons, adding that he had recruited a Malaysian sales agent and was seeking to hire another from Japan.[29] With an election imminent in NSW and the unpopular Labor government of Barry Unsworth about to be ejected from office, the Hawke government acted, imposing an outright ban on purchases of urban residential real estate by non-residents. Only companies with investments in Australia buying property for temporary residence by executives and approved migrants were exempted. Treasurer Paul Keating claimed the surge of foreign investment in Australian real estate was bringing no economic benefit. Asian Australians pointed out the contradiction. "You want to be part of Asia, yet suddenly you want to be separate. Have you ever heard of London or New York stopping foreign investment?" a Sydney-based, but Hong Kong-born lawyer, Edwin Mok, asked.[30] The blanket ban was softened somewhat over the next three years, making it easier for foreign investors to buy vacant land for development and purchase newly built apartments off the plan. Temporary residents could buy established property but must sell it on their departure from the country.

However, the rules were essentially unchanged for the next 20 years until the global financial crisis sparked a rethink. House prices were plunging in the United States, Britain and Spain, and prominent University of Western Sydney academic Steve Keen was predicting a 40 per cent fall in prices in Australia's capital cities. "We are in the middle of the biggest housing bubble we have ever had", he declared as house prices indeed started slipping in the latter half of 2008.[31] A stimulus package, launched four weeks after the collapse of US Lehman Brothers had caused global financial markets to seize, included generous new incentives for first home buyers. At the same time, the assistant treasurer, Chris Bowen, announced that temporary residents would no longer have to notify the FIRB of purchases of established property, new real estate or vacant land. A requirement that foreign developers sell at least half their units to Australian residents was dropped, and they were allowed to buy vacant land. The intent was to help bolster the sagging real estate market.

But by February 2009, as the new rule took effect, house prices had stopped falling and were starting to lift. The first home owners grant was working, encouraging that slice of the market to take on bigger debts than ever before while interest rates were at record lows. By March 2010, house prices in Melbourne had leapt 25 per cent while the Sydney gain was 18 per cent and, as in 1987, the finger was being pointed at Asian buyers.

"A large expectant crowd is gathered to bid on a property at auction. And yet, thousands of kilometres away, the auction is being watched via the internet in America, Britain, Eastern Europe, China and India. Suddenly there are phantom bidders competing furiously with the domestic bidders, pushing the price higher and higher via net or mobile phone. And often, they win the day. Everyone else goes home, doubly disappointed that not only did they fail to secure their dream home but they were outbid by someone who was half a world away", wrote Fairfax journalist Charles Purcell.[32] It was not, he said, a matter of economics. "Owning some place to call home appears to be an in-built territorial instinct for humans. Animals are the same way – whether it's a nest, a cave, a tree or a pond, everything needs a space that acts as a base and place of sanctuary."

Historian Marilyn Lake saw Australia's age-old anti-Chinese racism in the reaction. "No longer accused of augmenting the ranks of cheap labour, they are now attacked for their apparent wealth and blamed for the difficulties experienced by young white Australians in buying their own homes, in realising the Australian dream. The offence of the Chinese, it seems, is that they now have too much money. Increasingly, callers to talkback radio blame not just negatively geared investors exploiting Australian tax law, but Chinese buyers who speak Mandarin."[33]

The government was facing an election and did not want to do so facing a wall of talkback radio on how it was to blame for pricing young Australians out of the market. Reversing the 2009 changes, assistant treasurer Nick Sherry acknowledged there was no hard evidence that foreign buying was in fact pushing up house prices but said "there are anecdotal concerns to which we are responding". He announced tough new penalties for breaches and a "dob-in-a-foreign-bidder" hotline.

And yet the issue of foreign buying of real estate would not go away. After a quiet few years, house prices started lifting again in late 2013 following the Reserve Bank's decision to cut its cash rate to a historic low of 2.5 per cent, which was enough to bring the cheapest mortgage rates in the market below 5 per cent. Again, there was talk of Asian buyers driving the market and pricing local first homebuyers out of the market, a development which *Sydney Morning Herald* columnist Paul Sheehan described as "not culturally healthy". He said that "curbs on foreign ownership will become an inevitable public debate if a critical mass of locals believe they are being priced out of home ownership in their own cities".[34]

Left intellectual Clive Hamilton wrote in the *Guardian* that "Cash pouring in from China is one of the principal drivers" of rising Sydney house prices and this was "changing the city's social fabric in a way that will be felt for generations to come". Following a storm of online protest, the *Guardian* editors acknowledged that a reasonable person could have seen the article as racist and acknowledged there was insufficient evidence to support the claim in the headline that "Wealthy Chinese are making Sydney's housing problem worse".[35]

Investment bank Credit Suisse wrote a provocative report, predicting that Chinese investors would spend $44 billion on Australian real estate over the seven years to 2020. It estimated that Chinese were buying 18 per cent of new housing supply in Sydney and 14 per cent in Melbourne. "While Australia has some of the most unaffordable housing in the world, further strong Chinese demand can push prices even higher."[36] The note urged investors to cash in on the trend by buying shares in property development companies.

There were suggestions that non-resident Chinese were simply avoiding the foreign investment prohibition on them buying established real estate. It was said some were buying property for student children and then renting the houses out when the students returned home, while others were getting resident relatives to buy on their behalf or simply buying at auction and never registering with the FIRB. It was said the chances of getting caught were slight.

Treasurer Joe Hockey took these claims seriously enough to commission a parliamentary inquiry led by one of the brightest of the new generation of Liberal backbenchers, Kelly O'Dwyer. The chair of the FIRB, Brian Wilson, noted to the committee that one in ten Australians has one Asian parent and in the many parts of the state capitals, the proportion could be double that. He said the "dob-in" hotline established in 2010 often got calls along the lines of, "A Chinese has bought this house and my daughter was not able to do so", only to find that when the claims are investigated the purchasers are found to be citizens with as much right as anyone else to buy a property. He added that there were 450,000 legal temporary residents with an entitlement to buy a house, so it was not surprising that some did.

A study presented to the inquiry examined 74,000 home sales in Sydney over the decade to 2011 and identified that the proportion going to buyers with Chinese surnames rose from 6.5 per cent to 13.2 per cent over that period. However, it found that when controlling for variables such as suburb, housing quality and date, the Chinese buyers paid an average of 2 per cent, or $14,000, less than other purchasers, suggesting they are not the force driving up house prices.[37] This analysis was of established home sales. Another study of sales to foreign investors "off the plan" recorded through the FIRB found that the level of sales was related to movements in prices with a 12-month lag. This meant it was more likely that prices were generating sales volume than vice versa, although the author emphasised the conclusion was tentative.[38]

Figures presented to the inquiry showed there had only been 5100 applications for FIRB approval to buy established housing in 2012-13, against a total of 363,000 sales of established housing in that year – just 1.4 per cent. The committee concluded that the number was too small to cause distortions in the market, but O'Dwyer nonetheless introduced the report to parliament, saying it was responding to the reality that "many Australians now worry that home ownership may be out of reach for them, their children, or their grandchildren".[39]

With about 190,000 permanent migrant visas being issued each year, in addition to up to 20,000 or so arrivals from New Zealand, foreign demand is a factor in the property market, aside from the numbers of temporary residents required to seek foreign investment approval to buy established housing.

There is an increasingly global real estate market. In part this reflects the growing mobility of professionals and business people, with a United Nations study showing highly skilled migration has been rising about 50 per cent faster than migration overall since

1990.[40] People from Asia dominate the migration of people with tertiary qualifications globally. With its large migration program focused on skills, Australia is more exposed to these global influences than almost any other country. OECD figures show Australia has 40 per cent as many skilled migrants as skilled native-born residents, against an average across advanced countries of 11 per cent.[41] At least a third of skilled migrants come to Australia originally on temporary visas. These are, as the FIRB's Brian Wilson notes, people with a legitimate interest in acquiring real estate.

Even as the controversy about Chinese real estate purchases was running hot, the Labor government introduced a new class of residency visa for "significant investors", who could shortcut the normal bureaucracy if they invested at least $5 million in an approved investment. These, and the longer established business visas, are marketed squarely at wealthy Chinese who can be counted on to buy real estate.

The search for "safe haven" assets is a driving force behind the globalisation of residential real estate. A British study quantified this by looking at the foreign-born population in each of the 640 electoral wards in London and analysing what happened when there was a political shock in the home country of that population. The theory was that turmoil in, for example, Greece would result in appreciation of house prices in London boroughs with high Greek populations. The study found this was indeed the case, with turmoil in China strongly associated with house price appreciation in high-income wards with large Chinese populations, and turmoil in Southern Europe affecting low-income wards.

The parliamentary inquiry's report did not discuss any alternative strategy for governing foreign investment in residential real estate, accepting the proposition in the terms of reference set out by Hockey that "the overarching principle of Australia's foreign investment policy, as it applies to residential property, is that the investment should increase Australia's housing stock", and that otherwise permanent investment in established housing by non-residents should be banned. O'Dwyer was shocked that there had not been a prosecution for breaching the prohibition on non-residents buying established housing since 2006.[42]

University of Griffith economist Tony Makin has pointed out that there is no economic rationale for this prohibition. When foreigners buy existing Australian assets at higher prices than residents would pay, the Australian sellers make capital gains they would not otherwise have made. This can be used to create new assets or be spent on consumption – either way the economy is better off and there has been an inflow of capital.

Former analyst with the Centre of Independent Studies Stephen Kirchner has argued that the problems with housing affordability are not due to too much foreign demand but rather too little domestic supply. Restrictive planning meant that supply did not respond to increased demand and instead prices rose. The solution should be to accommodate both domestic and foreign demand by generating greater housing supply, with regulation of foreign direct investment a "second best solution".[43] The Reserve Bank takes a similar view. Its submission to the inquiry was sceptical that foreign investment would have much influence on housing markets other than in a few localised areas. In response to a question from O'Dwyer while testifying before the committee, governor Glenn Stevens noted that under current guidelines, most foreign investment in real estate was for newly built housing.

"That is where it is easiest for them to come in. It cannot be beyond our capacity over time to meet that demand and to meet the legitimate demands of our own citizens for structures as well, can it? If we cannot do that, if there is a supply side constraint, I would say that is an issue worth addressing in its own right."[44] Beyond that, it was not an economic question but one of how welcoming Australia wanted to be towards foreign investment generally. "That can be a vexed issue at times. With all due respect, that is a matter for our parliament to manage", he said.

The view in the foreign investment legal fraternity was that the government wanted a "head on a stick" to show the world it was serious about enforcing its rules on residential real estate. The head of China's Evergrande Real Estate group, Xu Jiayin – estimated by Forbes Magazine to be worth $7 billion – was perfect for the purpose. An Australian subsidiary, Golden Fast Food, had bought the Point Piper mansion of recruitment entrepreneur Julia Ross for $39 million – a Sydney record for a property without waterfront. It had been all over the papers in November 2014. "Golden Fast Foods is a foreign-owned company which failed to notify FIRB of its intended purchase. Under Australia's foreign investment policy, foreign investment should increase Australia's housing stock. Non-resident foreign nationals cannot buy established dwellings as homes or investments", said Treasurer Joe Hockey.[45]

The decision to force the sale received broad publicity in China. "Australia is like a crow standing on a pile of coal – it just sees the darkness of others and never sees itself", said one post on Weibo, China's version of Twitter.

The inquiry led to a new crackdown on foreign property purchases. Fines of $127,500 and three years' imprisonment would be imposed on foreign individuals and up to $637,500 on foreign companies caught buying established property without permission under a new regime of criminal penalties. To gain permission, a fee of $5000 would be due for properties worth less than $1 million. Beyond that, the fee would be a $10,000 per $1 million. The tax office was put in charge of enforcing the new regime.

Having taken the leap of putting fees on foreign purchase of real estate, the Coalition government went further, applying fees to all foreign investment that required FIRB approval, ranging from $10,000 to $25,000 for business takeovers. The 2015 budget booked revenue of $735 million from foreign investment applications. The best that trade and investment minister Andrew Robb was able to do was to grab $30 million of this to fund a foreign investment promotion campaign.

The Victorian government got in on the act, imposing a 3 per cent surcharge on stamp duty on property purchases by non-residents, adding $15,000 to the cost of a $500,000 apartment on top of the $5000 charged by the Commonwealth. It calculated the fee would raise $300 million.

But will the tide turn? When Sydney house prices are falling, as inevitably they will, will we be wanting the Chinese back, just as the Rudd government did in early 2009? Having avoided the big falls in house prices experienced in most of the advanced world during the global financial crisis, Australia's house prices are now among the highest in the world, while Australian households also have bigger debts than households anywhere else. In the senior executive suites of Australia's big banks, which hold the vast majority of housing mortgages, there are concerns that the crackdown on foreign investment in real estate might prove too successful and that the loss of foreign money coming into the housing market could precipitate a destabilising downturn in the housing market.

10

THE DISAPPEARING CORPORATION

Treasurer Joe Hockey had been entertaining an American friend at his North Sydney home. When the time came to go, his friend used the Uber app on his phone to order a car. The car arrived at the front door promptly. Hockey's friend had paid with his US credit card, which presumably went through Uber in the United States, or Bermuda, or somewhere else entirely, but not through Australia.

"As he was driving off I thought well, I am never going to see the GST out of that. I also thought to myself, Uber is not paying company tax in Australia."[1]

Hockey then reflected on the fact that it was destroying both the value of taxi licences and the revenue that cab companies pay to state governments.

"So, government misses out in three different areas: license fees for existing participants in the market, company tax, and probably GST. So, where is this taking us? How do you design laws where money is more mobile, goods are able to be delivered by drone from Google apparently, and there are disruptive technologies developed every day? So, that is the challenge. That keeps me awake at night."

Yet on Hockey's desk was a report he had commissioned, calling for regulatory barriers to Uber's entry into the Australian market to be demolished. The review of competition policy being led by Professor Ian Harper noted that regulatory agencies had been prohibiting Uber and fining its drivers, despite the evident public demand for its services. "This indicates existing regulation is more concerned with protecting a particular business model than being flexible enough to allow innovative transport services to emerge."[2] The failure to reform taxi regulation suggested governments weren't serious about competition policy. Regulation should "be consumer-focused and not inhibit innovation or protect existing business models", the panel urged.

The review argued that all other service industries were able to operate without regulatory caps being placed on the number of operators. Those caps created a scarcity value for licences that suggested rents were being extracted from ownership of cabs. This was at odds with the industry's claims that the system of taxi licensing matched market supply and demand. The limit on the number of cab licences dates from the depression, when taxi-driver unions and the taxi companies fought a combined campaign to stop their incomes being eroded by new cut-price entrants. The industry had called on the competition inquiry to crack down on "new market entrants ignoring or avoiding compliance with necessary regulatory requirements under the guise of Disruptive Innovation" and gaining an unfair advantage over the incumbents.

Uber is plainly an awkward entity for governments and regulators. Fares are booked through subsidiaries in low-tax countries and the business makes use of the same sort of tax minimisation strategies used by more established trail-blazers in the digital world such as Google and Apple. Its Australian footprint as a corporate entity may be tiny relative to the big operators in the taxi industry but their sense that their livelihood is under threat is shown by the vehemence with which they are fighting the new entrant and its peers.

In the 21st century, the nature of business is being transformed, and with it geographic location is becoming ever more incidental to the generation of profit. The dissemination of news no longer requires massive presses capable of churning 100,000 newspapers an hour consuming entire forests in the course of a night's work. The record store has almost disappeared, the video store is not far behind, and retailers generally no longer need to invest in shop-fronts. Banking is increasingly conducted online. Although the big banks are still the titans at the top of the share market listings, new "peer-to-peer" lending platforms, where individuals make loans and take deposits with each other, may evolve to threaten their dominance. Even at the pinnacle of the manufacturing industry, the auto industry worries that the future may belong to the owners of applications that deliver your driverless car to your door-step. As old businesses are being transformed, new businesses are emerging performing functions hitherto undreamt of, like Twitter, Google and Facebook.

The concern is no longer foreign investment as such, but rather how foreign companies are servicing Australian customers and what collateral damage are they causing to Australian businesses and government tax revenue, whether they have a physical presence and have invested capital in the country or not. It still generates many of the same responses from the same groups that have long had troubles with foreign investment. The left sees inequity in the low levels of tax paid by foreign companies doing massive volumes of business in Australia. Within business, incumbents challenged by the new order seek protection. The tradition of the free traders, carried into the 21st century by people like Ian Harper, calls for innovation to be given free rein, sorting out the tax consequences later.

Globally, the OECD has mounted a campaign to strengthen tax law so that taxes are paid in the country where the profit is earned, and to curtail the opportunities for tax arbitrage with havens and low-tax jurisdictions. However, identifying where profit is earned in the internet age is a challenge, while the technology that created stateless currencies like the bitcoin is evolving to make genuinely stateless enterprises possible.

Australia's first attempt to wrestle with the challenge that internet-based businesses posed to regulation designed for the bricks and mortar age ended in a dismal failure. When the Productivity Commission conducted a web search for "online gambling" in 1999, it yielded just 7000 hits, but there was a sense that it might be the next big thing. Prime Minister John Howard declared he wanted to ban it before it got going. "It is much easier to anticipate something and do something about it than try and close the stable door after the horse has bolted", he said.[3] The horse had already bolted as far as race-track and other sports betting was concerned; however, the Interactive Gambling Act passed in 2001 imposed an outright prohibition on any Australian company offering any form of online gaming such as poker, blackjack or roulette. Looking back on this ten years later, by which time a web search for "online gambling" yielded 12 million hits, the Productivity Commission estimated, on the basis of the number of active gambling accounts in the United States that have Australian addresses, that around 700,000 people were playing online casino-type games – a substantial share of the adult population. The commission acknowledged that many gamblers would have more than one account, however it also noted that the biggest two poker clubs in Australia have 800,000 members, most of whom would have gambled online at some stage.

The Productivity Commission concluded that the prohibition meant that Australian gamblers were more likely to be ripped off by unscrupulous stateless operators with no practical legal recourse, that domestic operators offering traditional forms of gambling had faced greater competition from jurisdictions with looser regulation, that Australian governments had been deprived of tax revenue and Australian businesses had been deprived of an export market.[4] Putting national fences around businesses selling services online doesn't work – the business service can be provided from anywhere on the planet.

Retailers, however, believed that their business selling physical goods rather than online services was different, and that they could raise the barriers somewhat against their global online competitors by forcing customers to pay GST on purchases as they came into the country through the post. The problem was that although the 10 per cent GST is charged on all sales of goods and services for domestic businesses with turnovers of more than $75,000, it was only charged on imported goods if they were worth more than $1000. For booksellers trading against Amazon, there was a clear competitive disadvantage. As the scale and scope of internet commerce grew, clothing and homewares retailers also started to complain.

Having witnessed the runaway success of the resources industry in doing away with the hated Resource Super Profits Tax, a group of 21 leading retailers, including Myer, Just Jeans and Harvey Norman, mounted an advertising campaign pleading for Australian retailers to be given "a fair go". Harvey Norman CEO Gerry Harvey claimed it was "un-Australian" to shop online without paying GST, while Myer threatened to set up online distribution from China to take advantage of the tax break. The government was sensitive to the campaign and asked the Productivity Commission to investigate the issue. The commission concluded that the retailers had a case, but that lowering the threshold to $20, as the retailers wished, would involve the processing of 30 million parcels a year at a cost of more than $2 billion. The additional revenue raised would be only $550 million.[5]

The local retailers did not give up their campaign. With the election of the Coalition government in 2013, they found an attentive ear to the proposal that online retailers should have to pick up the cost of having their parcels inspected for GST. However, as GST revenues went to the states, the Commonwealth left it up to the states to work out the formula. Western Australia refused to discuss any extension of the GST until its claim for a larger share of the GST pie was resolved.

The inequality of GST tax treatment was only the smallest symptom of a profound change sweeping retail worldwide. Brand manufacturers started entering retail directly in competition with traditional retailers. In retail, the bigger you are, the more profit you make. Companies like Zara, Ikea, Gap and Apple began launching themselves as global retailers. They were assisted by advances in the technology of distribution management, winning economies of scale over conventional retailers. Over the five years to 2013, foreign investment in Australian retail grew by more than 50 per cent, to $57 billion.

The entry of the foreign retailers brought opposition from incumbents. Not only did small independent retailers complain about German supermarket chain Aldi being given development sites, the giant Woolworths did too. It lobbied politicians over Australian Competition and Consumer Commission (ACCC) limits on its purchases of new sites, arguing it was losing market share to the foreign interloper.[6] Retailer Dick Smith, who has his own line of food products and has campaigned against foreign investment, argued that Aldi was driving local suppliers out of business with its loss-leading tactics.

However, it was the complaint that the new global retailers, along with many others of the new-generation global businesses, were not paying their share of tax that brought the sharpest political response. IKEA, for example, turned over $5 billion in Australia in the decade to 2013 but paid just $31 million in tax. Coffee retailer Starbucks, which entered the Australian market in 2000, has never paid tax, having been continuously in loss after paying large licence fees to its US parent. "It is hugely important for the globe that companies pay tax where they earn profits", Joe Hockey said at the G20 meetings in Brisbane in 2014, which agreed to an automatic exchange of information among tax authorities.[7] "It is theft when somebody does not pay the tax that is due to a nation and it undermines the ability of that nation to be able to deliver the sort of services that are essential to alleviate poverty, to reduce inequality."

Concern about foreign companies not paying their fair share of tax goes back to the introduction of company tax in the early 20th century. The Vestey family business, built on storing and shipping meat, was so outraged by the British imposition of a 9 pence in the pound tax on their entire international profits in 1915 (intended to help pay for the war) that they shifted their operations to Argentina. When they tired of their exile, they set up an arrangement under which their global operations were leased to a British company, which paid the lease fees into a France-based family trust where funds could accumulate untaxed. The Vesteys argued there should be no profit tax, only a sales tax on the meat they sold in England. As Sir William Vestey told a royal commission sparked by his tax affairs, "In a business of this nature you cannot say how much is made in one country and how much is made in another. You kill an animal and the product of that animal is sold in 50 different countries. You cannot say how much is made in England and how much is made abroad".[8] Until the early 1950s the Vestey cattle operations in Australia took advantage of a loophole, which the tax office unsuccessfully challenged, allowing primary producers resident in the Northern Territory to be exempt from income tax.[9]

The League of Nations made the first effort to tackle tax evasion by international companies in the early 1920s. The league had been trying to resolve double taxation – when a company was headquartered in one country but had manufacturing or marketing in another, there was potential for both to try taxing the same profits. While this could be dealt with by a bilateral treaty between the two countries, the league concluded that battling tax evasion would require an agreement among all countries; otherwise, it would be in the interests of a minority of countries with low taxes to become the transit point for capital and profits. While an agreement was reached that tax authorities could exchange information about companies and their directors on a reciprocal basis, it was not binding and was largely ignored.

By the early 1950s, the belief that multinational companies were avoiding Australian tax was driving the Labor left's criticism of foreign investment. As Labor left luminary Clyde Cameron argued when the double tax agreement with the United States was being debated in parliament in 1953, "as a Labour man, I derive no pleasure from the passage of a measure which, in the main, proposes to make financial hand-outs to organisations and individuals who could well do without them".[10] He proceeded to list the Vacuum Oil Company, the Goodyear Tyre and Rubber Company, General Motors Holden and the picture theatre interests among the businesses that would benefit from tax breaks as a result of the deal.

As economic nationalism and the backlash against multinationals developed through the 1960s and 1970s, it drew on the claim that multinationals were avoiding tax by overcharging their Australian subsidiaries for supplies and intellectual property, or 'transfer pricing'. Left academic economists Ted Wheelwright and Greg Crough explained: "intra corporate transactions now represent a very considerable proportion of world trade and the scale of these transactions clearly gives tremendous scope for the manipulation of prices with their resultant effects on profits, and thus both taxable and national income."[11] They highlighted the rise of global accounting firms to help their multinational customers arrange their affairs in a way to minimise tax.

A case that made its way to the High Court illustrated the problem. The aluminium group Comalco was shipping bauxite to Japan via a Hong Kong business which it jointly owned with its Japanese customers. The bauxite was sold to the Hong Kong company for 33 shillings a ton, which it then onsold to the Japanese customers for 40 shillings a ton, although no value had been added and the Hong Kong company had no operations. Profit was accumulated in Hong Kong where the tax rate was 12 per cent, rather than Australia's 46 per cent. The tax office's case was rejected by the High Court, which, under its chief justice Garfield Barwick, repeatedly found in favour of those exploiting tax loopholes that were contrary to the clear intent of the legislation. The court's stance inflamed the anger of the anti-multinational left. The seventies also brought attention to the use by multinationals of tax havens and of the use of debt rather than equity to fund their subsidiaries. Interest is deducted from taxable profits, whereas dividends were paid after tax. Following the passage of the Whitlam government's Foreign Acquisitions and Takeovers Act in 1975, the FIRB would not approve investments if the debt was more than three times the equity.

The advent of the internet in the mid-nineties was immediately seen as a threat to the tax base. The Australian Tax Office prepared a paper on it in 1997, at a time when less than 10 per cent of businesses used email and barely 50,000 Australians had bought anything online. The ATO concluded that "key taxation principles relating to the source of income, residency and permanent establishments are seriously challenged by electronic commerce".[12] At the heart of the Australian tax system for international businesses was the principle that profits are taxed at their source, so profits made in the country are taxed there. But this assumes a foreign business has a permanent establishment in the country. "Universal access to a web site, automation and high mobility mean that most electronic commerce activities may generate considerable revenue without necessarily being located in close physical proximity to the market and without significant use of any infrastructure anywhere", the report said.

Google was incorporated a year later in 1998 and started selling advertisements linked to search words in 2000. It soon became the poster-child for global tax avoidance, courtesy of its use of a tax minimisation strategy known as the "double Irish with Dutch sandwich". Google sells the right to use its intellectual property to an Irish subsidiary, which is managed and controlled by another subsidiary in Bermuda. The Irish subsidiary licenses rights to use the intellectual property to a subsidiary in the Netherlands, which sub-licenses it back to another Irish company. By the time the flat-footed tax authorities have caught up, hardly any tax appears to be due anywhere. Challenged in 2012 by Bloomberg over his company's tax practices, Google chairman Eric Schmidt was unapologetic.

"We pay lots of taxes; we pay them in the legally prescribed ways. I am very proud of the structure that we set up. We did it based on the incentives that the governments offered us to operate ... It's called capitalism. We are proudly capitalistic. I'm not confused about this."[13] A Bloomberg investigation estimated that Google had cut the effective tax rate on its global profits to just 2.4 per cent.[14]

Under pressure from the OECD, Ireland moved in 2014 to curb use of its tax system for tax strategies such as the "sandwich", but the challenge to the tax base posed by business delivering services online remains. Under Google's strategy, the sale of advertising from its Irish subsidiary into Australia is not subject to Australian tax. The head of Treasury's tax division, Rob Heferen, is not convinced that it should be. "Some of [the] questions that run through my head include, is the sale of the advertising, in substance, really a service provided by Ireland to Australia. Does it really look like an import? ... What if the transaction involved a tangible business input such as a tractor? What if an Australian farmer bought a tractor from a manufacturer in Ireland and the tractor maker had no presence in Australia. Should the profits from the sale of the tractor be taxed in Australia? I think the answer is clearly no."[15]

And yet there is a perceived unfairness when, as an *Australian Financial Review* article noted, the wholly Australian-owned website Carsales.com paid $27 million in tax on sales of $184 million while Google Australia paid just $780,000 on sales of $1 billion.[16] The problem is not so much the delivery of a service over the internet – although there can, as Heferen says, be ambiguity about exactly which jurisdiction that is – as the attribution of profit to intellectual property which can be located wherever it is most tax efficient.

A US academic Edward Kleinbard has popularised the idea of "stateless income", which he says is income subject to tax only in a jurisdiction that is not the location of the customer, the internet server (or however else the service or good is produced) or the location of company headquarters.[17] The OECD has mounted a campaign, backed by the G20, to halt the erosion of the corporate tax base by the shifting of profits to low-tax regimes. It is working on more than a dozen strategies, including tightening transfer pricing rules to make sure they trap transactions that do not reflect the creation of value and demanding greater transparency and cooperation between tax administrations. Several strands of work tackle "hybrid securities", which are debt instruments that can be converted into equity or vice versa. Because interest on debt is tax deductable but dividends on profit are not, hybrids play a key role in profit shifting. The OECD wants to revisit tax treaties to ensure that in their effort to prevent the double taxation of the same income they do not provide for the double "non-taxation" of income across countries.

A number of business groups have voiced concern about these efforts. The US Business Roundtable is concerned it may "result in the imposition of new, unprecedented taxes on trade and investment that will freeze business investment and slow economic growth".[18] The Confederation of British Industry is worried about the additional administrative burden. The Business Council of Australia (BCA) supports the OECD's project while warning that "International tax laws should not be an obstacle in the unstoppable evolution of the global economy. They should not be so excessive or complex such that they hinder trade, investment and innovation".[19]

The US has an ambiguous role in the global pursuit of multinational taxes. Unlike most of the rest of the world, it believes companies should be taxed where their headquarters are resident, not where the profits are derived. As the home country for so many of the world's multinationals, that obviously suits the US, but means it has little interest in helping other countries to trap profits at their source. However, efforts by US companies, including Burger King and Pfizer, to shift headquarters to lower-tax jurisdictions has encouraged greater US cooperation with the OECD's efforts.

On the left, many argue that the OECD's approach is completely wrong-headed and doomed to failure. The OECD is trying to tie down a physical location for profits by strengthening rules about how goods and services that are transferred within a corporate group should be priced and how companies fund their subsidiaries. With as much as 70 per cent of world trade occurring between companies and their subsidiaries, rather than between different enterprises, critics argue this is impossible. Instead, they suggest, the final profit of a corporate group should be taxed and the proceeds should then be split up according to where its sales, staff or assets are located. As the OECD has said, this approach would be flatly rejected by the US.

Corporate tax law is being tightened. Companies are facing new limits on the amount of debt they can use to fund their subsidiaries. The United Kingdom has pioneered a so-called "Google tax" which withholds 25 per cent of sales income if it is transferred to an entity in another country without profit being declared in the UK. Treasurer Joe Hockey considered following suit, but did not get Cabinet backing for introducing a new tax. The Coalition government instead pursued a group of 30 multinationals suspected of having transferred profits out of the country to low-tax Singapore and other jurisdictions with an intense tax audit. However, there is as yet no material increase in the company tax revenue being collected.

While there are debates about the OECD's approach, there is close to a political consensus in Australia, from the Greens to the Nationals, Liberal and Labor, that something needs to be done about the low levels of tax paid by companies like Google, Apple and Starbucks. The BCA frames its reservations about the OECD's work in the most cautious of terms. When RMIT's Professor Sinclair Davidson suggested the whole endeavour was misguided, it was as though he had uttered a heresy. The Association of Chartered Certified Accountants (ACCA), who published his critique, included a prominent disclaimer that while it was a worthwhile contribution to the discussion, the ACCA did not share his views.

Davidson sees the crackdown on the tax of international companies as a revenue grab by high-taxing governments that will choke investment. "Tax havens add value by allowing multinationals to reduce their tax liabilities while increasing their investments in high-tax economies. An increase in their tax burdens would reduce those levels of investment, leading to reduced employment opportunities, reduced consumption and reduced innovation."[20] He says the OECD and advocates of its work, such as Kleinbard, undervalue the intellectual property on which so much business is now based. He cites the case of Starbucks. "The consumer is not simply consuming a coffee – an inexpensive, easily manufactured, homogeneous product. Rather consumers are consuming an experience where the coffee is only one component of a branded product. Drinking a Starbucks coffee is either a form of conspicuous consumption or a reduction in information and search costs for consumers in a strange city who wish to consume a product of known quality." This begs the question of whether the other 17,000-odd cafes and restaurants around the country paying $300 million in tax could similarly be reducing this sum by claiming licence fees for their intellectual property.

However, Davidson argues there is no such thing as stateless income – all income is generated and reported somewhere. There is income that governments such as the US and the UK do not tax because, under their own legal tax systems, the income is not sourced in their economy. He says there is no evidence that the corporate tax base is being eroded, with company tax having trended slowly higher from 2.2 per cent of global GDP in 1965 to reach a peak of 3.8 per cent in 2006, before the global financial crisis cut it back to 2.9 per cent.

It is possible that the future may bring income that is truly stateless. Central bankers and tax authorities scoff at bitcoins – they do not "nearly fulfil the essential criteria for a currency and are more an object of speculation, the risks of which should be fully understood by investors", says Deutsche Bundesbank president Jens Weidmann.[21] Yet it represents a revolution in payments systems, enabling transactions to be concluded among anonymous parties without the intermediation of a central bank to underwrite the value of the medium of exchange or a bank to verify the transaction. Although still a curiosity largely confined to technerds, it could provide the next big leap forward in global corporate organisation.

The essential feature of the bitcoin system is the trust it engenders so that anonymous parties can deal with each other confident that the transaction is not fraudulent or duplicated anywhere else in cyberspace. The hallmark of the digital world is the ease of copying (hence all US State Department confidential cables could wind up on Chelsea Manning's CD). The trust that is essential to the functioning of a traditional payments system is delivered by bitcoin, first by use of cryptography, but crucially by the incentives built into the system for members of the network to verify that transactions are valid. The system was designed so that the amount of computing power needed to fool the system is so great that it would be more profitable to use it to earn money verifying than defrauding. The ability to generate the trust required for unknown counterparties to deal with each other is also the defining feature of the limited-liability corporation.

A Bank of England paper exploring the bitcoin's development starts with the creation of paper money in the 17th century. A merchant lodging gold at a bank is given a receipt for it. The merchant can exchange that receipt for goods with someone else. If that person goes to the bank to get the gold, the bank can verify that the receipt matches the record in its ledger. With bitcoin, the ledger is public and distributed on the network. The details of the people transacting may be anonymous, but their computer addresses, and the history of their transactions are on the public ledger.

Bitcoin may be tiny relative to traditional currencies but it is not small – on a random day, its turnover was around $13 million while the value of all the bitcoins in circulation was $5 billion. Between one and two million people are using it.

The Australian Tax Office has delivered a series of tax rulings on bitcoin transactions, declaring they should be treated like barter. It says that bitcoins (and the several hundred rival virtual currencies, all of which are far smaller) are "neither money nor a foreign currency, and the supply of bitcoin is not a financial supply for GST purposes. Bitcoin is, however, an asset for capital gains tax purposes". The ATO will let people conduct transactions of up to $10,000 without having to pay GST, providing a ready incentive for its use.

There is economic history behind the bitcoin, with libertarian economist Friedrich Hayek arguing in the mid-1970s (as inflation seized the world) that money should be privatised and "denationalised", with the private interests in a competitive market for money likely to produce a better result than government-controlled central banks.

A devotee of Hayek and the Austrian school of libertarian economics, Ross William Ulbricht, claimed them as inspiration for establishing by far the most ambitious, and for a time successful, enterprise based on the stateless bitcoin, the online marketplace, Silk Road. Established on the "dark" web, which is not indexed or covered by search engines, Silk Road was a trading platform where willing buyers and sellers of everything from heroin to cigarettes, hitmen to essay-writing services, could do business with each other. All transactions were in bitcoins. Ulbricht was eventually caught by the FBI and sentenced to life imprisonment. Following that, the servers on which the platform was based were located and shut down.

Dozens of start-ups are devising ever more elaborate business models for using the bitcoin. The history of technology is full of innovations that start as curiosities before becoming indispensible tools of the economy, ranging from the motor vehicle to the personal computer and Google. It is entirely plausible that the same technology that gives people sufficient confidence to deal with each other anonymously and without the legal backing of a state in the bitcoin system could also be the basis for the genuinely stateless corporations of the future – networked entities that are both everywhere and nowhere, without the need for so much as a brass plaque in the Cayman Islands. In such a world, there would be no foreign investment and company taxation would not exist.

11

CO-INVESTING IN CARS

The staging was simple – a handful of Holden cars lined up with Lake Burley Griffin in the background as Prime Minister Julia Gillard, industry minister Greg Combet and General Motors' Australian chief executive Mike Devereux performed for the cameras and reporters.

"When we see a co-investment that means jobs, means the continuation of manufacturing here, means that what is an icon manufacturer in Australia, like Holden, continues with all of the feed in to the economy, the supply chain, skills and innovation that that makes possible, then we are prepared to be involved", Gillard said. It was March 2012 and she was announcing that the federal and South Australian governments would grant General Motors a further $275 million to keep operating in Australia. The company, for its part, had promised to invest $1 billion, with plans to manufacture two new cars in Australia. "This partnership will see GM Holden continue making cars in Australia until at least 2022." Devereaux said the package was vital to GM's survival. "[We] have to be able to have a profitable business model for the long-term with the set of economic conditions that we've got right now."[1]

On his company's video-blog, the American Devereux explained that the trouble with Australia was that it needed a business plan.

"Australia cannot just become a hole in the ground for raw materials. If you're going to make things – high value things – the automotive industry is the bedrock."[2] From the motor industry came the skills you needed for a vast range of manufacturing, he said. But for today's global car companies to invest, a "co-investment" was required.

"The Australian government needs to be competitive and needs to look at what's happening around the world and see what it takes to attract more than a billion dollars of investment from a company. This game gets played in one of two ways. Either countries protect with high tariff walls or in some way, they co-invest. Sometimes they manipulate the currency to promote exports. In Australia's case, we don't think raising a big tariff wall is the way to go – we think the answer is co-investment."

It isn't an investment in any equity sense. The government gets no cash dividends from any profits the company may make and it has no seat on the board. It is just a subsidy. Devereux was right – countries around the world do offer them. Indeed, South Australia's manufacturing industry – Australia's second largest after that of Victoria – was built on the back of the generous tax breaks offered since the mid-1930s by its premiers Richard Butler and Thomas Playford to attract investment to the state. However, not many advanced countries offer their motor industry aid on the scale of Australia. The Productivity Commission added up the cost to the taxpayer of the subsidies and the tariff protection that the motor industry had received over a 15-year period and came up with a figure of $30 billion. About 45 per cent of this total was direct subsidies.

The industry had been in trouble for much longer than that. Tariff protection of 35 per cent for Australian-built motor vehicles was proving insufficient by the mid-1960s as Japanese cars began to be imported in large numbers. The Menzies government lifted the tariff to 45 per cent in 1964, to give local manufacturers greater competitive advantage, but the Japanese onslaught continued. Between 1964 and 1974, the market share of the fully locally manufactured vehicles fell from 84 per cent to 58 per cent.

The component industry was also being offered support. Local manufacturers had been allowed to import components tariff-free provided no local product was available. But in 1964, the Menzies government included a requirement that high-volume manufacturers had to move towards 95 per cent local content over a five-year period while a lesser requirement was imposed on low-volume producers (a move which encouraged the low-volume producers to remain small).[3]

In the early 1970s, with Toyota and Nissan seeking permission to join General Motors, Ford, Chrysler and Leyland as local manufacturers, the Whitlam government commissioned its new Industries Assistance Commission (IAC), which had replaced the Tariff Board, to investigate the industry's need for protection. It concluded that much of the industry was not viable because production runs were too small, and recommended that local content schemes be abandoned completely and that tariffs on imports be cut to 25 per cent. There was uproar from unions, manufacturers and the South Australian government, with the result that the government instead resolved to guarantee the local manufacturers 80 per cent of the market, with import quotas (said to have been proposed in caucus by a young back-bencher Paul Keating[4]) to be introduced should their share drop below that. It was, the industry minister Kep Enderby said, not simply a matter of economics, but also "pollution, safety and quality of life".[5]

After the global oil crisis in 1974, however, this market share proved unattainable as consumer preferences shifted to smaller cars, which were not made locally. Tariffs, which had been trimmed to 34 per cent under the Whitlam government's across-the-board tariff cut, were raised by the Fraser government to 58 per cent. Another (IAC) inquiry in 1981 repeated the recommendations of the first, saying the level of support to the motor vehicle industry, which it put at $1 billion a year or about $3000 per vehicle, could not be justified. Amid bitter division within the Liberal Party between the "wets", favouring further support, and the "dries", backing the IAC's report, the Fraser government's industry minister Philip Lynch resolved to keep the system as it was, while adding punitive 150 per cent tariffs for companies that exceeded their import quotas. Companies were also able to reduce their local content if they exported. Lynch argued, as had Menzies in the late 1930s, that the industry was essential for defence purposes, providing half the defence force's capacity for large-scale production of military equipment and 20 per cent of its engineering capacity.[6] Consumers, paying as much as double the price of motor vehicles in other markets, received no consideration.

The Hawke government, elected in 1983, diagnosed the industry's problem as too many manufacturers chasing too small a market with too many models. The industry was receiving six times the support given to the rest of manufacturing. Hawke's industry minister John Button developed a plan that would see quotas abolished and tariffs reduced in return for incentives for exports. The aim was to reduce the number of models and manufacturers, ideally to three manufacturers and five models.

For a time, the fall in the value of the Australian dollar made local production highly competitive with imports, but the steady erosion of market share never stopped, while the industry plans kept coming. The first formal scheme of subsidies was the Howard government's Auto Investment and Competitiveness Scheme in 1998, which offered $2 billion over five years to support business investment. This was boosted by another $4.2 billion in 2002 with the scheme extended to 2015.

The industry was changing, partly in response to the incentives provided in government policies. General Motors and Toyota started exporting, finding a good market in the Middle East after modifications to Australia's large cars to give them an extended life in the harsh desert climates. There were also several efforts to market Australian-built models in the United States. By the early 2000s, a third of Australian production was being exported, earning $3 billion a year (roughly the same as wool exports). Component makers were achieving sales of $6.5 billion, of which a quarter were exported. The goal of concentrating the number of manufacturers and models was achieved with Nissan closing in 1992 and Mitsubishi in 2008, which left three manufacturers making five models.

However, the industry's total output peaked in 1974 at just under 500,000 units, at which time it held an 85 per cent share of the local market. By the beginning of the 2000s, its share of the local market was down to half and production had dropped to about 350,000 units. By 2010, as Gillard was announcing her government's "co-investment" to guarantee Holden's presence for the next decade, total production was down to 250,000 and the share of the domestic market was down to 15 per cent. Among motor-vehicle-producing nations, Australia had dropped from 10th in the world in the early 1970s to 33rd, behind Uzbekistan. Its share of global production dropped from around 1.5 per cent to 0.3 per cent.

By early 2013, Ford concluded that it was not going to turn around the losses in its Australian production and announced it would stop manufacturing in 2016. Its plant in Geelong, opened in 1925, and its 1950s plant in Broadmeadows would both close. Sales of its Falcon model, which had peaked at just under 100,000 in the mid-1990s, had dropped to little more than 10,000 a year, while its

Territory was selling 15,000. For new assembly lines around the world, production runs of 200,000 or 300,000 were considered the minimum economic size for mass-market cars. "Manufacturing is not viable for Ford in Australia in the long term", the American head of the Australian operation Bob Graziano said. Holden was also cutting production levels, notwithstanding its deal with the federal and South Australian governments of the previous year.

The motor industry manufacturers were suffering on all fronts. The mining boom – still going strong – had raised the value of the Australian dollar and enabled importers to cut their prices while making exports from Australia uncompetitive. Their core product remained the big six-cylinder car, while consumer tastes were moving first to small cars from the 1960s through to the '90s and then to the SUVs. And the diseconomies of the small scale for a small market, which seemed bearable behind the wall of tariff protection, simply looked bizarre in a world where massive production lines were being rolled out in Thailand, China and elsewhere. Holden calculated that it cost twice as much to manufacture a motor vehicle in Australia as in Europe and four times as much as in Asia.

But the remaining manufacturers, Holden and Toyota, had not entirely given up in the lead-up to the 2013 election. The motor industry commissioned a study showing the economy would be $7.3 billion smaller by 2018 without a motor industry, billions of dollars of foreign investment would cease, the economies of Melbourne and Adelaide would shrink by around 1.5 per cent and would take until 2031 to recover. Moreover, the motor industry brought benefits to the rest of manufacturing by introducing research and development and the latest management and manufacturing techniques to the broader economy.

Asked by the new Abbott government to investigate these claims, the Productivity Commission concluded that attempts to multiply the investment of the government to arrive at a net figure for the value of the industry to the economy failed to consider the value that might flow from other uses of the government's money. It did not justify special support for the motor industry. The "spill-over" benefits from the introduction of research and development or management techniques were impossible to quantify and, in a world of global information, were mainly in the public domain in any case.[7] Toyota had claimed that its introduction of "lean manufacturing" techniques, with the elimination of waste and "just-in-time" inventory, had spread throughout its supply chain and was an example of the benefits which the motor industry brought to manufacturing in Australia more generally. The Productivity Commission noted that while Toyota had certainly been the innovator, there was a vast management literature on the subject that was available to any manufacturer. There was nothing special about the broader benefits conferred by the motor industry compared to, say, pharmaceuticals or the mining machinery industry, that warranted the extraordinary public support that had been lavished on the motor industry for decades.

The OECD, which tries to set "best practice" for the economic policies of advanced countries, says incentives for foreign investors are warranted only when they bring something unique to an economy that delivers greater benefits to local firms and the society in general than the cost of the subsidy. It cautions that because subsidies of any sort attract businesses simply looking to profit from the handout, incentives should be offered on equal terms to all investors, irrespective of industry and nationality.[8]

Labor's industry minister Kim Carr declared the 2013 election to be a "referendum on the future of the car industry", as he promised to lift government assistance over the next five years from $1.5 billion to $2 billion, while the Coalition was saying it would cut assistance back to $1 billion. Tony Abbott said his government would support the motor industry but was not "running down the road after Holden waving a blank cheque at them".[9] Devereux commented that 2013 "would be the year that Australia decides whether it wants to have an auto industry or not".

Within weeks of the Coalition's election victory, the media was full of reports of Holden's imminent demise. General Motors announced that Devereaux was being transferred to run the company's sales and marketing in China. A visiting senior General Motors executive declined a meeting with the new industry minister Ian Macfarlane. His predecessor, Kim Carr, revealed that the future of the Australian operation was on the agenda at the latest board meeting in Detroit. Appearing before the Productivity Commission inquiry launched by the new government in early December 2013, Devereux was emphatic that no decision had been made; however, Hockey was not convinced he was telling the truth. In parliament, he challenged the company to be honest about its intentions. "Either you're here, or you're not." That night, Devereux telephoned head office and a decision was made. The company would cease its Australian operations in 2017, 69 years after the first Holden had rolled off the production line at Melbourne's Fishermans Bend.

Two months later, in February 2014, Toyota decided it too would leave. The departures of Ford and Holden had made it harder for Toyota to continue, as it would be supporting the network of suppliers alone. As the scale of the suppliers' market contracted, their costs would rise. But Toyota also made no secret of the contribution which difficulties in dealing with their unionised workforce had made to their decision. The company had sought a number of concessions in return for a pay increase in excess of inflation, among them cutting back the three-week shutdown over Christmas, reducing long-weekend sickies and loadings for overtime and shifts. The union won a court order, delivered around the same time General Motors was announcing its withdrawal, preventing the offer being put to the employees.

By the end, there were about 40,000 employees across the last three manufacturers and their major suppliers. While metalworkers union secretary Dave Smith forecast a "recession all along the south-eastern seaboard", Tony Abbott, while acknowledging the "devastation" felt by the affected employees, promised "there will be better days in the future".

"The important thing to remember is, while some businesses close, other businesses open, while some jobs end, other jobs start."[10]

The residents of Elizabeth in South Australia and Geelong in Victoria do not see it this way. There are few new jobs starting for skilled and semi-skilled manufacturing workers. But it is another step in the steady transformation of the economy that has been underway since the early 1980s, when Australia still manufactured televisions, washing machines, tyres and shirts. There were telex technicians and linotype operators, and Newcastle bustled in the smog of the steel-works. And the launch of the latest model from Holden was front-page news in the way that the unveiling of the latest offering from Apple is today.

12

THE NATIONAL INTEREST

The national interest is a slippery concept that achieved prominence in the policy sphere to justify the global exercise of American power in the 1950s. The US political thinker who popularised it, Hans Morgenthau, saw global politics as a struggle for power, rather than of moral values, and said that nations were bound to pursue their national interest, which "encompasses the integrity of the nation's territory, of its political institutions and of its culture". Although Gough Whitlam, the most idealistic of Australian prime ministers, would have taken the opposite side in this debate, the national interest was nonetheless the concept to which the drafters of his Foreign Acquisitions and Takeovers Act turned in 1975.[1]

Any foreign investment will be prohibited under the act if the treasurer deems it to be "contrary to the national interest". It is a strange piece of business regulation. There is no definition of what the national interest encompasses. It is left entirely up to the treasurer to determine and the decision cannot be appealed through the courts. The treasurer takes advice from the Foreign Investment Review Board, which is a panel comprising mainly business people supported by a secretariat provided by the Treasury department. The FIRB does not appear in the legislation and has no statutory existence. It has no formal accountability, although it files an annual report to parliament and the Treasury officers in charge may be grilled in Senate committee hearings. Not only does the legislation not mention the FIRB, it also does not mention the thresholds, or the sensitive areas for which special rules apply, such as agricultural land or residential housing, and industries like the media and telecommunications. There is a statement of policy, but investors wanting to be sure they are up to date with the latest requirements are referred from the FIRB website to the treasurers' press releases. The Abbott government embarked on the first rewrite of the act since the Hawke government's changes in the 1980s, but left much of this ambiguity intact.

For the most part, transactions get waved through – defenders of the system highlight that it requires a negative test, with proposals rejected only when they are against the national interest – but when there are difficulties, companies feel they are shadow-boxing with no real idea of how judgements are being made.

By the standards set down by the OECD, it is a travesty. Australia's investment policy lacks transparency, predictability and accountability. Our regulations are regularly queried by other advanced countries in the OECD's annual foreign investment roundtables. Under an OECD treaty, the only grounds for restricting foreign investment are "maintenance of public order, health, morals, safety and the protection of essential security interests". Australia has signed the treaty but included a reservation for its foreign investment policy.

To all this, the government replies that the lack of definition to the national interest actually facilitates the flow of investment: "What is contrary to the national interest cannot be answered with hard and fast rules. Attempting to do so can prohibit beneficial investments and that is not the intention of our regime."[2]

The policy statement posted on the FIRB's website tries to help would-be investors by citing examples of the issues considered by the FIRB. National security is at the top of the list, and the FIRB does take advice from the security agencies. There is no elaboration of the sorts of issues that might raise national security concerns.

Competition is also emphasised, with the government considering whether an investment would deliver control over market pricing or production. The Australian Competition and Consumer Commission would also examine the competition issues of any takeover; however, the FIRB does its own assessment. In 2009, when the Chinese state-owned business Chinalco was trying to raise its stake in Rio Tinto, the FIRB told it that investing in Rio's aluminium assets would be a problem because it was already China's biggest aluminium producer. Chinalco responded that the ACCC and all other international competition bodies had approved that aspect of the transaction and that aluminium was a highly competitive market. The FIRB, however, was unmoved, and was not required to provide any explanation of its position.[3]

The policy is vague about broader issues, saying the government "considers the impact of the investment on the general economy". The FIRB will look at how an investment is being funded and at the level of Australian participation. The extent to which an investor will develop the assets they purchase in Australia will be considered, while the investment should also ensure Australia "remains a reliable supplier to all customers in the future".

Decoding some of this, the concern about the "extent to which an investor will develop the asset" appears to be a reference to the 2001 decision to block Shell's takeover of Woodside, reflecting fears that the Australian assets would disappear into Shell's portfolio of gas assets and would not necessarily be developed first. As noted in Chapter 7, there was a furore when the head of the FIRB secretariat,

Patrick Colmer, gave a speech to a business audience saying that the government preferred that foreign investments in new resource projects should be kept to no more than 50 per cent and stakes in existing major producers should be capped at 15 per cent. It was taken as a new statement of policy. However, the speech was never posted on the Treasury website (Centre for Independent Studies researcher Stephen Kirchner obtained it under Freedom of Information) and it appeared to be an embarrassment to the government, which had never intended to state a bald Australian equity policy.[4] Several FIRB decisions during that period suggested that it might be a "covert" policy, with a number of transactions for 100 per cent ownership of resource projects rejected.

The reference to Australia "remaining a reliable supplier to all customers" looks like a warning that Chinese investors should not market only to Chinese customers. This was the reason given for barring the consolidation of Chinese ownership of a new iron ore province near Geraldton in Western Australia. It had never previously applied in the resource sector where, for example, companies with alumina refineries sold their produce derived from their wholly owned bauxite mines exclusively to their own overseas smelters.

The guidance says the FIRB will also consider the "character" of the investor and whether it operates on a transparent commercial basis.

Government-owned investors are a particular concern, with FIRB considering whether the investor "may be pursuing broader political or strategic objectives that may be contrary to Australia's national interest".

The Foreign Acquisitions and Takeovers' Act does spell out that all investments by foreign state-owned enterprises must receive approval from the treasurer, with no minimum monetary threshold. The policy explains that this applies to any business with as little as

15 per cent government shareholding. This can go to absurd lengths. In 2009, China's sovereign wealth fund CIC bought a 14.9 per cent stake in the Singapore-based resource investment company Noble Resources. Because a small part of Noble's portfolio included minority stakes in some Australian coal mines and an iron ore venture, CIC had to seek FIRB approval. Quite how a minority stake in a minority stake could conceivably influence Australia's national interest was never explained.

However, the fear that behind the corporation with a government shareholding lies a manipulating state pursuing broad strategic rather than purely commercial motives goes beyond Australia. A World Bank report on China's outlook comments: "There is some concern that government influence over the large state-owned enterprises (SOEs) may encourage unprofitable, but politically important, foreign takeovers."[5]

As detailed in Chapter 7, these concerns loomed large for the Rudd government when its 2007 election coincided with a wave of investment by Chinese state enterprises in the Australian resource sector.[6] The FIRB threw obstacles in front of several transactions. It told the Chinese rare-earths miner, China Nonferrous Metals Company that it could only acquire 49.9 per cent of Australia's major rare-earths producer, Lynas, not the 51.7 per cent it was seeking, which led it to withdraw its offer.

One of the strangest decisions concerned the effort of China's Minmetals to buy a struggling Australian copper-gold miner, OZ Minerals. It had a number of assets, but the prize was the Prominent Hill mine, located in the vast Woomera defence zone. Covering 130,000 square kilometres, or roughly the size of England, it is the largest military zone in the world and covers the "Gawler Craton", a geological formation rich in copper, gold, iron ore, nickel, lead and zinc. Although OZ Minerals had been told defence had no objection to the sale, Treasurer Wayne Swan announced that the FIRB had found otherwise, saying it was a matter of national security. The Woomera testing zone is 160 kilometres away from the mine and there was scepticism that the Chinese, who were in any event proposing to keep the Australian management and staff, could learn anything of its operations from the bowels of an underground mine that far away. The outcome was that Wayne Swan allowed Minmetals to buy all the OZ Minerals assets except the Prominent Hill mine.

Was there really a national security concern? Was it, as some foreign investment lawyers suspected, a means of imposing a 50 per cent limit on a Chinese resource takeover? Some involved in the transaction wondered if the defence department, which was very unhappy with its minister, Joel Fitzgibbon, was happy to see him embarrassed by the rebuff of a Chinese investment on defence territory one week after he had been outed for having too close a relationship with a Chinese businesswoman.[7]

Another Chinese state-owned enterprise was barred from entering an iron ore exploration joint venture in the Woomera zone, notwithstanding the fact that, as the Australian partner Western Plains pointed out, defence retained the ability to inspect operations at all times, the Stuart Highway and the Adelaide to Darwin rail traverse the zone carrying countless tourists while opal miners had free rein of the territory. (These deals later led to a review of mining rights in the Woomera zone, although the issue of foreign investment was not addressed.)

The Abbott government's belief that it has brought a radical change in Australia's stance towards foreign investment by state-owned enterprises highlights the extent to which foreign corporations are playing blind man's bluff in negotiating Australia's investment regime.

In 2012, as Tony Abbott prepared for government, he went on a trip to China where he adopted a hard line towards Australia's biggest trading partner, speaking about the country's need for political liberalisation and promising a much tougher stance on foreign investment than had been implemented by the Labor government.

"It would rarely be in Australia's interests to allow a foreign government or its agencies to control an Australian business", he said, noting that Chinese investment was dominated by state-owned enterprises. "That's because we don't support the nationalisation of businesses by the Australian government, let alone a foreign one."[8]

Journalists had been briefed that under a Coalition government, Chinese state-owned companies would be allowed to establish their own start-up operations or "greenfields" investments in Australia but would be barred altogether from the purchase of existing businesses.

On his first trip to China as prime minister two years later, in mid-2014, Abbott shifted both his own and Australia's stance on China's state-owned enterprises.

"Australia hopes for much more Chinese investment – on the same basis that we welcome investment from our other FTA [Free Trade Agreement] partners such as the United States", he said, following a meeting with China's premier Li Keqiang. "We now appreciate that most Chinese state-owned enterprises have a highly commercial culture. They're not the nationalised industries that we used to have in Australia."[9]

Treasurer Joe Hockey says this marks a new position on foreign investment, and reverses Labor's stance on state-owned enterprises. "I've consulted with our security agencies about the risks and formed the view that some SOEs in general were no greater risk to Australia's national interest than investment from private companies, some of which are more closely wedded to the interests of a foreign state than the state company might be."[10] Hockey says this new stance, which he says has been "generally unrecognised", lay behind the government's approval of the $6 billion purchase of electricity group, SP AusNet and its related Jemena business, which has electricity, gas and water assets. A condition was imposed that at least half the directors must be Australian citizens.

The change of heart was not just brought about by the realities of government and the assessment of the intelligence agencies. Abbott had set an objective of concluding the ten-year-long negotiations with China on a free trade agreement in his first year of government. Australia did not have much it could trade for greater access to China's markets, as its tariffs were already close to zero. Concessions on investment were what the Chinese were seeking. They wanted the same threshold for foreign investment that applied in Australia's free trade agreement with the United States – over $1 billion rather than the standard $230 million – and they wanted it applied to their state-owned enterprises.

Abbott's trade and investment minister Andrew Robb – whom he had entrusted with the task of completing trade deals with China, Japan and Korea – made it clear Australia's insistence on vetting all investments by state-owned enterprises needed to change. Abbott's comments in China signalled that he was ready to move.

The Business Council of Australia commissioned a study that highlighted the growing competition to attracting investment from China. Australia had slipped from being the largest destination to second spot behind the United States , while Canada had raised its thresholds before foreign investment scrutiny to $1 billion for private companies and $330 million for state companies. Britain, which has no foreign investment screening at all, simply requiring that foreign companies have at least one British resident on the board, was attracting a growing share of Chinese investment.

The Business Council commented that, "We need to accept there may be some risks associated with the operation and governance of SOE investors in Australia and acknowledge these risks are manageable. If we do not adopt a risk management mindset with SOEs and continue to rely on the existing FIRB screening regime to satisfy community concerns, we run the risk of losing out on the opportunities these new sources of capital provide".[11]

The paper suggested a number of options, including treating state companies the same as private companies or establishing an accreditation scheme that exempts state companies from FIRB scrutiny if they already have a commercial track record in Australia, or if they operate on private sector principles.

When the free trade agreement with China was finally unveiled on the eve of the G20 summit in Brisbane in November 2014, it raised the threshold for FIRB scrutiny of investments by private Chinese companies from $250 million to just under $1.1 billion, but the state-owned businesses that are responsible for about 90 per cent of China's offshore investment were left having to seek FIRB approval for every single transaction. Announcing the free trade deal alongside China's president Xi Jinping, Abbott indicated that the issue would be looked at again when the agreement is reviewed in three years. Australia would also want improved access to China's rice, sugar, wheat and cotton markets.

Hockey says the need for FIRB approval of all state-owned investments is a second-order issue to the government's change in attitude towards them. He says the need to obtain approval is just about bringing a transaction to the government's attention. "What matters is the outcome", he says, flagging that the government is happy to approve major investments by state-owned companies. However, the fact that the government's change of attitude towards state-owned enterprises is not written down in any formal way, and that nobody seems to have noticed it, highlights the vagueness surrounding the foreign investment regime.

In all of this, it was never really explained what a Chinese state-owned mining group might do in the country that was inimical to the "national interest". The Australian Tax Office had ample power under the transfer pricing rules to stop anyone selling produce back to China at less than the market price. The ACCC could stop any collusion between companies, while ASIO should be able to detect any illicit intelligence gathering.

An OECD study examined the threats to national security that might plausibly be presented by foreign investment. Three were proposed:

- A foreign investment might make a country dependent on a foreign supplier for goods or services essential to the functioning of the economy.
- The investment could facilitate espionage or sabotage.
- Technology or other expertise could be transferred to a foreign-controlled entity that could be used by its government in a manner harmful to national interests.[12]

Wayne Swan as treasurer would argue the conditions he placed on the sale of rare-earths miner Lynas to a Chinese state-owned company was driven by the first of these – China has a dominant position in rare earths with about 85 per cent of world supplies. Australia is not a consumer, exporting its entire output, but its US ally would have had strong views about retaining a non-Chinese-owned producer.

Companies directly supplying defence or intelligence services have their own protections, with the government requiring contracts to include clauses that they can be voided if there is a change of ownership. However, Singapore Telecommunications' takeover of Optus in 2001 represented the most serious potential threat to national security as it gave a foreign state-owned company control of Australia's communications satellites.

The company was previously owned by the British private sector company Cable & Wireless, so control was passing from one foreign company to another, but the fact that Singtel was state-owned elevated concerns. These were dealt with in an agreement between Singtel and the defence department which sectioned off the defence communications, required personnel to obtain security clearance, and gave Australia the ability to resume control of the satellite network in a national security emergency. The transaction also required the support of the US authorities who supply the satellite equipment.

The fact that this deal could be consummated in the face of resistance from defence analysts and some economic nationalists within the business community, led by the Seven Network chief executive Kerry Stokes, shows how flexible the barriers to state-owned enterprise can be when the political will is there.

The Chinese communications company Huawei, which is the world's largest telecommunications equipment supplier, encountered greater resistance when it emerged as a potential tenderer for work on the National Broadband Network in 2011. This was not a foreign investment consideration – the company had already built a thriving business in Australia – and nor did it concern a state-owned enterprise. Huawei was private, although there were suggestions that its founder – a former People's Army colonel – was too close to the state. But the intelligence agencies advised the government that Huawei should be excluded from NBN tenders because of the intensity of monitoring required to ensure that no silent bugs were inserted into the telecommunications system. "As a strategic and significant government investment, we have a responsibility to do our utmost to protect [NBN's] integrity and that of the information carried on it", a spokesperson for Attorney-General Nicola Roxon said.[13]

Huawei had gone to great lengths to assuage security concerns around the world. It appointed the British government's former chief information officer to be its global cyber-security advisor. It appointed Australia's former foreign minister Alexander Downer to its Australian board. The company's standing in Australia gained some support in 2013 from the Coalition in opposition, with shadow communications minister Malcolm Turnbull questioning the government's decision. Turnbull noted that Huawei had been made the lead contractor for Britain's broadband roll-out and had presumably passed their security concerns. "We will review that decision in the light of all the advice in the event of us coming into government", he said. The ban was confirmed following the Coalition's victory in September 2013 by Attorney-General George Brandis.

Huawei was later barred from tendering for US government work in 2013. Although no evidence of Huawei spying has ever been made public, the former head of both the CIA and the US National Security Agency Michael Hayden told the *Australian Financial Review*'s Christopher Joye that US agencies had hard evidence that Huawei had "shared with the Chinese state intimate and extensive knowledge of the foreign telecommunications systems it is involved with".[14] However, a 2015 investigation led by Britain's head of cyber security concluded there was no evidence Huawei's involvement in critical UK networks posed any threat to national security.

National security concerns of a very different order led to the scuttling of the Singapore Stock Exchange's proposed takeover of the Australian Securities Exchange in 2011. The takeover, which had the support of the ASX, would have created Asia's fourth-largest exchange. Wayne Swan said the advice from the FIRB to reject the deal was unanimous and was based on two main reasons. Part of it was the economic nationalist desire to build Sydney as the financial centre of Asia. There was concern that the takeover of the ASX by the smaller SGX would see the financial centre move to Singapore, with the loss of jobs. "This is not a merger, it's a takeover that would see Australia's financial sector become a subsidiary to a competitor in Asia", Swan said.[15]

However, the rejection also drew on the advice of the Reserve Bank, ASIC and the Treasury, who were concerned about the ASX's clearance and settlements functions. The banking regulator, the Australian Prudential Regulation Authority, took a different view, arguing that the change of control could be managed without jeopardising national interests. The ASX is not only the clearing house for equities, but also for futures trading, while it also runs the securities and depository and settlement system, Austraclear, for government bonds and corporate debt securities. Austraclear is linked to the Reserve Bank's settlement system for real-time clearing of bank transactions. The regulators believed that in the event of a financial crisis, it would be vital to have no ambiguity about the sovereignty of regulation of this system.[16] On the list of national security threats detailed in the OECD study, this was an example of the sovereignty of market regulation moving offshore in a way that could jeopardise the national interest.

Both Labor and the Greens believe free trade and international investment agreements can bring a serious loss of regulatory sovereignty, by providing for independent arbitration in a third country of disputes between companies and governments. Known as "investor–state dispute settlement procedures", they first appeared in a trade deal between Germany and Pakistan in 1959 and had the intent of encouraging foreign investment by providing protection against expropriation and discrimination. There are over 3000 bilateral and multilateral investment treaties and free trade agreements with these clauses. Australia is party to about 25 clauses. Until 2000, they were rarely used, but over the past decade, there have been roughly 60 cases a year as companies have discovered they can be used to win compensation from governments whose regulation in fields such as environment or health have curtailed their ability to operate.

Most claims are brought against developing countries by investors from the United States and Europe. According to the United Nations Commission on Trade and Development, there have been a total of 274 known cases concluded, of which 43 per cent were decided in favour of the state, 31 per cent in favour of the investor and 26 per cent settled. Measures relating to renewable energy, patents, sovereign bonds and the revocation of licences have been the subject of numerous actions in recent years.

Germany's decision to phase out nuclear power has brought action from one of the operators, while a US company has taken action against a Canadian province for banning "fracking" of gas. The scope is broad. The television network Al Jazeera is using a bilateral investment agreement between Qatar and Egypt to claim US$150 million damages through arbitration from Egypt over the harassment and imprisonment of its journalists, including Australian Peter Greste. There have been some large awards, with the biggest a US$2.3 billion payment to Occidental Petroleum from the Ecuadorian government over the termination of an oil concession.

The Howard government had resisted the inclusion of an investor–state dispute settlements clause in the Australia–US Free Trade Agreement, arguing they were not necessary in treaties between two nations with mature legal systems. However, Philip Morris has used Australia's investment treaty with Hong Kong to seek compensation over Australia's legislation on plain packaging for cigarettes. A year after the Labor government had announced it would legislate to remove brand advertising from packaging but nine months before the law was passed, the US company sold its Australian subsidiary to its Hong Kong subsidiary so that it would be covered by the investment treaty. The company claimed the plain packaging law was an expropriation of its brand property without compensation. This was rejected by the High Court, which concluded that depriving rights to use a property is not the same as its expropriation. However, the case is now before a tribunal in Singapore, with Philip Morris seeking billions in compensation. The action caused Labor to reject investor–state dispute settlement procedures for the remainder of its term; however, the Coalition took a more flexible approach. The free trade agreement with Korea includes an investor–state dispute clause, with exclusions allowing the government to regulate in fields of health, welfare, environment and public morals without fear of second-guessing by an international tribunal. The High Court chief justice Robert French, who was aggrieved by the Philip Morris action, has called for investor–state agreements to include clauses that preclude their use to challenge decisions of the courts.

A Productivity Commission report argues there is no robust evidence that investor–state dispute settlement procedures lead to greater investment flows and says there is a danger that they will discourage governments from regulating in areas such as health and environment. It says companies worried about investing in an emerging economy should simply take out some insurance against political risk. However, a dissenting report from trade expert Andrew Stoler, who was an associate commissioner for the study, said this was equivalent to saying fire brigades should be disbanded because people had household insurance.[17] He argued that governments should simply be more careful about how they regulate to ensure they did nothing that affected the existing contractual rights of foreign businesses operating in Australia. "There is reason to believe that a little bit of 'regulatory chill' might be a good thing, even in Australia." Defenders of the provisions argue they not only act as a check against capricious regulation, but also serve both states and companies – settling disputes in third nations ensures they are not clouded by domestic political issues. However, the concern that these agreements bring a loss of legal sovereignty remains, not only among the environmentalists and opponents of globalisation but also among jurists such as Chief Justice French.

Much of the policy debate about foreign investment has nothing to do with national security or sovereignty. The limits on investment in housing, agricultural land and agribusiness respond to political sentiment. The resistance to Chinese investment in the resource sector through the resources boom appeared to be little more than the same economic nationalism that had driven resistance to earlier waves of investment from Japan and the United States.

The foreign investment policy statement explicitly allows for this. "The Government also recognises community concerns about foreign ownership of certain Australian assets. The review system allows the Government to consider these concerns when assessing Australia's national interest." This was the element of the policy cited by Joe Hockey in his rejection of Archer Daniels Midland's bid for GrainCorp.

This leaves decisions about foreign investment firmly in the political arena, where the National Party can find common cause with the Greens, while the holders of economic portfolios in the Labor and Liberal parties believe themselves above the nationalist fray, welcoming any investment proposal that can find its way through the fog of Australia's regulatory policy. It remains highly contentious ground.

13

POLITICAL VOICES

There were 160 speeches and interventions referring to foreign investment in the parliamentary debates of the Abbott government's first year. Foreign investment in Qantas, agricultural land, residential real estate, GrainCorp and Warrnambool Cheese, along with the foreign investment policy implications of free trade agreements, state-owned enterprises and the motor industry, engaged politicians from all sides in both the House of Representatives and the Senate. Hansard records over 2000 separate speeches on foreign investment since the Hawke government last amended the act in the late 1980s. Although Paul Keating pushed back the economic nationalist tide during the 1980s and reclaimed political ground for advocates of free trade, the boundaries in this debate are far from settled, as is shown by the fresh restrictions imposed by the Abbott government in 2015 on investment in the rural sector, the tightening of regulation on real estate and the imposition of fees on all foreign investment.

The era of globalisation sparked by the 1980s led to a 30-year stretch during which global trade grew twice as rapidly as global economic growth, while cross-border investment rose even faster. This era of intense trade and investment accompanied the rise of the emerging nations led by China and pulled billions of people out of subsistence into the modern economy. But since the financial crisis, growth in both trade and global capital flows has more than halved and barely matches global growth. The forces of globalisation are proving to be weaker than many, including their opponents on both the right and the left, may have thought. Interviews with political leaders conducted in late 2014 reveal that the themes that have echoed through Australia's history still find political traction today.

"Globalisation and climate change have changed everything when it comes to issues around foreign investment" says the outgoing Greens leader and Tasmanian senator Christine Milne.[1] With globalisation, multinationals and giant state-owned enterprises have the power to appropriate whatever they want, wherever it is, for their own benefit, while climate change is putting a new premium on Australia's resources of agricultural land and scarce water.

The Qatari state-owned company Hassad Foods is the sharpest illustration of what is wrong with our foreign investment regime, she says. "Hassad are open in saying they have a strategy of buying agricultural food production and water resources in all countries in the world so that they'll have a secure source of food for their people. They see food as the major scarce commodity of the 21st century because of the climate challenge."

Hassad, which supplies about 60 per cent of Qatar's food imports, has purchased about a dozen large farm properties in Australia for sheep and wheat production.

"It makes no sense for us to allow another country to use us to outsource their food production", Milne says. Her concern is that our food exports will be channelled directly to the companies of the countries that own our land, rather than being sold on the open market. "It is grossly unfair, when a lot of developing countries are going to be starving or suffering major food shortages, if we have sold our land and water in outsourcing arrangements. We won't be supplying our food surpluses into global commodity markets that would enable those countries to feed themselves at a fair price."

Because foreign governments are buying land for strategic reasons, they are paying prices which push local companies out of the market. She worries about Chinese investment in Tasmania's dairy country. "If they end up buying the land and then the processing facilities and then bring in their own workers to work it and shift the produce out, there is zero benefit to Australia. We'll have outsourced some of the best dairy country in the world for the sake of the food security of a foreign government."

Milne believes there should be more black-letter law governing foreign investment, rather than it being left up to the treasurer to decide. "The discretion at the moment is purely what the government of the day determines should be in the national interest and that's an ideological position. It should be codified." Where the current regime imposes a negative test – something will be allowed unless it is expressly ruled as against the national interest – Milne believes it should be a positive test where the law expressly states what investment is allowed, and where.

Governments are allowing Australia's national interests to be made subservient to those of global corporations, Milne says. The Greens see this in the new generation of bilateral trade agreements, with large investment chapters. "The free trade agreements of today are not about what the Nationals argue for on the improved access for sugar or commodities. They are being used to standardise the laws by which multinational corporations intend to operate, anywhere in the world they want." Free trade agreements impose constraints on regulations over digital rights, patent protection, environmental regulation, or labour standards. "We're losing our national sovereignty as a government that governs for Australia."

The Greens have strongly opposed the international dispute settlement clauses in free trade and investment agreements that, as Greens trade spokesperson Peter Whish-Wilson says, "allow corporations to access shady international tribunals where nobody knows what happens, there is no right of appeal, and they have the right if anyone finds against you to fine you billions".

Milne says the basis of the national interest against which foreign investment should be judged should be "the vision for the nation – what do we want to see in ten or 100 years. It is not just about economic decisions. It is about the bigger picture for Australia, its place in the world and how does it contribute to maintaining freedoms, the landscape, and the opportunities for people. It should also be about where the money comes from, and about corruption and human rights".

For the National Party too, pure economics do not tell the story. "The purpose of a nation is to make sure the dominant owner of its assets and the means of producing its wealth are its people. Ultimately the control of those assets is control of the destiny of the nation", says Barnaby Joyce.

"If you just talk pure dry economics, it would be superior to have a single large organisation own all the farm land, but it just wouldn't be a nation."

Joyce recalls that when he was young, he used to get irritated with hunters coming onto his father's property because it limited what he could do. His father told him to make allowances. "As a returned serviceman, he would say it is very hard to get someone to love their nation if you never let them set foot on it. It's just as hard to get someone to love their nation if they don't have any ownership of it."

Joyce traces the tradition of the soldier settler back to Roman times. "They brought soldiers back from Gaul and gave them a farming block because they wanted them to love the Roman empire. It's not because it is efficient." Land may have value because of what it can produce, but it also has a deeper value. "The dominant currency through the history of man is land. If you've got free title on land and you can enforce your ownership, you've got the best asset in the country."

And for Joyce, it grates that foreign investors own land equivalent to two-and-a-half times the size of Victoria. "Australia remains the most liberal country on earth for foreign investment", he claims. Like Milne, he believes the onus of proof should not be that an investment is against the national interest but that it advances it. His concern is not just the quantity of land being sold, but its quality. The best land is going to foreigners. "They don't own the rubbish – they own the good stuff. You're creating two classes – the busted-arse farmer in one area and the foreign owner in another. You'll create social heat down the track and you won't see the benefit. It's like houses – you can say there are 1.2 million houses in Sydney and only 100,000 of them are owned by people from overseas, but they're all the ones near the harbour. They're the good ones. They don't own any houses in Blacktown and no Australians have access to the houses where they want to be."

Joyce rejects the idea that Australia is short of capital and needs vast flows of foreign investment. "We're a nation with $1.6 trillion in superannuation – it is bigger than our economy but they don't seem to want to invest it in land. It's peculiar because everyone else does. We've got access to massive amounts of capital."

Joyce fears for the impact on food prices if Australian farmland and its agricultural businesses are sold off to foreigners. "We've got to make sure that the Australian public in general has access to one of the greatest benefactions of this nation, which is affordable food." He understands that many people take a purely economic argument that national output will be increased if untrammelled foreign investment is allowed. "But the purely economic argument is this: it's a lot cheaper for me to have a prostitute than a wife, but that's not what I want."

Labor's Chris Bowen was for several months of 2013 in charge of Australia's foreign investment system. He endorses the discretion it leaves to the Treasurer, while acknowledging it has its failings, saying "It's the worst system apart from all the others – someone has to take responsibility and I think there has to be political accountability for big decisions like that. I don't think it's an appropriate decision for a non-elected body. The FIRB plays an important advisory role but at the end of the day the most senior minister responsible for the economy should be making that call".

"Most treasurers exercise power pretty carefully and given that treasurers in the modern era come from the Liberal Party or the Labor Party, they're both pro-foreign-investment parties. In the old days when [the Country Party's] Artie Fadden or Earle Page was treasurer I might have been more sceptical about the system, but I'm not aware of any plan to return the Treasury portfolio to the National Party."

Bowen readily accedes to the proposition that foreign companies might not be acting in the national interest but adds, "nor will Australian companies. They'll act in the best interest of their shareholders whether they're Australian or foreign owned – that's their fiduciary duty".

Bowen accepts the reasons given for Peter Costello blocking Shell's takeover of Woodside and Wayne Swan's blocking of the Singapore takeover of the ASX, though he believes the takeover of GrainCorp by ADM raised no national interest concerns and should have been allowed to go through.

He believes foreign state-owned enterprises do need the level of screening provided under Australia's system of regulation, with all investments subject to vetting. "The question should be answered to the satisfaction of the treasurer of whether the state-owned enterprise is operating as a policy arm of government or as a profit-making company that happens to have a majority government-owned shareholding. It is a legitimate question to be asked."

However, he does not have concerns about foreign ownership of resources, including by state-owned enterprises, if he's satisfied they're working on a commercial basis. "The fact of the matter is that extracting resources is very expensive and requires a big capital injection, which involves foreign capital." He harks back to the time when nationalism reigned. "There was the memorable period with John Gorton and Rex Connor out-bidding each other on nationalism saying 'don't sell the farm'. It only really changed in the 1980s with Keating and the foreign banks at the forefront."

Labor's quandary was exposed at the federal conference of July 1984 when Keating was pushing for a policy change to allow foreign ownership of banks. The leader of the left, NSW deputy premier Jack Ferguson, was leading the charge against it, saying he would choose Australian banks over foreign ones every time. "Here was the left wing of Labor embracing the big Australian banks", says Bowen.

Labor's traditional hostility to the power of capital – "money power" – has not entirely been shaken: Bowen says Labor is a "broad church, as are the conservatives". But he says the debate about foreign investment, whether in shadow cabinet or a branch meeting, is a world away from the early 1980s and earlier.

"It is part of a broader shift in Labor thinking, from means to ends. The old Labor style was change the means – the new Labor style is change the ends. It doesn't matter how we get there – how we have a bigger and better economy. Modern Labor thinking is let's use the market for good ends. If we have the ends and we get there, and if a company is going to invest and employ and grow, it doesn't matter if the shareholders are Canadian or English or Chinese."

With this lens, Bowen does not have a problem with foreign investment in agricultural land. "Foreign companies may be buying up our land to improve their own food security but the essential point is we are going to be exporting food – we've got to export it somewhere. We always have and we always will."

But Bowen says the system of foreign investment review still serves a purpose. "The FIRB fulfils two roles: it gives good advice to the treasurer of the day but, importantly, it provides the treasurer with a narrative and some reassurance to the population that these issues are properly considered and the national interest is weighed up."

"John Hewson wanted to abolish the FIRB in the 1993 election. I think that would be problematic because it would make the debate harder for those of us who promote foreign investment and argue for it. It is easier to do it with FIRB there to say, in the very rare occurrence that foreign investment is not in our national interest, that there is a process to deal with it, for it to be independently considered and advice given to the treasurer. If that process didn't exist, it would be easier for those to argue that foreign investment is not in our national interest to make their case."

Joe Hockey takes a very similar view. "The national interest test is essential as a safety valve for community concerns given that the legislation has a disposition in support of foreign investment. Australians know they've got a very lucky country. They never want to feel as though they're being taken advantage of or exploited, and therefore having a rarely used provision that ensures that the treasurer can invoke the national interest in order to protect Australia's best national interests is of comfort to the Australian people". He does not support codification of the national interest test, saying it would simply result in a "re-litigation of the justification or otherwise of foreign investment decisions every time the justification or otherwise of a foreign investment decision gets into dispute".

Hockey sees the views of the Greens and the nationalists within the National Party as outliers. He says there is a large measure of bipartisanship in the policy, and endorses the decision former treasurer Wayne Swan took to block the Singapore Stock Exchange's takeover of the ASX. He is disappointed that Labor did not back him on blocking the takeover of GrainCorp: "They failed to make a decision on it [the bid by ADM for GrainCorp was made in October 2012, well ahead of the 2013 election] when they could have, lacking the courage, but I think overall there is a maturity about the debate. Australians instinctively know we've got a large country with a small population and we need a huge amount of resources to develop our economy to its capacity. That's why we need foreign investment."

The radical free trader perspective – the voice of John Hewson, who once called for the abolition of the Foreign Acquisition and Takeovers Act – no longer finds expression in mainstream politics. The regulation and barriers to foreign investment was, astonishingly, not mentioned in the otherwise comprehensive review of the financial system conducted for the Coalition government by David Murray in 2014, despite terms of reference which required it to investigate how the Australian economy is funded. The libertarian think-tanks – the Centre for Independent Studies and the Institute of Public Affairs – still make the case for deregulation, but no one in either the House of Representatives nor the Senate advocates that view. However, if the United Kingdom can operate with no screening of foreign investment at all beyond a requirement that companies have at least one director resident in the country, there is no reason why Australia should not as well. While the UK's openness to foreign investment might lure a few unsavoury Russian oligarchs to its shores, it has enabled the country to preserve its position as the unrivalled centre of global finance. The UK also maintains a vibrant manufacturing industry with technological leadership in many fields and a wide range of services exports beyond finance. A laissez faire attitude to foreign capital has not led to the hollowing out of its economy.

Australia has largely accepted the arguments of free trade regarding physical goods – there is no political constituency for re-erecting the tariff walls that surrounded the country for almost a century. Nor is there pressure to reimpose the capital controls that prevented Australian companies and financial institutions from investing offshore and regulated the amount and kind of capital that could come into the country. But politically, nobody on the left, the right or the economic centre wants to let go of the system of vetting foreign investment.

Yet, neither can any side of politics escape the circularity of argument in which the system of vetting is there to satisfy the public that there is a system of vetting. The argument that no harm is done while the vast majority of deals are approved misses the deterrence that the system imposes to businesses and investors who simply decide not to look at Australia. But, more importantly, it gives a legitimate place to the nationalists during the periods when there is an upsurge of direct investment, whether it is the Japanese in the 1970s, the Chinese in the 2000s or, indeed, the Americans in the 1950s and 1960s. During such peaks of foreign investment interest, governments become susceptible to nationalist pressure, and the presence of the foreign investment screening mechanism gives them the tools to exercise the control that the nationalists – whether from the left or the right – are seeking. There is less Chinese investment in Australia's resource industry than there might have been. While we can look back and wonder at the folly of those who wished to curtail Japanese investment in building Australia's tourism industry in the 1980s, it is no different in character to the efforts now to restrict foreign investment in Australia's agricultural industry. That industry will be poorer and less productive as a result. While we maintain a system of vetting which gives legitimacy to these voices, we'll never learn.

ACKNOWLEDGEMENTS

Many thanks to all those who freely gave me their time and thoughts in the course of researching this book. It draws on the research of many others, particularly Christopher Pokarier's marvellous 2001 thesis, "Politics of foreign direct investment in Australia, 1960-96", and also papers and books by Peter Drysdale, Murray Goot, Mal Harop, Stephen Kirchner, Peter Love, Raymond Markey, Narelle Morris, Ian McLean, Greg Melleuish, among many others. I also thank the Parliamentary Library for access to their wonderful resources and the brilliant Trove archive of newspapers managed by the National Library of Australia. This book owes much to the constant support of Hilary Russell during the writing, and also to her first edit. Finally, my thanks to Black Inc. for its faith in this endeavour.

ENDNOTES

CHAPTER 1 STRANGE BEDFELLOWS

1. Yoshihiro Toyama, "Japanese tourists and tourism investment in Australia and Queensland", *Otemon Economic Studies*, vol 24, 1991
2. From *Courier Mail* 1988, cited in Narelle Morris, "Last Post for the Gold Coast", *Journal of Australian Studies*, vol 28, no 8, 2004
3. Ted Wheelwright & Abe David, "Japanese Global Economic Strategies and Australia", in Gavan McCormack (ed), *Bonsai Australia Banzai*, 1991
4. John Hood, "Australian high wages cost free trade multinationals profit", Australia First Party website, www.australiafirstparty.net, 14 April 2014
5. Occupy Australia home page, www.occupyaustralia.net
6. Christine Milne, National Press Club Address, 13 September 2013
7. Warren Truss, 2013 Coalition campaign launch, QPAC Brisbane, 25 August 2013
8. Gabrielle Chan, "Foreign investment makes explosive entry into election campaign", *Guardian*, 29 August 2013
9. Joe Kelly, "Food for thought", *The Australian*, 30 June 2011
10. Andrew Robb, "Australia: a land of investment and opportunity", speech to Credit Suisse Asian Investment Conference, Hong Kong, 27 March 2014
11. Penny Wong, "Australia's future is in the world and there is no turning back", speech to Economic and Social Outlook Conference, Melbourne, 3 July 2014
12. Doug Cameron "Free traders are at it again", published on www.dougcameron.com.au, 8 October 2013
13. Christine Milne, "Old parties flip-flopping on foreign ownership", 26 August 2013
14. "KGB Interview: GrainCorp's Alison Watkins", *Business Spectator*, 8 July 2013
15. Sid Maher, "Warren Truss slams GrainCorp takeover", *The Australian*, 29 November 2013
16. Joe Hockey, media release, 29 November 2013
17. Australia, House of Representatives 2014, Debates, Qantas Sale Amendment Bill 2014, Second Reading, 6 March 2014

18. Australian Services Union submission, Senate Economics Legislation Committee Inquiry, Qantas Sale Amendment Bill 2014, 14 March 2014
19. Rochelle Belkar, Lynne Cockerell & Christopher Kent, "Current Account Deficits: The Australian Debate", Reserve Bank discussion paper 200702, March 2007
20. United Nations Conference on Trade and Development, *World Investment Report 2014 – Investing in the SDGs: An Action Plan*, 2014
21. Ted Evans, "Economic nationalism and performance: Australia from the 1960s to the 1990s", Colin Clarke Memorial Lecture, University of Queensland, 1999
22. Stephen Kirchner, "Foreign Direct Investment in Australia following the Australia–US Free Trade Agreement", *Australian Economic Review*, vol 45, no 4, December 2012
23. The Lowy Institute Poll, 2014
24. Murray Goot, "How much? By whom? In what? Polled opinion on foreign investment 1958–1990", *Australian Journal of International Affairs*, vol 44, no 3, November 1990
25. The Lowy Institute Poll, 2012
26. Tom Switzer, "Public attitudes toward foreign investment", Institute of Public Affairs Research Paper, December 2008

CHAPTER 2 **KEEPING OUT THE FOREIGNERS**

1. Geelong correspondent, *Argus*, 1 December 1851
2. "The farmers of Bellarine", *Geelong Advertiser and Intelligencer*, 19 March 1856, p2
3. Letter to editor, *Geelong Advertiser and Intelligencer*, 29 May 1856, p2
4. Letter to editor, *Geelong Advertiser and Intelligencer*, 23 May 1856, p3
5. "Free trade and protection", *Argus*, 25 March 1856
6. "Protection to Native Produce", article from *Geelong Advertiser* reprinted in the *Argus*, 15 March 1858
7. Tariff Reform League, *Argus*, 1 June 1859, p5
8. John Stuart Mill, "American Protection", *Sydney Morning Herald*, 5 July 1866, p3
9. Martin Shanahan & John Wilson, "Do good institutions result in good trade policy? The evolution of tariff protection in the colony of Victoria 1880–1890", paper for Asia Pacific Economic and Business History Conference, 18–20 February 2011, Berkeley, California
10. "Anti-Chinese meeting in Melbourne", *Geelong Advertiser*, 12 May 1880
11. Adam Smith, *Wealth of Nations*, book 4, chapter 2, 1776
12. *Sydney Morning Herald*, 5 July, 1860. George Melleuish has a good discussion of the humanism in the free trade movement in his book *Cultural Liberalism in Australia* (Cambridge University Press, 1995)
13. John West, "The Friendly Intercourse of Nations", lecture to Mechanics School of Arts, reported in the *Sydney Morning Herald*, 8 July 1857
14. *The Age*, 24 October 1865; cited in Stuart Macintyre, *A Colonial Liberalism*, Oxford University Press, 1991, p106
15. "Population and Protection", *Empire*, 6 September 1851, p2
16. Lecture on Richard Cobden, *Sydney Morning Herald*, 28 July 1865, p5

17. Paul Pickering, "Loyalty and Rebellion in Colonial Politics", in Philip Buckner & Douglas Francis (eds), *Rediscovering the British World*, University of Calgary Press, 2005
18. Stuart Macintyre, *A Colonial Liberalism*, Oxford University Press, 1991, p106
19. Cited in Philip Griffiths, "The making of White Australia", PhD thesis, ANU, 2006, p246
20. Edmund Rogers, "Free trade versus protectionism: NSW, Victoria and the tariff debate in Britain, 1881–1900", *Australian Studies*, vol 1, 2009
21. *Sydney Morning Herald*, 3 November 1900, p13
22. "Pre-sessional Speech of Mr Alfred Deakin to his constituents", Melbourne, 24 June 1905, cited in James Walter, *What Were They Thinking?*, UNSW Press, 2010, p110
23. Hansard, House of Representatives, Immigration Restriction Bill, Second Reading, 12 September 1901
24. Hansard, 12 September 1901
25. H.V. McKay, "Profits on Harvesters", letter to the editor, *Argus*, 9 December, 1905
26. W.K. Hancock, *Australia*, Ernest Benn, 1930, p89
27. Hancock, 1930, p228
28. Sibylle Lehmann & Kevin O'Rourke, "The Structure of Protection and Growth in the late 19th Century", NBER Working Paper 14493, November 2008
29. There were fierce arguments between Dutch free trading merchants and financiers and Belgian manufacturers seeking protection from Britain in the first half of the century; see C.P. Kindleberger, "The Rise of Free Trade in Western Europe, 1820–1875", MIT Working Paper 133, July 1974
30. Darren Gray, "Mallee wheat farmer backs proposed ADM takeover of GrainCorp", *Sydney Morning Herald*, 12 November 2013
31. And GrainCorp is also majority owner of Australia's largest flour miller, Allied Mills.

CHAPTER 3 **THE MONEY POWER**

1. "Run on the savings bank – wild and criminal statements", *Goulburn Evening Penny Post*, 13 February 1892
2. "The Savings Bank", *Evening News*, Sydney, 24 April 1893
3. Arthur Desmond, "The Robbers of Today", *The Worker*, Brisbane, 4 November 1893
4. Ray Markey, "Explaining union mobilization in the 1880s and early 1900s", *Labour History*, no 83, 2002, p25
5. "The Coming Revolution", *Bulletin*, 11 August 1888, p1
6. From William Lane's novel, *Workingman's Paradise* (1892), cited in Humphrey McQueen, *A New Britannia*, University of Queensland Press, 1970, p193
7. Cited in Harry Cole, "The right of Labour to its produce", PhD thesis, University of Western Sydney, 2007
8. Nick Dyrenfurth, "A 'Terrible Monster': From 'Employers to Capitalists' in the 1885–86 Melbourne Wharf Strike", *Labour History*, May 2008

9. Robin Gollan, *Radical and Working Class Politics*, Melbourne University Press, 1960, p171
10. *The Worker*, 16 January 1892
11. *The Worker*, Melbourne, 10 March 1894, cited in Peter Love, *Labour and the Money Power*, Melbourne University Press, 1984
12. *The Worker*, Sydney, 4 March 1893, cited in Peter Love, 1984
13. *New Order*, 8 September 1894, cited in Peter Love, 1984
14. *The Worker*, Brisbane, 2 December 1911
15. Frank Anstey, *Money Power*, 1921, p59
16. "Australian finance, Text of Agreement. Budgets must be balanced. Sir Otto Niemeyer's review", *Argus*, 22 August 1930, p7–8
17. Reported in "Coming down to earth", *Argus*, 26 August 1930, p6
18. "Deliberately Organised: Present depression the work of international financiers", *The Worker*, 3 September 1930
19. *Labor Daily*, 23 August 1930, cited in Peter Love, 1984, p103
20. "Mr Lang, speech at Forbes", *Sydney Morning Herald*, 7 October 1930
21. John Curtin, "Money Power and the 55,000,000 pound interest bill", *Westralian Worker*, Perth, 1930
22. Report of the Royal Commission appointed to inquire into the Monetary and Banking Systems, cited in Peter Love, 1984, p147
23. Hansard, 9 May 1940
24. Hansard, 18 September 1947
25. *Australian Worker*, 17 September 1947, cited in Peter Love, 1984
26. Chifley speech, September 1948, cited in John Hawkins, "Ben Chifley, True Believer", Treasury Round-Up, Issue 3, 2011
27. "Control of Banks, Wartime Measures", *West Australian*, 27 November 1941
28. *Lateline*, ABC Radio National, 17 November 2011
29. Kevin Rudd, "The Global Financial Crisis", *The Monthly*, February 2009

CHAPTER 4 **MIDWIFE TO THE MOTOR INDUSTRY**

1. Hansard, 22 May 1936
2. Hansard, 1 December 1936
3. Mal Harrop, "Corio 1940: Triumph for John Curtin but Stillbirth for an Australian Motor Car", *Labour History*, no 91, November 2006, p131–149
4. Harrop, 2006
5. Hansard, 22 May 1940
6. "Full Cabinet Agendum 588A", 24 May 1944, cited in Sydney Butlin, *Australia in the War of 1939–45*, vol IV, ch 24, p755
7. "Australia's first mass-produced car launched", *Argus*, 30 November 1948, p3
8. D. Copland, *Inflation and Expansion*, Cheshire, 1951, p46
9. Hansard, 19 May 1949
10. Speech to NSW ALP Conference, 1949, cited in H.W. Arndt, "Foreign Investment", in P. Nieuwenhuysen and P.J. Drake (eds), *Australian Economic Policy*, Melbourne University Press, 1977, p133

CHAPTER 5 HERE COME THE YANKS

1. Don Brash, *American Investment in Australian Industry*, ANU Press, 1966, p9
2. Cited in Brash, 1966, p35
3. Brash, 1966, p36
4. Hansard, House of Representatives, 2 August 1945
5. "Statement of policy in relation to overseas investment in industry in Australia", Commonwealth Treasury, 25 August 1952
6. "Reds employ inflation", *Canberra Times*, 2 October 1950, p1
7. "No alteration to pound in plans to fight inflation", *Daily Advertiser*, 7 October 1950, p1
8. "Menzies and Evatt clash on issues", *West Australian*, 10 October 1950
9. Hansard, House of Representatives, 19 October 1950
10. Hansard, House of Representatives, 23 November 1953
11. "General Motors seeks Australian Pref Shares", *Canberra Times*, 23 December 1959
12. *Sydney Morning Herald*, 4 July, 1960, cited in Harold Bell, "Attitudes to Overseas Investment", *Australian Quarterly*, September 1960
13. Hansard, Senate, 28 November 1951
14. Cited in Bell, 1960
15. "Foreign money curb advised", *Canberra Times*, 28 July 1965
16. Hansard, House of Representatives, 12 October 1961
17. "Withdrawal of takeover bid questioned", *Canberra Times*, 16 October 1961
18. Kosmas Tsokhas, *A Class Apart?: Businessmen and Australian Politics, 1960–1980*, Oxford University Press, 1984
19. Brash, 1966, p14
20. Brian Fitzpatrick & Ted Wheelwright, *The Highest Bidder*, Landsdowne, 1965, p40
21. Fitzpatrick & Wheelwright, 1965, p40
22. Hansard, House of Representatives, 21 September 1965
23. Hansard, Senate, 29 August 1963
24. "No danger control from abroad", *Canberra Times*, 18 February 1965
25. Hansard, House of Representatives, 12 September 1968
26. Cited in Ian Hancock, *John Gorton: He Did it His Way*, Hodder, 2002
27. "Australia Club Address", Department of Prime Minister and Cabinet transcript, Dorchester Hotel, London, 17 January 1969
28. Hansard, House of Representatives, 20 May 1970
29. Hansard, House of Representatives, 26 September 1972
30. Harold Bell, "New approach on foreign investment", *Sydney Morning Herald*, 10 October 1972

CHAPTER 6 SYMBOLS FOR SALE

1. "The buck stops at Chiko roll", *The Age*, 4 May 1972
2. Hansard, Senate, 9 May 1972
3. "Question on notice, answered", Hansard, House of Representatives, 15 August 1972

4. "US bid for Frozen Foods under fire", *The Age*, 27 April 1972
5. Hansard, Senate, 9 May 1972
6. Following IT&T's withdrawal, Frozen Foods was subject to a bidding war between two Australian-owned companies, Lifesavers and Provincial Traders. Brisbane-based Provincial Traders won, but was swallowed by the US-owned George Weston two years later. In 2013, the privately owned US corporation Simplot celebrated its manufacture of the billionth Chiko Roll.
7. "Arnott clan urges small investors to put bite on Campbell", *Canberra Times*, 15 December 1992
8. Hansard, Senate, 14 October 1992
9. "Should we give a cracker about who owns Arnotts?" *Green Left Weekly*, 4 November 1992
10. "Arnotts deal approved", *Canberra Times*, 15 May 1985
11. John Dawkins, media release, 7 December 1992
12. Bijit Bora, "Implications of globalization for Australian foreign investment policy", Centre for International Economic Studies Discussion Paper, University of Adelaide, 1995
13. Richard Gluyas, "VB goes flat as tipplers turn to boutique brews", *The Australian*, 16 August 2014
14. Wayne Swan, media release, 25 November 2011

CHAPTER 7 **MONEY FROM ROCKS**

1. Minerals Council of Australia, Henry Tax Review submission, November 2008, p14
2. Ray Vernon, *Sovereignty at Bay*, Longman, 1971
3. Associated Press report, *Canberra Times*, 30 September 1969
4. "Mutual distrust as talks begin on iron ore", *Canberra Times*, 24 January 1966
5. Hansard, House of Representatives, 19 April 1966
6. "London look at Hamersley ore prospects", *Canberra Times*, 30 September 1969
7. Harold Holt, Election Speeches, Museum of Australian Democracy
8. "Liberal opposes AIDC", *Canberra Times*, 20 May 1970
9. "Legislation to limit overseas holdings", *Canberra Times*, 18 September 1970
10. "Cairns spells out aims of AIDC", *Sydney Morning Herald*, 8 March 1973
11. "Minerals bill under attack", *Sydney Morning Herald*, 28 March 1974
12. "Five-point plan for resources", *Canberra Times*, 30 October 1973
13. "Tension runs high in the mining clash", *Sydney Morning Herald*, 17 June 1973
14. Hansard, House of Representatives, 9 July 1975
15. "Utah and Australia", *Four Corners*, ABC, 4 Nov 1977
16. *Four Corners*, 1977
17. Hansard, House of Representatives, Phillip Lynch Ministerial Statement, 1 April 1976
18. Christopher Pokarier, 'Politics of foreign direct investment in Australia, 1960–1996', PhD thesis, ANU, October 2000
19. Hansard, House of Representatives, 16 August 1977

20. "Resources ownership essential", *Canberra Times*, 29 March 1981
21. Hansard, House of Representatives, 14 November 1979
22. Patrick Walters, "Labor plan to replace states' tax on mining", *Sydney Morning Herald*, 22 April 1982
23. "Evans defends oil tax regime", *Sydney Morning Herald*, 1 May 1987
24. "Howard's policy speech", *Canberra Times*, 26 June 1987
25. Cited by David Cox in Hansard, House of Representatives, 4 April 2001
26. Hansard, House of Representatives, 8 March 2001
27. John Howard, interview with Laurie Oakes, *Sunday*, Channel 9, 11 February 2001
28. Peter Costello, media release, 23 April 2001
29. Cited in David Uren, *The Kingdom and the Quarry*, Black Inc, 2012, p97
30. *Lateline Business*, ABC, 6 May 2010
31. Dominique Strauss Kahn, preface to Philip Daniel & Michael Keen (eds), "Taxation of petroleum and minerals, principles, problems and practice", IMF, 2011

CHAPTER 8 EMBRACING GLOBALISATION

1. Alan Bond & Robert Mundle, *Bond*, HarperCollins, Sydney, 2003, p44
2. Australian Financial System, Final Report of the Committee of Inquiry, AGPS, 1981
3. Cited in Max Walsh, "Libs manifesto is doomed by history and by Cocky corner", *Sydney Morning Herald*, 17 April 1984
4. Hansard, *House of Representatives*, 12 October 1978
5. Hansard, *House of Representatives*, 15 September 1977
6. Edward Shann, *An Economic History of Australia*, Cambridge University Press, 1948, p410
7. Gregory Moore, "The campaign to arrest Ed Shann's influence in Western Australia", paper at 21st Conference of the History of Economic Thought, 2008
8. Keith Hancock, *Australia*, Ernest Benn, 1930
9. Tariff Reform Leagues were founded in the United Kingdom in the 1890s in opposition to the free trade that followed from the abolition of the corn laws. In Australia by the 1920s, Tariff Reform Leagues were strenuous critics of protection.
10. Peter Drysdale, "The Relationship with Japan", in L.T. Evans and J.D.B. Miller (eds), *Policy and Practice: Essays in Honour of Sir John Crawford*, ANU Press, 1987
11. Andrew Leigh, "Trade Liberalisation and the Australian Labor Party", *Australian Journal of Politics and History*, vol 48, no 4, 2002, p487
12. Hansard, House of Representatives, 5 June 1975
13. Malcolm Fraser, election speech, 27 November 1975
14. Malcolm Fraser, "Pacific Community: Further Steps" from Robert Downen & Bruce Dickson (eds), *The Emerging Pacific Community: A Regional Perspective*, Westview Press
15. "19th century laissez faire philosophy with safety net", *Canberra Times*, 28 April 1982
16. Wolfgang Kasper, "A generation of reform", *Quadrant*, 1 April 2011
17. "Financial review", *Canberra Times*, 1 June 1983

18. "The dollar floats free: bankers rocked", *Sydney Morning Herald*, 10 December 1983
19. "Decision to float criticized", *Canberra Times*, 12 December 1983
20. "Keating hints at six new banks", *Sydney Morning Herald*, 12 January 1984
21. Wolfgang Kasper, "Capital Xenophobia", CIS Policy Monograph 6, December 1984
22. Max Walsh, "Libs manifesto is doomed by history and Cocky Corner", *Sydney Morning Herald*, 17 April 1984
23. Interview with author, November 2014
24. Andrew Leigh, "Trade Liberalisation and the Australian Labor Party", *Australian Journal of Politics and History*, vol 48, no 4, 2002
25. Bob Hawke "Australia and Japan", 3 February 1984, cited in Leigh, 2002
26. Hansard, House of Representatives, 25 May 1988
27. Hansard, House of Representatives, 12 March 1991
28. Hansard, House of Representatives, 12 March 1991
29. Gareth Evans, "Trade policy into the 21st Century", speech to Sydney Institute, 15 November 1989
30. Takeshi Terada, "The genesis of APEC: Australian–Japan political initiatives", Pacific Papers No 298, December 1999
31. Kenichi Ohmae, "Managing in a borderless world", *Harvard Business Review*, May 1989

CHAPTER 9 OUR LAND

1. World Bank Press Conference, Washington, 16 April 2011
2. "World Investment Report 2009: Transnational Corporations, Agricultural Production and Development", UNCTAD, 17 September 2009
3. Steve Lewis & Nick Christensen, "Foreign land grab on Aussie farms and brands to secure local food supply", *The Daily Telegraph*, 15 November 2010
4. Cited in Tom Cowie, "Foreign ownership of Aussie land: the peril of selling the farm", *Crikey*, 16 June 2011
5. Hansard, Senate, 15 November 2010
6. Hansard, Senate, 24 November 2010
7. AAC remains Australia's largest landholder, controlling 1.1 per cent of the landmass or about 75,000 square kilometres. Although still owned by overseas interests, it has not been afraid to make appeals to national interest to pursue its own cause. In 2012, as the company was competing with a Chinese consortium for an interest in the Ord River, its chief executive David Farley warned that Australia's interests were being jeopardised by Chinese investment. "Australian agriculture is a very attractive investment to a lot of offshore players at the moment and I think if the sale investments were analysed there would be a lot of surprise about what size properties are being purchased and by who", he told the ABC's *Background Briefing* program. "We need to focus on making sure the investments are productive and are in the national interests of Australia." (Stephen Crittenden, "Selling the Farm", *Background Briefing*, ABC, 5 May 2011)
8. "The Country Party Platform Discussed: principles of state finance and scope of private enterprise", *The West Australian*, 14 March 1913

9. Cited in Les Carlyon, "Rush to fill our empty north", *The Age*, 17 March 1967
10. Ian Davis & Carol Sides, "PM acts on land buys", *The Age*, 20 August 1981
11. "Hallam wants a rural voice on FIRB", *Canberra Times*, 8 July 1981
12. "More land owned abroad", *Canberra Times*, 29 July 1981
13. "Retain FIRB says Cattle Council", *Canberra Times*, 20 May 1989
14. "Treasury should have FIRB tasks, say Nationals", *Canberra Times*, 28 May 1989
15. "Japanese could take over cattle industry", *Canberra Times*, 13 January 1989
16. Andrew Stewart, "Factions not leaving Ahern in peace", *Canberra Times*, 31 May 1988
17. Natasha Bita, "Chinese mine giant snaps up 43 NSW farms", *The Australian*, 27 June 2011
18. Cited in Lanai Vasek, "Nationals Senator Barnaby Joyce says farming land should be off-limits to all mining companies", *The Australian*, 30 June 2011
19. Barnaby Joyce, "Cubbie station now in Wayne's world", *Sydney Morning Herald*, 6 September 2012
20. Cited in David Crowe & David Uren, "Politicians told not to play the crowd on Cubbie", *The Australian*, 6 September 2012
21. "Greener pastures: The global soft commodity opportunity for Australia and New Zealand", *ANZ Insight*, 9 October 2012
22. Mick Keogh, "An overview of the challenges and opportunities associated with foreign ownership of Australian agricultural land and agribusiness", speech to University of Western Australia, 19 July 2012
23. Alan Jones, National Press Club Address, 19 October 2011
24. "Australian Collaborative Land Use and Management Program", data downloaded from www.agriculture.gov.au/abares/aclump
25. Submissions 037 and 056 to "Inquiry into foreign investment in residential real estate", House of Representatives, September 2014
26. *Boomerang*, 14 April 1888
27. Max Walsh, "The 'export' to Japan which helps maintain our lifestyle", *Sydney Morning Herald*, 24 July 1989
28. Letter to editor, *Bellarine Echo*, 26 September 1989, cited in *On Target*, vol 25, no 41, League of Rights, October 1989
29. Rosanne Robertson, "Elizabeth Bay home set to catch the record price", *Sydney Morning Herald*, 8 October 1989
30. Cited in Bernard Lagan, "Foreign buyers ban 'step backward'", *Sydney Morning Herald*, 1 October 1987
31. *Lateline*, ABC, 1 November 2008
32. Charles Purcell, "Terrible time to relax foreign ownership of housing laws", *Sydney Morning Herald*, 6 April 2010
33. Marilyn Lake, "'Yellow Peril' racism rears its ugly head", *The Age*, 3 April 2010
34. Paul Sheehan, "Cashed-up Chinese are pricing the young out of the property market", *Sydney Morning Herald*, 10 March 2014
35. Clive Hamilton, "Foreign demand is making Sydney's housing problem worse", *The Guardian*, 18 February 2014

36. "The Chinese Property Boom Down Under", Investment note from Credit Suisse Equity Research, 4 March 2014
37. Lorenzo Casavecchia & Adrian Lee, "Chinese demand for Sydney Residential Property", Submission 10 to House of Representatives for the "Inquiry into Foreign Investment in Residential Real Estate", University of Technology, Sydney, 2014
38. Angelo Karantonis, "Is Australia selling off its real estate?" University of Technology Sydney, Pacific Rim Real Estate Society Conference, 2011
39. Hansard, House of Representatives, 27 November 2014
40. Theo Dunnewijk, "Global Migration of the Highly Skilled", United Nations University Working Paper 070, 2008
41. "The Global Competition for Talent", OECD presentation to Lisbon Council, Brussels, 13 November 2008
42. "Report on Foreign Investment in Residential Real Estate", House of Representatives Economics Committee, 27 November 2014
43. Stephen Kirchner, "Regulating Foreign Direct Investment in Australia: A discussion paper", Financial Services Institute of Australia, February 2014
44. Hansard, House of Representatives Economics Committee, 7 March 2014
45. Joe Hockey, "Treasurer orders foreign investor to sell illegally purchased $39 million Sydney mansion", media release, 3 March 2015

CHAPTER 10 THE DISAPPEARING CORPORATION

1. Joe Hockey, Q&A Bloomberg Summit, Sydney, 16 September 2014
2. Competition Policy Review, Draft Report, 22 September 2014
3. John Howard, *A Current Affair*, Channel Nine, 16 December 1999
4. "Gambling", Productivity Commission Inquiry Report, 26 February 2010
5. "Economic Structure and Performance of the Australian Retail Industry", Productivity Commission, 4 November 2011
6. Lucy Battersby, "Familiar faces lobby for supermarkets", The *Age*, 6 March 2013
7. Joe Hockey, "Doorstop interview, Brisbane", G20, 13 November 2014
8. Royal Commission into Taxation, 1920, United Kingdom, cited in Sol Picciotto, "Constructing Compliance: Game-playing, tax law and the state", Centre for Tax System Integrity Working Paper 81, ANU, 2005
9. Phillip Knightley, *The Vestey Affair*, Macdonald Future, 1981, p137
10. Hansard, House of Representatives, 26 November 1953
11. Greg Crough & Ted Wheelwright, *Australia: A client state*, Penguin, 1982, p143
12. "Tax and the Internet", Discussion report of the ATO Electronic Commerce Project, 1997
13. Brian Womack, "Google chairman says Android winning mobile war with Apple", *Bloomberg Business*, 12 December 2012
14. Jesse Drucker, "Google 2.4 per cent rate shows how $60 billion US revenue lost to tax loopholes", *Bloomberg Business*, 21 October 2010
15. Rob Heferen, "Implications of digitisation for the Australian tax system", Speech to Economic and Social Outlook Conference, Melbourne, 4 July 2014

16. David Bassanese, "Gaping loopholes mean huge losses in tax revenue", *Australian Financial Review*, 20 June 2013
17. Edward Kleinbard, "Stateless income", *Florida Tax Review*, vol 11, no 9, 2011
18. "BRT Letter to Treasury Secretary Lew on OECD BEPS Project", Business Roundtable, 30 May 2014
19. Jennifer Westacott, "Speech to BCA-Clayton Utz BEPS Workshop", 6 November 2014
20. Sinclair Davidson, "Multinational corporations, stateless income and tax havens", Association of Chartered Certified Accountants, March 2014
21. Jens Weidmann (President Deutsche Bundesbank), "Outlook for 2014", Speech, Berlin, 16 January 2014

CHAPTER 11 CO-INVESTING IN CARS

1. Julia Gillard, "Transcript of joint doorstop interview, Canberra", 22 March 2012
2. Mike Devereux, "Exclusive interview with Holden MD Mike Devereux on co-investment announcement", www.videoatgm.com, 22 March 2012
3. This history draws on Lindsay Smyrk, "The political economy of, and modelling the demand for, Australian passenger motor vehicles", PhD thesis, Victoria University of Technology, 2000
4. "Australia's auto industry: from military paranoia to dreams of modernity", *Rear Vision*, ABC Radio National, 9 July 2013
5. Cited in Gay Davidson, "10 year plan for car industry", *Canberra Times*, 15 November 1974
6. Commonwealth Record, 1981, p457; cited in Smyrk, 2000
7. "Australia's automotive manufacturing industry", Productivity Commission Inquiry Report, 31 March 2014
8. Magnus Blomström, "The economics of international investment incentives", OECD, 2002
9. Interview with Samantha Hawley, *PM*, ABC Radio National, 21 August 2013
10. Tony Abbott, "Doorstop interview, Canberra", 10 February 2014

CHAPTER 12 THE NATIONAL INTEREST

1. The "national interest" is rarely used as a test in legislation. It does not appear in the anti-terrorism or treason legislation and is only a minor test in the ASIO Act, enabling officers to communicate with ministers when the national interest requires. The Coalition government's crackdown on migrants seeking asylum in 2014 gave the minister the power to reject visa applications if they are deemed contrary to the national interest.
2. "Australia's foreign investment policy", statement by Treasurer, 2013, on FIRB website, www.firb.gov.au
3. David Uren, *The Kingdom and the Quarry*, Black Inc, 2012, p107
4. Stephen Kirchner, "More inscrutable than the Chinese", *The Australian*, 19 February 2010
5. "China 2030: Buiding a modern, harmonious, and creative society", World Bank, 2013, p388

6. For a fuller account of the Rudd government's management of these issues, see my book, *The Kingdom and the Quarry*, 2012
7. Barry Fitzgerald, "Swan's Prominent Hill decision is absolute nonsense", *Sydney Morning Herald*, 28 March 2009
8. Cited in John Garnaut, "Abbott talks tough during China visit", *Sydney Morning Herald*, 25 July 2012
9. Tony Abbott, "Address to Australia week in China lunch, Shanghai, China", 11 April 2014
10. Joe Hockey, interview with author, December 2014
11. "Discussion Paper on Foreign Investment and State-owned Enterprises: managing the risks to maximise the benefits", Business Council of Australia, August 2014
12. Theodore Moran, "Foreign Acquisitions and National Security: What are the genuine threats? What are implausible worries?", OECD Global Forum on International Investment, 2009
13. Lucy Battersby & Peter Cai, "China company ban puts trade relations at risk", *Sydney Morning Herald*, 27 March 2012
14. Christopher Joye, "Huawei spies for China, says ex-CIA head", *Australian Financial Review*, 19 July 2013
15. "Why the ASX-SGX merger failed", *Sydney Morning Herald*, 21 April 2011
16. Laura Tingle, "Security risks killed the deal", *BRW*, 7 April 2011
17. "Bilateral and regional trade agreements", Productivity Commission Research Report, November 2010

CHAPTER 13 **POLITICAL VOICES**

1. All quotations in this chapter based on interviews with the author conducted between October and December 2014.

INDEX

A

AAC 145, 146, 154, 229
Abbott, Tony 152, 153, 154, 155, 191, 192, 199
Abbott government 3, 4–5, 15, 119, 194, 198, 199–202, 209
Aboriginal land rights 101, 148
Aboriginal stockmen's strikes 148
Active Services Brigade 36
Adventures of Barry McKenzie, The [film] 90
Aeroplane Jelly 86
Age, the [newspaper] 22, 29
agribusiness 155–6
agricultural land
  and climate change 210
  degree of foreign ownership 145, 152
  emotional argument over 175
  historical hostility to foreign investment in 145–51
  political flashpoint over ownership 143–4, 209, 216
  purchased for mining ventures 151–2, 154
  quality over quantity 213
Al Jazeera 206
Albanese, Anthony 10
Alcoa 17
Aldi 172
all-Australian car, desire for 53–7
Allende, Salvadore 75, 84
Allen's confectionery 86
American Challenge, The (Servan-Schreiber) 76
Ansett, Joan 59
Ansett, Reg 59
Anstey, Frank 44
Anthony, Doug 79, 126
anti-Chinese campaigns 24–5, 28, 157, 159–60
anti-communism 66, 67
Anti-Corn Law League 25, 26, 27
anti-Semitism 37, 42, 46, 71
ANZUS Treaty 80
Apple 168, 172, 179
Archer Daniels Midland (ADM) 8–9, 33, 208, 214, 217
Argus, the [newspaper] 21, 22, 31, 71
Argy, Fred 127
Arndt, Heinz 78
Arnott, William 87, 88
Arnott's biscuits 86, 87–9
Asia, enmeshment with 140–1, 157
Asia Pacific Economic Cooperation (APEC) 141
Asia Pacific region, integration of Australia 138, 139–40
Asian immigration 157
Associated Chambers of Manufacturers 74, 79
Association of Chartered Certified Accountants (ACCA) 179
Atlantic Charter 130
Austraclear 205
Australasian League against Transportation 27
Australia–China relations 114
Australia–USA free trade agreement 13, 80–1
Australia at the Crossroads (Kasper et al.) 133
Australia China Investment Forum 114

Australia First Party 4
Australia Reconstructed (ACTU) 140
Australia–US Free Trade Agreement 13–14, 80, 206–7
Australian Agricultural Company (AAC) 145–6, 154
Australian Cattlemen's Union 150
Australian Citizens Against Foreign Ownership 2
Australian Competition and Consumer Commission (ACCC) 172, 195, 202
Australian Consolidated Industries (ACI) 55–6, 57, 58
Australian Democrats 87–8
Australian dollar, floating of 122, 123, 135
Australian equity requirements, calls for 73
Australian Farm Institute 153
Australian Industry Development Corporation (AIDC) 99–100, 101–2, 111, 136
Australian Joint Stock Bank 35, 36, 37
Australian Mining Industry Council 103
Australian Petroleum Exploration Association 108
Australian Prudential Regulation Authority 205
Australian Republican [newspaper] 41
Australian Resources Development Bank 99
Australian Securities Exchange (ASX) 204–5, 217
Australian Security and Intelligence Organisation (ASIO) 202
Australian Tax Office 175, 182, 202
Australian Wheat Board (AWB) 34
Australian Workers Union (AWU) 115
Auto Investment and Competitiveness Scheme 187–8

B

balance of payments crisis 137–8
"banana republic" 138
Bank of England 44
bank nationalisation 43–4, 48, 49–51, 102
Bank of NSW 35–6, 46–7, 128
Banking Act 127
banks/banking
  crashes in 1890s 35–6
  deregulation 51–2, 123, 125, 126–7, 137, 215
  royal commission into 48
  vilification by labour movement 41–3
Bartholomew, Harry 71
Barton, Edmund 29
Barwich, Garfield 51, 175
bauxite 103, 112, 120, 175, 196
Bavin, Thomas 46
"Bazza McKenzie" comic strip 90
beef exports 149, 150
beer 90-1
Bell, Harold 73, 80
Bellamy, Edward 40
Berry, Graham 24–5
BH South 73
BHP 70, 97, 98, 108, 109
BHP Billiton 110, 112, 115, 118, 121
Billabong 86
Bishop, Julie 6, 152
bitcoin 170, 180–3
Bjelke-Petersen, Joh 2, 95
Blainey, Geoffrey 157
Blunt, Charles 150
Bond, Alan 88, 122
bond rates 126
Boomerang [newspaper] 39, 157
Bora, Bijit 89
Boral 17
Bourke, William 67
Bowen, Chris 15, 158, 214–16
Brandis, George 204
Brash, Don 64, 66, 74
Brisbane Courier [newspaper] 44–5
Brisbane Worker [newspaper] 43–4
British Colonial Office 145
British East India Company 145
Broadcasting Act 1956 77–8
Brodie-Hall, Laurence 102
Brown, Bob 151
Brown, John 2
Bruce, Stanley 47
Bulletin [magazine] 38–9
Burns Philp 66, 123
Burns, Tom 2
Bush, George W. 80
Bushells 86
Business Council of Australia (BCA) 155, 178, 179, 200–1
business elite, concerns about foreign takeovers 73–4

Butler, Richard 185
Button, John 89, 148–9, 187

C

C. Itoh 97
Cable & Wireless 203
Caesar's Column (Donnelly) 43
Cairns Group 138–9
Cairns, Jim 101–2, 103
Calwell, Arthur 64–5, 69, 70, 72–3, 148
Cameron, Clyde 50, 69–70, 174
Cameron, Donald 30
Cameron, Doug 8
Campbell Report 125–6, 127, 135, 138
Campbell Soup Company 87–9
Canada, regulation of foreign investment 11
capital controls, removal of 123
car exports 188
Carling 90
Carlton & United Breweries 90
Carlyon, Les 83–4
Carr, Kim 190, 191
Carreras 66
Carsales.com 177
Casey, Richard 53, 56, 66
Cass, Moss 103
Cattle Council of Australia 6, 150
cattle industry 146–51
Centre for Independent Studies 133, 164, 217
Century [newspaper] 52
Chifley, Ben 48, 49, 50, 59–61, 66, 68, 104–5, 125
Chiko Rolls 83–5
China
  free trade agreement with Australia 13–14, 112, 154–5, 199, 200–1, 201
  industrialisation 112, 210
  internationalisation of economy 143
  trade with Australia 112, 121, 154–5
China Nonferrous Metals Company 197
Chinalco 112–13, 115, 195
Chinese immigration 24–5, 28
Chinese investment in Australia
  in coal industry 151–2
  growing competition to attracting 200–1
  in residential property 159–62
  in resource industry 112–16, 196–8
  via state-owned enterprises (SOEs) 113–14, 197–202
Chrysler 186
CIA 75
CIC 197
Citibank 135
climate change 8, 210
Club of Rome 103
co-investment in motor vehicle industry 185–92
coal industry
  Chinese investment 151–2
  foreign domination 126
coal prices 111–12
Cobb, John 153
Cobden, Richard 26
Coca-Cola 64
Cold War 65–6
Colebatch, Hal 128
Colmer, Patrick 114, 196
Colonial Sugar Refinery (CSR) 66
Comalco 175
Combet, Greg 184
Commercial Bank of Australia 35
commodity prices 111–12, 120
Commonwealth Bank 43–4, 47–8
Communist Party of Australia 66, 67
company tax 167, 173, 180
competition policy review 168
competitiveness, decline in 137–8
Conciliation and Arbitration Court 31
Confederation of British Industry 178
Connor, Rex 76, 98, 102, 104, 215
constitutional crisis in Victoria 23
Conzinc Riotinto 97
Cooperative Bread Society and Bakery 18
Copland, Douglas 60
Corden, Max 129
Corn Laws (UK) 25
corporate tax law 179
Costello, Peter 111, 112, 214
Cottee's jams 86
Country Party 6, 79, 133, 147
Courage 90
Cox, David 111
CRA 107, 109
Crane, Gordon 73
Crawford, John 71, 130
Crean, Frank 68
Credit Suisse 161

Crossroads Group 133–4
Crough, Greg 174–5
Cuban revolution 73, 74, 75
Cubbie Station 152–3
current account deficits 11–12, 137
Curtin, John 44, 47, 48–9, 51, 54, 56–7, 62, 104–5, 130

D

Daily Mirror [newspaper] 71
"dark" web 182
Davidson, Sinclair 179–80
Dawkins, John 89
Dawn [journal] 37
Dawson, Sandy 87
Deakin, Alfred 29–32, 127, 142
Deloitte Access Economics 119, 120
Democrats, Australian 87–8
Dennis, Charles John 20
depression
  in 1890s 37
  in 1930s 44–7
deregulation of financial market 90, 109, 122, 135, 136
deregulation of foreign investment 137–8, 149
Desmond, Arthur 36, 37, 42, 52
Devereux, Mike 184–5, 191
Dibbs, George 36
Donnelly, Ignatius 43
"double Irish with Dutch sandwich" 176
Downer, Alexander 204
"dries" (Liberal Party) 132, 187
drought 37, 127, 142, 152
Drysdale, Peter 130

E

economic nationalism 21, 33, 76–8, 95–6, 146, 148, 174, 215
economic rationalism 140
economic reform 138
economic statistics, on protection versus free trade 28
economy
  contribution of mining industry 120
  impact of specific foreign investments 195
  internationalisation of 121
  mining boom in 1960s 96–7
  royal commission into 75
  supplying US war machine in Pacific 62
Electric Power Development Corporation 106
electronic commerce, threat to tax base 175–7
Elliott, John 90, 122
Emerson, Craig 5
Empire [newspaper] 26
Enderby, Kep 186
English Chartism 38
environmental impact statements 103
environmental protection 103
equity investment abroad 123
Esky ice-boxes 86
Eta peanut butter 86
Eureka rebellion 38
European Union, regulation of foreign investment 10–11
Evans, Gareth 108–9, 140
Evans, Ted 13
Evatt, HV "Doc" 51, 68
Evergrande Real Estate group 165
exchange rate, abolition of controls 122, 123, 125, 135

F

Fadden, Arthur "Artie" 67, 214
"Faintly Interested Review Board" 87
Fairbairn, David 98
Farley, David 229
farm sector, deregulation 6–7
Farmers Cooperative and Protective Association 19
farmers and settlers associations 146–7
Ferguson, Martin 118, 119
financial capital, Labor suspicion of 51
financial market
  deregulation 90, 109, 122, 135, 136
  regulation 52, 122
financial system inquiry (Campbell Report) 125–6
Fisher, Andrew 43, 47
Fishermans Bend GMH plant 59
Fitzgibbon, Joel 198
Floyds Ice Works 84
food prices 143–4, 213
food production 143, 151–2, 154, 210–11
food security 144
Ford Canada 56

Ford, Henry 48
Ford Motor Company 17, 53–7, 64, 66, 186, 188–9
Forde, Frank 44
Foreign Acquisitions and Takeovers Act 1975 175, 193, 196, 217
foreign investment, *see also* regulation of foreign investment
  deregulation 137–8, 149, 217
  forces shaping Australian approach to 3, 15–16, 143
  grounds for restricting 194
  public attitudes to 14–15
  Foreign Investment Advisory Committee 106
foreign investment debate 15–16
Foreign Investment Review Board (FIRB)
  accountability 194, 214
  composition 193
  "covert" policy 196
  Howard's vow to abolish 110
  national interest test 109
  policy and operation 194–7
  political purpose 14
  raising of thresholds for approval 138
  rejection of SGX takeover bid for ASX 205
  representation of agricultural interests 4, 152
  role 193–4, 216
  on Shell's hostile takeover bid for Woodside 110–11
  on Sinosteel's bid for Midwest Minerals 112
  on Sinosteel's bid for Murchison Metals 114
  threshold for approval 13
  threshold for US companies 81
  threshold for agribusiness 155
  treatment of state-owned enterprises 113–14, 197–201
Forrest, Andrew 117
Fortescue Metals 117
Foster's 90–2, 122
Fraser, Malcolm 106, 126, 131
Fraser government 106–8, 126, 131, 136, 149, 187
free trade
  as doctrine of Victorian ruling establishment 22–4, 27
  as libertarian philosophy 25
  radical perspective 217
  struggle between Rattigan and McEwen 129
free trade agreements
  with China 13–14, 112, 154–5, 199, 200–1, 201
  with Japan 151, 200
  and national sovereignty 205–8, 211–12
  partners in 7, 155, 200
  with South Korea 151, 200
  with United States 13–14, 80, 206–7
free trade movement
  in colony of NSW 26
  internationalist aspect 25
  loss of political base 32
Free Trade Party 127, 142
free traders view of foreign investment 3, 16
free-market fundamentalism 52
French CJ, Robert 207, 208
Friedman, Milton 124, 132, 133
Frozen Foods 83–6
FX Holden 59

G

Game, Philip 47
Garnaut, Ross 138
"Gawler Craton" 197
Geelong 17, 56–7
Geelong Advertiser [newspaper] 21
Geelong Loan Company 18
Geelong People's Association 18
Geelong Union Mill Company 18
General Agreement on Tariffs and Trade 139
General Motors Holden 53, 54–5, 56, 58–9, 66, 69, 70, 184–5, 186, 188, 189, 191
George, Henry 28
Gibbons, Andrew 158
Gibson, Robert 47
Gillard, Julia 118, 184
Gillard government 118, 145, 188
Glasson, Bill 148
global accounting firms 175
global capital markets, rise of 123–4
global financial crisis 52, 158, 180, 210

global real estate market 162–3
global tax avoidance 176
globalisation 8, 141, 143, 146, 209–10
Golden Circle pineapple 86
Golden Fast Food 165
Golding, Peter 72
Google 168, 176, 199
"Google tax" 179
Gorton Government, foreign investment policy 78
Gorton, John 71, 76–8, 100, 215
GrainCorp 8–9, 33, 34, 156, 208, 209, 214, 217
Grassby, Al 85, 86
Graziano, Bob 189
Green Left Weekly [journal] 88
Greens [political party] 4, 8, 115, 144–5, 151, 179, 205, 210–12, 217
Greenwood, Ivor 86
Greste, Peter 206
Griffith, Bryce 108
Griffiths, Bryony 87
Grindlays 135–6
Gruen, Fred 131
GST, and online purchases 167, 171–2
Gullett, Henry 54
Gurindji people 148

H

Hallam, Jack 148, 149
Hamersley Iron 97
Hamilton, Clive 160
Hancock, Keith 32, 128
Hanson, Pauline 2
Hard Cash [newspaper] 36, 42
Harper, Ian 168, 169
Harrison, James 21–2, 27
Harrop, Mal 57
Hartnett, Lawrence 58
Harvey, Gerry 171
Harvey Norman 171
Hassad Foods 210
Hawke, Bob 124, 135, 138, 157
Hawke government 108–9, 134–41, 149, 158, 187, 194, 209
Hayden, Michael 204
Hayek, Friedrich 124, 132, 133, 182
Heart of the Nation 2
Heferen, Rob 177
Heffernan, Bill 144
Heinz 64
Henry Jones IXL 90
Henry, Ken 93–4, 116
Henry Tax Review 116, 120
Hewson, John 127, 216, 217
Higgins, Henry 31
Hockey, Joe 8–9, 33, 34, 152, 153, 156, 161, 163, 165, 167, 173, 199–200, 216–17
Hocking, Doug 133
Hodgson Vale 154
Hogan, Paul 90
Holden, *see* General Motors Holden
Holman, William 42–3
Holmes à Court, Robert 122
Holt, Harold 72, 76, 96, 99
Holt Government 76, 98
hostile takeovers 73
Howard, John 80, 106–7, 110, 111, 125, 126, 157, 170
Howard government 6, 187, 206
Howell, M.W. 103
Huawei 203–4
Hughes, Billy 37, 42, 56
Hummer [newspaper] 39
Humphries, Barry 90
Hutchinson, Bill 59
hybrid securities 177–8
Hyde, John 132

I

Iceland, regulation of foreign investment 10, 11
IKEA 173
immigration, post-war program 64–5
Immigration Restriction Act 30
import quotas 186
industrial disputes 40–1, 147–8
Industries Assistance Commission (IAC) 186, 187
industry assistance plans 139, 140
"infant industry" defence 33–4
inflation 66–7, 124, 131, 132, 141
Institute of Public Affairs (IPA) 133, 217
intellectual property 80, 81, 180
Interactive Gambling Act 2001 170
interest rates, regulation of 125
international business, unethical nature of 75–6

international capitalism, "money power" critique 42–4, 45–6, 48, 50, 68
International Harvester 17, 30–1
international investment flows 123
International Monetary Fund (IMF) 118
International Packers 148
International Workingmen's Association 40
internationalism 40
internet-based businesses, regulatory challenges of 170, 175–7
investment banking 73
investment opportunities, abundance of 13
investment policy liberalisation 137–8
"investor–state dispute settlement procedures" 205–8
iron ore exports 97–8, 121
iron ore marketing, shift to spot markets 115–16
IT&T
- bid for Frozen Foods 83–6
- involvement in CIA plot in Chile 75, 84, 85

Iwasaki, Yohachiro 1

J

Japan
- friendship treaty with Australia 130
- regulation of foreign investment 10–11
- trade with Australia 72, 97, 98, 121, 130

Japanese investment in Australia
- in cattle industry 149–51
- in Queensland tourism ventures 1–3
- in residential property 157–8

Japanese steel industry 98–9
Japanese tourists 2, 3
Jemena 200
Jensen, John 58
Johnson, Bob 135
Johnson, Lyndon 74
Jones, Alan 152, 154, 155
Joyce, Barnaby 5, 91, 95, 115, 151, 153, 156, 212–14
Joye, Christopher 204
Just Jeans 171
"just-in-time" inventory 190

K

Kaiser Steel 97
Kane, Jack 85
Kasper, Wolfgang 133–4, 136
Keating, Paul 15, 51–2, 88, 100, 105, 108, 125, 126–7, 141, 158, 186, 215
Keating government 109–10, 141
Keen, Steven 158
Kellogg's 64
Kelly, Bert 129, 132
Kelly, Chris 33
Kelly, Stan 129
Kemp, Charles 133
Kemp, Rod 133
Keogh, Mick 153–4
Kernot, Cheryl 88
Keynesianism 132
King Ranch 148
The Kingdom of Shylock (Anstey) 44
Kirchner, Stephen 164, 196
Kiwi Boot Polish 123
Kleinbard, Edward 177, 180
Kodak 64
Kogas 111
Korea, regulation of foreign investment 10, 11
Kraft Foods 86–7
Kurrumbede 154

L

Labor Daily [newspaper] 46
Labor Party 32, 205, 214–16
labour movement
- commitment to socialism 41
- vilification of the banks 41–3

laissez-faire policy on foreign investment 65, 70–1, 74–5, 76, 80
Lake, Marilyn 159
Lan-Choo tea 86
land ownership 4–5
Land Society 18
land taxation 28
Lane, Don 3
Lane, William 40, 42, 157
Lang, Jack 37, 46–7, 51–2
Law Reform Society 18
Lawrence, Neil 117
Lawson, Henry 37, 39
Lawson, John 55–6
Lawson, Louisa 37
League of Nations 174

"lean manufacturing" techniques 190
leftist view of foreign investment 3, 15–16, 37
Leigh, Andrew 138, 140
Lend-Lease program 62, 63
Levitt, Theodore 141
Leyland 186
Liberal Party 132, 142, 187
Liberals 32
libertarianism 25, 133–4, 136
licence fees 167
Life Offices' Association 77
life-insurance industry 77
Limits to Growth (Club of Rome) 103
Lindemans 92
Lindsay, Greg 133
Linkletter, Art 148
Looking Backward (Bellamy) 40
Love, Peter 42
Lynas 197, 202
Lynch, Phillip 106, 107, 187
Lyons, Joseph 53

M

MacArthur, Douglas 62
Macarthur, John 145–6
McEnroe, Frank 84
McEwen, John 5, 6, 71–2, 76, 99, 129–30
"McEwenism" 72
Macfarlane, Ian 191
Macintyre, Stuart 27
McKay, Hugh Victor 30–1
McMahan, Ken 100
McMahon, William 77, 78, 79–80, 83, 99
McMahon government 78–80, 83, 94
McNamara, Bertha 37
McNamara, William 37
Macquarie Broadcasting Network 71
MacRobertson's confectionery 86
Makin, Tony 164
manufactured exports 142
manufacturing
  dependence on protection 17
  dislocation following tariff reductions 141–2
  foreign investment in post-war years 60–1
  impact of war-time production 63
  post-war boom 63
  share of GDP 142
  in South Australia 185
  'time and motion' methods 69
  US investment in post-war period 64
  in Victoria 185
Marks, John 73
Marshall, Adam 151
mass consumer market 63
media ownership 71
Melrose, Ian 115
Melville, Leslie 129
Menzies, Robert 5, 49–50, 53, 54–7
Menzies government 65, 66, 70–1, 74–5, 76, 186
Mercantile Bank of Australia 35
Midwest Minerals 112, 114
Mill, John Stuart 21, 24, 28, 33–4
Milne, Christine 4, 8, 144, 210–12
mineral exports, federal control over 98
Mineral Securities (Minsec) 100
mineral wealth 120–1
Minerals Council 94, 116, 119
minimum wage determination 31
mining booms 96–7, 111, 119–20, 189
mining industry
  campaign against RSPT 117
  contribution to national economy 120
  growth driven by foreign investment 121
  internationalisation 110–11
  operations on agricultural land 151–2, 154
Minmetals 197–8
Mirror newspaper group 71
Mitsubishi 188
Mitsui 97
MLC life insurance company 77
Mok, Edwin 158
Molson 90
Money Power (Anstey) 44
monopolies 43, 55–6, 57, 58–9, 67–8, 85, 126
Mont Pelerin Society 133
Morgenthau, Hans 193
motor vehicle component industry 186
motor vehicle industry 17, 53–9, 184–92
multinationals, depriving Australia of tax revenue 78, 174
Murchison Metals 114
Murray, David 217
Myer 171

N
Nabarlek uranium mine 100
Nabisco 88
national brands, debate over ownership 86–90
National Broadband Network (NBN) 203–4
National Farmers' Federation (NFF) 6–7, 133
national interest
  codification of test 216–17
  concept of 193
  and foreign investment 212
  and foreign ownership 10
  and foreign takeovers 79–80
  lack of definition 194
  negative test 193–7, 194, 211
  positive test 211, 213
  and prohibition of foreign investment 193–7
  as test in legislation 232
National Party 4–5, 6, 8–9, 33, 145, 212–14, 217
national register of agricultural land owners 155
national register of foreign ownership of land 148, 152
national security, and foreign investment 197–8, 202–5
National Security Committee 113, 114
nationalism 40
neo-liberalism 52
Nestlé 76
"New International Economic Order" 103
The New Order [newspaper] 42–3
New Zealand, regulation of foreign investment 10, 11
Newton, Max 129
Niemeyer, Otto 44–6, 47
Nissan 186, 188
Nixon, Richard 123
Noble Resources 197
Non-Aligned Movement 75
Norman, John 102
North West Shelf gas project 110–11

O
Occidental Petroleum 206
Occupy movement 4
O'Dwyer, Kelly 161, 162, 164
Officer, Bob 127
Ohira, Masayoshi 102–3
Ohmae, Kenichi 141
oil crises
  in 1973 95–6, 131
  in 1979 107
oil embargo 95–6
oil industry, resource rent tax 108–9
oil prices 107, 131
Old, Dick 148
One Nation movement 2
online gambling 170–1
open-door policy 76
opinion polls on foreign investment 13–14
Oppen, Alice 87
Optus 203
Organisation for Economic Co-operation and Development (OECD) 10, 177–9, 180, 194
Organization of the Petroleum Exporting Countries (OPEC) 95–6, 103, 107, 111
O'Sullivan, D. 156
OZ Minerals 197–8

P
Page, Earle 214
Parkes, Henry 26, 27, 28, 29
Peko-Wallsend 107
Penfolds 91, 92
Peters ice cream 86
Petroleum and Minerals Authority 102, 104
Pharmaceutical Benefits Scheme (PBS) 81
Philip Morris 206–7
Playford, Thomas 185
Pokarier, Christopher 73, 107
political convergence 8
Political Labour League Conference 41
Popper, Karl 133
portfolio investment abroad 122
Potter, Ian 73
privatisation 124, 136
Productivity Commission 170, 171, 185, 189–90, 191, 207
profit shifting 177–8
profiteering 67, 68
Prominent Hill mine 197, 198
property market, foreign demand 162–3
protectionism, *see also* tariff levels
  association with liberalism 22

erosion of political base 129
influence on framing of Constitution 29
links to land and electoral reform 23, 27
links to working hours and conditions 29–31, 33
origins in Victoria 17–22
role in economic policy 15
stance on foreign investment 33
and White Australia policy 24–5, 30
Protectionist Party 26, 29, 127, 142
Purcell, James 159

Q

Qantas 9–10, 209
Queensland, Japanese investment in tourism ventures 1–3

R

radical movement, in colonial Australia 38–41
rare-earths industry 197, 202
Rattigan, Alf 129, 131
Reagan, Ronald 124
regional economic assistance 140
regulation of financial market 52, 122
regulation of foreign investment, *see also* national interest
arguments for and against 12–13
beginnings of 86
convergence of political support for 218–19
current political debate over 7–8
establishment of regulatory structure 7
extension under Fraser government 106
McMahon's proposals 79–80
measuring impact of 13–14
in OECD advanced countries 10–11
state-owned company proposals 113–14
under Howard government 110
under Whitlam government 101, 106
winding back under Hawke/Keating governments 109–10
Reid, George 28–9, 32, 127, 132, 142
rent-seekers 107
Reserve Bank 164, 205
residency visas, for "significant investors" 163
residential property
Asian buyers blamed for high prices 159–60, 162
ban on purchases by non-residents 158
Chinese investment in 159–62
crackdown on foreign purchases 165–6
"dob-in-a-foreign-bidder" hotline 160, 161
fees on foreign purchases 165–6
foreign investment policy 163–6
inquiry into foreign investment 156–7, 161–2, 163–6
Japanese investment 157–8
relaxation of regulations 158–9
resource industry
expansion in 1960s and 1970s 96–7
hostility towards foreign investment 95
politics of 95
state power over 95–6
state royalties 94–5, 116, 119, 120
resource rent tax
considered by Fraser government 107–8
government desire for 93–5
Minerals Council support for 94
negotiated by Gillard government 118–19
on oil industry 108–9, 119
Resource Super Profits Tax (RSPT) 93, 117, 119
resource sector
Australian ownership 76–7, 134
desire for greater Australian participation 99–101
Resource Super Profits Tax (RSPT) 93, 117, 119
Restucci, Raoul 110
retail industry
barriers against global online competitors 171
campaign for "a fair go" 171–2
tax evasion by foreign retailers 172–3
Returned Services League (RSL), in Rockhampton 1–2
Revolutionary Ring for the Liberation of Queensland 1
revolutionary socialist movement 38–41
Ricardo, David 25
Ricketson, Staniforth 73
Riddle, Thomas Crosby 18–20, 23, 27, 34, 53
Rilington, Mitchell 156
Rio Tinto 98, 100, 107, 109, 110, 112, 113–14, 115, 118, 121, 195

R.M. Williams 86
The Road to Serfdom (Hayek) 124
Robb, Andrew 6, 7, 8, 154, 156, 200
Robinson, Joan 133
Rockefeller oil interests 75
Ross, Julia 165
Roxon, Nicola 204
Rudd, Kevin 5, 52, 112–13, 117
Rudd government 49, 112–14, 197
rural businesses
  foreign shareholding 152
  government-controlled marketing 146–7
rural politics
  pastoralists versus small farmers 6, 146–7
  protectionists versus free traders 6
rural sector 4–9
Ruxton, Bruce 157
Ryan, T.J. 147

S

SABMiller 91–2
"safe haven" assets 163
Sakhalin gas project 111
Samuel, Saul 28
Santamaria, B.A. 68
Schmidt, Eric 176
Scullin Labor government 47
Secondary Industries Commission 58
Senate report on foreign investment 79
Servan-Schreiber, Jean-Jacques 76
Shandong Ruyi 153
Shann, Edward 128
Shareholder Action Organisation (SAO) 87
shearers' strikes of 1890s 40–1, 147
Sheehan, Paul 160
Shell Australia 133, 214
Shell, hostile takeover bid for Woodside 110–11, 195
Shenhua Watermark 151, 152
Sherry, Nick 160
Silk Road 182
Sinclair, Ian 126
Singapore Stock Exchange 204–5, 217
Singapore Telecommunications 203
Singtel 203
Sinosteel 112, 114
Skase, Christopher 122
Sladen, Charles 23
Sloan, Alfred 59
Smith, Adam 25
Smith, Bill 55–6
Smith, Dave 192
Smith, Dick 86, 144, 172
soldier settlers 212–13
South African Breweries (SAB) 91
Southcorp 91
sovereignty issues 205–8, 211–12
SP AusNet 200
Spalvins, John 122
Speedo 86
Spence, William 42
Starbucks 173, 179, 180
state intervention 29
state-owned enterprises (SOEs) 113–14, 197–202
"stateless income" 177, 180
Stevens, Glenn 164
Stokes, Kerry 203
Stoler, Andrew 207–8
Strauss-Kahn, Dominique 118
Streets ice cream 86
subsidies, co-investment 185–92
Sunshine Harvester 30
Sutherland, Joan 105
Swan, Peter 127
Swan, Wayne 92, 112, 116, 118, 119, 153, 198, 202, 205
Switzer, Tom 15
Syme, David 22, 26, 27, 29, 34

T

Tariff Board 128, 129, 186
tariff protection
  Australia compared to other countries 32–3
  cuts by Hawke/Keating government 139–40
  dismantling of 138–40
  Fraser's opposition to cuts 131
  for motor vehicle industry 185–91
  relationship of levels to effectiveness of lobbyists 24
  in United States 32
  Whitlam's desire to reduce 131
Tariff Reform Leagues 22, 128, 132, 228
tax law, and online trading 169–70

tax minimisation 168
tax treaties 178
taxi licensing 167–8
Taylor, Rod 105–6
telecommunications industry 203–4
Thatcher, Margaret 124
The Australian [newspaper] 146
Theophanous, Andrew 135
Thompson, Albert 69
Thornton, George 35
"tiger economies" 140
Tocsin [newspaper] 39
tourism industry 1–3
Toyota 186, 188, 189, 190, 191–2
trade
  bondage to Britain 71–2
  with China 112, 121, 154–5
  free trade agreements 7, 8, 155
  with Japan 72, 97, 98, 121, 130
  linked to foreign policy 140
  with United Kingdom 121, 130
  with United States 62–3, 80–2
trade liberalisation 139, 141
trade ministry, National Party incumbency 5–6
trade policy, differences between colonies 27
trade unions
  growth in 1880s 38
  militancy 40–1
  support for industry assistance plans 140
trading companies 66, 123
Treasury 43, 65, 77, 79, 94, 116, 119, 125–6, 135, 194, 205
Treasury Wine Estates 92
Trewin, Gordon 85
Truss, Warren 4, 6, 9, 33, 152
Tsingdao 91
Turnbull, Malcolm 115, 204

U

Uber 167, 168
Ulbricht, Ross William 182
United Fruit 75
United Graziers Association 150
United Kingdom
  deregulation of banking 123
  imports from Australia 121
  investment in cattle industry 146, 147–8
  privatisation program 124
  regulation of foreign investment 11, 217–18
  tariff levels 32
  trade with Australia 121, 130
United Nations Commission on Trade and Development 206
United States
  balance of payments deficits 74, 123
  controls on outgoing investment and bank loans 74–5
  deregulation of banking 123
  floating of US dollar 123
  free trade agreement with Australia 13–14, 80, 206–7
  imperialism, Marxist critique of 75
  Lend-Lease program 62, 63
  multinationals, activities in developing countries 75
  regulation of foreign investment 11
  role in global pursuit of taxes 178
  tariff levels 32
  trade with Australia 62–3, 80–2
  troops in Australia 62, 63
United States investment in Australia
  in cattle industry 148
  in manufacturing during post-war period 64
  share of total foreign investment in Australia 82
Unsworth, Barry 158
uranium exports 134
uranium mining 100, 110
US Business Roundtable 178
Utah Mining 105–6, 109
utopian idylls 40

V

Valentine, Tom 127
Vegemite 86–7
Vernon, Ray 96
Vernon Report 75
Vestey family 147–8, 173
Vestey, William 173
Victa lawnmowers 86
Victoria Bitter (VB) 91
Victorian Association for the Protection of Native Industry 22

Victorian Chamber of Manufacturers 73
Victorian Legislative Council (colonial) 22–3
Vietnam War 74, 75, 123
Virgin Australia 9
von Mises, Ludwig 133
Vosper, Frederick 41

W

Walker, Fred 87
Walsh, Max 157
Ward, Eddie 69
Wardel, Robert 146
Warrnambool Cheese 209
Wave Hill Station 148
Weidmann, Jens 181
Wentworth, William 146
West, John 25
West Australian Farmers and Settlers' Association 147
Western Mining 107
Western Plains 198
"wets" (Liberal Party) 187
wheat industry 8–9, 33–4
Wheelwright, Ted 3, 78, 136, 174
Whish-Wilson, Peter 212
White Australia policy 24–5, 28, 30, 69, 130
Whitlam, Gough 78, 85–6, 101, 130–1
Whitlam government 78, 95, 101–6, 130–1, 136, 148, 186, 187
WikiLeaks 114
Williams, R.M. 154
Wilson, Brian 161, 163
wine business 91
Wolf Blass 92
Wong, Penny 7–8, 155
Wood, Alan 129
Woodside 110–11, 195, 214
wool industry 145–6
wool-combing 17
Woolworths 172
Woomera defence zone 197–8
Worker [newspaper] 40, 41, 46
Workman [newspaper] 39
World Bank 96
Wright, Keith 150

X

Xenophon, Nick 144–5
Xi Jinping 155, 201
Xstrata 118
Xu Jiayin 165

Y

Yeppoon, bombing of tourist resort 1–2

Z

Zoellick, Robert 80–1, 143–4

Lightning Source UK Ltd.
Milton Keynes UK
UKHW04f1016090718
325432UK00003B/606/P

9 781863 957540

Protein Shakes

Top 50 Protein Shake Recipes for Building Muscle

By

Bring On Fitness